DE GAULLE TO MITTERRAND

It has been claimed that the President of the French Republic is the most powerful liberal democratic political leader in the world. Under closer scrutiny, however, this bold generalisation needs to be qualified at many points. Historically, the office emerged from a prolonged and bitter confrontation between the assertiveness of absolute monarchy and a countervailing desire to eliminate a head of state altogether. Hence, the stability of legitimacy was a long time coming after 1789.

Despite the importance of the subject, this searching scrutiny of the four Presidents of the Fifth Republic by six of Britain's leading specialists in French politics has no predecessor in any language. After examining France's institutional legacy in the matter of supreme executive power, *Jack Hayward* makes a critical examination of how the principles of the constitution established by General de Gaulle on becoming President in 1958 have since worked in practice under the presidencies of Georges Pompidou. Valéry Giscard d'Estaing and François Mitterrand. *Anne Stevens* examines the role of the President's staff, and *Vincent Wright* explores the tensions between Presidents and their Prime Ministers. *Howard Machin* then considers the crucial matter of President-party relations. The President's role in foreign and defence affairs is investigated by *Jolyon Howorth* and in cultural and broadcasting policies by *Martin Harrison*.

In the conclusion on presidential court politics, Jack Hayward returns to the theme of the personal role of the head of state, which remains of pivotal importance, despite the many domestic and foreign constraints upon the President's freedom of action.

All the co-authors hold academic posts at universities in the United Kingdom. *Jack Hayward* (also the editor) was Professor of Politics at the University of Hull until January 1993, when he became Director of the newly-established European Studies Institute at the University of Oxford, and a Professorial Fellow of St. Antony's College. He is also the editor of *Political Studies*. *Martin Harrison* is Professor of Politics at the University of Keele. *Jolyon Howorth* is Professor of French Civilization at the University of Bath. *Howard Machin* is Senior Lecturer in Government at the London School of Economics. *Anne Stevens* is Professor of European Studies at the University of Kent at Canterbury. *Vincent Wright* is Fellow of Nuffield College, Oxford, and co-editor of *West European Politics*. More biographical information on the authors is provided in the front of the book.

De Gaulle

to

Mitterrand

Presidential Power

in France

MARTIN HARRISON
JACK HAYWARD *(editor)*
JOLYON HOWORTH
HOWARD MACHIN
VINCENT WRIGHT
ANNE STEVENS

NEW YORK UNIVERSITY PRESS
WASHINGTON SQUARE, NEW YORK

First published in the U.S.A. in 1993 by
NEW YORK UNIVERSITY PRESS
Washington Square
New York, NY 10003

Library of Congress Cataloging-in-Publication Data

De Gaulle to Mitterrand: presidential power in France/Martin
    Harrison . . . [et al.]: Jack Hayward, editor.
        p.   cm.
    Includes bibliographical references and index.
    ISBN 0-8147-3355-7 (cloth)   — ISBN 0-8147-3356-5 (pbk.)

    1. Presidents—France.   2. France—Politics and government—1958–
I. Harrison, Martin, 1930–   II. Hayward, Jack Ernest Shalom.
JN2665.D39   1993
354.4403′13—dc20   92–40931
                                                                   CIP

CONTENTS

v

PREFACE

In his introduction to Vincent Auriol's unprecedented and (unfortunately) unemulated diary of his presidency, Pierre Nora declared in 1970 that 'the bibliography on the presidency is poor . . . because the lack of serious sources condemns its study to rely either on journalistic anecdotes or law theses.'[1] This stricture by a scholar, accustomed to more reliable documentation than France's fifty-year rule for access to public papers or the reticence of French public figures has placed at the disposal of political scientists, would seem to preclude a study of the Fifth Republic presidency that is not confined to legalistic formalities, yet provides a more systematic assessment of institutional practice than is yielded by the flashes of insight that the best anecdotes can offer.

The political scientists who have collaborated in this study of the French President do not adopt so defeatist a standpoint. The interaction between approaches that are state-centred (focussing upon the executive) and society-centred (focussing upon the party system), usually presented as alternatives, provide the dynamics of our analysis of the presidency. Intersecting this false dichotomy, the analysis is conducted simultaneously at three levels, which themselves interact: identifiable realities, the ways they are presented and the ways they are perceived. All this makes for a complexity that is simplified thanks to the constraints of partial knowledge and practical necessity. Relatively stable constitutional provisions are considered in this study as the point of departure for the scrutiny of political behaviour, while the day-to-day findings of investigative journalism are not spurned as indications of how practice has varied. Nevertheless, by combining the temporal depth that comes from a knowledge of the historical background with analytical comparison of how the first four Presidents of the Fifth Republic have managed their relations with their staff, the government, the parties, parliament and the mass media, as well as their role in policymaking and how all these facts are reflected in public perceptions, we endeavour to show that a serious albeit incomplete political analysis of the presidency is possible. To understand the scale of de Gaulle's Fifth Republic achievement in restoring the authority of the head of state, we start from the rejection of the personal power personified in the *Ancien Régime* monarch.

1. Vincent Auriol, *Journal du Septennat, 1946–54*, Paris, 1970, I, p. xviii.

First drafts of the papers that make up this book were discussed at a conference held at the Maison Française in Oxford on 28–29 June 1991, with the support and hospitality of its then Director, Professor Monica Charlot, and of the Nuffield Foundation. They have our warmest thanks, as do the discussants Roland Cayrol, Jean Charlot, Samy Cohen, Olivier Duhamel, Jean-Luc Parodi and Bernard Tricot, who contributed to vigorous exchanges from which we all derived deeper insights into a complex and protean political phenomenon: the political power of the French President of the Republic.

University of Hull   JACK HAYWARD
March 1992

'*Trait libre*'
(from *Le Monde*, 30 November 1991)

NOTES ON THE CO-AUTHORS

MARTIN HARRISON is Professor of Politics at the University of Keele. He is the author of numerous studies of French politics, notably (with Philip Williams) *Politics and Society in de Gaulle's Republic*, and a book on British media politics, *TV News: Whose Bias?*

JACK HAYWARD was Professor of Politics at the University of Hull until January 1993, when he became Director of the newly-established European Studies Institute at the University of Oxford, and a Professorial Fellow of St. Antony's College. He is also the editor of *Political Studies* and a Fellow of the British Academy. He is the author of *Governing France: the One and Indivisible Republic, After the French Revolution: Six Critics of Democracy and Nationalism* and editor (with Peter Hall and Howard Machin) of *Developments in French Politics*.

JOLYON HOWORTH is Professor of French Civilization at the University of Bath and former co-editor of *Contemporary France*. He is the author of a biography of *Edouard Vaillant* and numerous contributions to books and periodicals on French defence and foreign policy.

HOWARD MACHIN is Senior Lecturer in Government at the London School of Economics. He is the author of *The Prefect in French Public Administration* and co-editor (with Vincent Wright) of *Economic Policy and Policy-Making under the Mitterrand Presidency, 1981-84*.

ANNE STEVENS is Professor of European Studies at the University of Kent at Canterbury. She has written extensively on the subject of French public administration and is co-author of *Hostile Brothers: Competition and Closure in the European Electronics Industry*.

VINCENT WRIGHT is Fellow of Nuffield College, Oxford, and co-editor of *West European Politics*. He is the author of *The Government and Politics of France*, editor of *Continuity and Change in France* and co-editor (with Yves Mény) of *Centre-Periphery Relations in Western Europe* and (with John Vickers) *The Politics of Privatisation in Western Europe*.

1

FROM REPUBLICAN SOVEREIGN TO PARTISAN STATESMAN

Jack Hayward

The centuries preceding the French Revolution can be characterised by the manifest emergence in France of a centralised state power embodied in the absolute monarch, and by the latent emergence of a decentralised societal socio-economic power of the middle classes unrepresented by the parliamentary institutions that had developed in England. The seventeenth-century struggle for power between King and Parliament led in Britain to the compromise of a constitutional monarchy, which from the eighteenth century was to witness a growing predominance of parliamentary sovereignty. In France, the seventeenth-century apotheosis of arbitrary royal absolutism, personified in Louis XIV, meant that state power lacked the auxiliary legitimacy of representative oligarchy and relied solely upon the legitimacy of hereditary monarchy. Louis XIV's successors were ultimately unable to resist the demands of the liberal aristocracy and the increasingly assertive middle classes. The ensuing revolutionary process failed to establish the British model of constitutional monarchy which, combining hereditary and representative legitimacy, confided sovereignty to the King-in-Parliament. The result was 170 years of constitutional conflict before the Fifth Republic was at last able to achieve an enduring *modus vivendi*. This involved the 'restoration of the state' by Charles de Gaulle in the shape of a powerful President, elected by the people, ensuring that republican institutions ceased to be identified with weak, 'headless' government. Before we consider how the presidency has evolved during the Fifth Republic, we shall examine how the institution developed in the years between the collapse of one uncontested supreme political authority and before the emergence of another one.

From Impersonal to Personal Power

The French determination to avoid a return to royal absolutism after the Revolution proved less successful than the American concern to prevent the re-emergence of another George III. The unwillingness of Louis XVI to accept the constitutional monarchy as

1

provided for in the 1791 Constitution launched France upon a series
of republican experiments characterised by a determination to avoid
having a head of state at all, much less one capable of using and
abusing concentrated political power. Popular sovereignty having
been proclaimed as 'one and indivisible', it was essential to prevent
it being usurped by a single individual. The solution adopted from
1792–9 was to make the ministers collectively forming the government dependent upon a single-chamber legislature representative
of the popular will. However, because it was impossible for a large
assembly to control ministers suspected of seeking to be more than
a mere 'executive' of the will of the people's representatives, various
expedients were developed. From 1793–4, the Convention concentrated the arbitrary power wrenched from the King in the hands
of a twelve-member Committee of Public Safety, which was itself
dominated by Robespierre.[1] This brief period of Jacobin dictatorship, while it demonstrated that the forceful exercise of political
power did not require a formal head of state, simultaneously
showed that its absence was no guarantee against the arbitrary exer-
tion of unlimited power maximising political insecurity.

The liberals who came to power after the overthrow of the
Jacobins sought salvation in an elaborate separation of weakened
legislative and executive powers. Insofar as any body had the
authority to govern under the 1795 Constitution, it was the five-man
Directory, whose chairman changed every three months. The experiment in preserving a republican regime (in which only a minority
were republicans) continued till 1799, when the leading Director,
Sieyès – who had played a key part in the revolutionary process
from 1789 – sought what he thought was the temporary expedient
of calling upon General Bonaparte to replace the five-man Directory
with the three-man Consulate. However, the General quickly took
command as First Consul, proceeding by stages, each legitimised by
plebiscite, to make himself Consul for life and then hereditary
Emperor in 1804. The Napoleonic First Empire embodied the hyper-
personalisation of political power, in reaction against the forlorn
attempts in the 1790s to depersonalise it. Thereafter, France was to
lurch between these extremes, as well as trying to resuscitate constitutional monarchy as the antidote to both personal despotism and
impersonal anarchy.

The 1815 Bourbon Restoration offered an opportunity to
establish a British-style constitutional monarchy, the Charter
'accorded' by Louis XVIII marking a decisive break with the
pre-Revolutionary absolute monarchy. Nevertheless, the violation

1. R. R. Palmer, *Twelve Who Ruled*, Princeton, 1941.

of the Charter by his successor Charles X, in his attempt to retrieve lost royal autocracy, led to the 1830 Revolution. The July monarchy of Louis-Philippe, while it made an even more determined attempt to follow the British model, involved much more personal intervention by the head of state in day-to-day politics than could ever occur in Britain. Not only did the French King (unlike his British counterpart) preside over meetings of the government, but he made sure that the *de facto* Prime Minister acted in accordance with his policy. Some early critics of the Fifth Republic were to point to analogies with the July Monarchy as a way of creating a guilt-by-association with a discredited non-republican regime. For example, in 1959 Duverger claimed that the Fifth Republic sought to return to the 1875 'Orleanist Republic', itself linked to the July Monarchy. 'Orleanism is typically characterised by two fundamental features: the head of state does not govern himself but plays the role of supreme arbiter, exercising a "moderating power"; the Cabinet must have his confidence as well as that of Parliament, so he can dismiss ministers even if they have not been defeated in Parliament.'[2] Insofar as such parallels may be said to exist, what they indicate is the retrieval of a liberal continuity between the pre-1848 constitutional monarchy and the post-1958 constitutional republic, a continuity that the Second, Third and Fourth Republics failed to achieve.

The Second Republic, by instituting the direct election of the President and then electing Louis-Napoleon to the office by an overwhelming popular vote of 74 per cent, subsequently embodied for republicans the anti-model of personal presidential power. By first personalising executive power and then precluding the President from seeking re-election after completing his four-year term, it prepared the way for the 1851 *coup d'état* which led to the establishment of the Second Empire. Once again, a republic had made way for a Napoleonic dictatorship. This was helped by the fact that the monarchical majority in the one-chamber parliament was split between Legitimists and Orleanists, so the President's intrigues were facilitated by a dual threat of monarchical restoration. The republicans did not know whether to support the President against an Assembly that had restricted universal suffrage or the monarchists against an imperial restoration. Louis-Napoleon, who inaugurated the practice of French Presidents of the Republic making the Elysée palace their official residence, planned his *coup d'état* there, the very

---

2. Maurice Duverger, 'Les Institutions de la Cinquième République' in *Revue Française de Science Politique*, March 1959, IX, p. 107; cf. Jean Gicquel, *Essai sur la Pratique de la Ve République. Bilan d'un Septennat*, Paris, 1968, pp. 123, 187.

place where his uncle had abdicated in 1815.[3]

However, the powers of the Second Republic President were formally not very different from those of his republican successors. Apart from appointing and removing ministers, he required ministerial countersignature for his acts. He presided over the Council of Ministers but could not dissolve the National Assembly if it rejected legislation presented by the government. Nor could he veto laws passed by the Assembly, although he could require that they be reconsidered.[4] Nevertheless, Louis-Napoleon's personal popularity and the divisions of his opponents allowed him to use his control of the army to seize power in face of minimal resistance. Those, such as Proudhon, who had warned in forthright terms from 1849 that Louis-Napoleon was planning to overthrow the Republic were imprisoned for 'insulting the President'. Subsequent plebiscites massively approved both the *coup d'état* and the establishment of the Second Empire. Republicans, such as Jules Grévy, who had opposed the direct election of the President in 1848, were determined that a future republic would avoid this mistake. If there was to be a President at all, he should be elected by parliament, not by the people, because he could then be immediately replaced if there was conflict between parliament and the President.[5] Ironically, this was what happened to Grévy in 1887.

The Parliament-centred Third Republic

The 1870s witnessed the failure to restore monarchy in France owing to the intransigence of Chambord (the Legitimist pretender) and divisions with the Orleanists. Taking advantage of his prestige as the head of the government that had repressed the 1871 Paris Commune and his standing as a conservative champion of the dominance of the bourgeoisie, Thiers no longer favoured constitutional monarchy, of which he had been a champion for most of his life. Returning to power thirty years after being excluded from office by Louis-Philippe in 1840, he acted upon the principle he had enunciated during the Second Republic in 1850: 'The Republic . . . is of all

3. Charles de Gaulle, *Mémoires d'Espoir*, Paris, 1970, 1980, paper edn, p. 34, and Claude Dulong, *La Vie Quotidienne à l'Elysée au temps de Charles de Gaulle*, Paris, 1974, pp. 10, 250-1.
4. Jean Massot, *L'Arbitre et le Capitaine. La Responsabilité Présidentielle*, Paris, 1987, pp. 22-3, and Adrien Dansette, *Histoire des Présidents de la République*, Paris, 1953, 1981 edn, pp. 18, 29. More generally, see Paul Bastid, *Doctrines et Institutions de la Deuxième République*, Paris, 1945, 2 vols.
5. Odile Rudelle in Léo Hamon and Guy Lobrichon (eds), *L'Eléction du Chef de l'Etat en France de Hugues Capet à nos jours*, Paris, 1988, p. 141.

governments that which divides us least.'[6] Democracy having become unavoidable, a republic alone could establish the necessary legitimate authority, and he saw himself as its personification. To institutionalise his precarious position as provisional head of the executive, Thiers was designated 'President of the French Republic' on 31 August 1871 by 553 votes to 68 in an overwhelmingly anti-republican Assembly.

His title was doubly misleading. The Republic as such did not yet exist and Thiers had been put in power in the belief that he would restore monarchy. (In 1958, de Gaulle was helped to power and the founding of the Fifth Republic by the supporters of *Algérie Française* and they were also to discover their error too late.) Thiers did not formally declare his support for the Republic as the conservative basis of public order until December 1871. Furthermore, Thiers was responsible to the Assembly, and in this respect he was like de Gaulle in the period 1944–6 before the establishment of the Fourth Republic, i.e. a Prime Minister rather than a President. He was to learn this to his cost when, apart from sending messages to parliament, the President was denied the right to speak to the Assembly without giving twenty-four hours' notice, being crippled in answering attacks by having to leave the Assembly to debate in his absence.[7] He was forced to resign in 1873, the royalists resisting his attempt to establish a strong republican presidency which would block the way to a monarchical restoration. This was the first of several failures at *cohabitation* between a would-be powerful President and a hostile parliamentary majority.

The Right having used their parliamentary majority in 1873 to prevent the emergence of a strong President, the Left was to repeat this performance in 1877 against Thiers' successor, with much more enduring success. Once Thiers had been forced from office – itself an ominous precedent – the Right sought to strengthen the President pending the planned monarchical restoration. The transition was to be facilitated by giving Marshal MacMahon a seven-year term of office in November 1873. (Ironically, this improvisation was to become a permanent feature of the Republican presidency, not merely when he was reduced to the role of 'arbitrator' during the Third and Fourth Republics but when he became the supreme arbiter during the Fifth Republic. The length of the presidential term provided a 'legitimacy of continuity', derived from symbolising

6. Adolphe Thiers, *Disours parlementaires de M. Thiers*, Paris, 1879–89, VIII, p. 609, a speech delivered in the debate on the *Loi Falloux* on 13 February 1850.
7. Maurice Deslandres, *Histoire Constitutionnelle de la France. L'Avènement de la Troisième République*, Paris, 1937, pp. 138–59; cf. 173 and Dansette, pp. 35–40.

permanent France over and above changing French governments, which has since been supplemented by the democratic appeal to popular choice.[8]) MacMahon reversed his stand on presidential-parliamentary relations for purely tactical reasons between 1873 and 1877. On being elected to office thanks to a Right-wing Assembly majority, he had declared: 'The post in which you have placed me is that of a *sentry* who stands guard over the integrity of your sovereign power.' However, when the Left won control of the Chamber of Deputies, he sacked Prime Minister Jules Simon on 16 May 1877, claiming: 'Unlike you, I am not responsible to parliament, I am responsible to France.'[9] The logic of such a claim was to lead de Gaulle to adopt the popular election of the President.

In 1875 the provisional arrangements had finally to be given greater permanence. Hereditary monarchy's appeal had waned in a country where no monarch had inherited the throne from his father for more than a century. Thanks to the support of the Right-Centre, enough constitutional monarchists voted for the Wallon motion that 'The President of the Republic is elected for seven years' in January 1875, to allow the republican nature of the regime to be narrowly established by 353 votes to 352. The President was to be elected by the Assembly of the two houses of the future parliament, the Chamber of Deputies and the Senate. The acceptance of the second chamber in February 1875 was part of the historic compromise whereby the moderate republicans agreed to this bulwark against the dangers of the popularly-elected first chamber, particularly because the Senate would have a major influence in preventing the election of a dangerous radical as President.

The three piecemeal constitutional laws amounted to France's shortest constitution. As became a parliamentary system in the British manner (which it was intended to be), there was no special amending procedure, so when the republicans won an overwhelming victory at the 1876 general election, the stage was set for a trial of strength between a royalist President and the republican majority on where sovereign power would lie. Dissolution of the Chamber of Deputies in 1877, followed by the re-election of a (reduced) republican majority, produced a decisive shift of power from President to Assembly by discrediting the use of the dissolution power and ensuring that the government would no longer be accountable to the President. As Jules Ferry warned, the balanced constitution

8. Odile Rudelle in Hamon and Lobrichon, p. 140.
9. Quoted in Pierre Miquel, *La Troisième République*, Paris, 1989, pp. 162, 235.

had given way to government by Assembly.[10] Faced with the choice of submitting to the Chamber of Deputies majority or resigning, MacMahon first submitted in 1877 by forming a government enjoying the confidence of parliament, and then resigned in January 1879 over his right to appoint and remove generals. Such appointments were to be restored by the Fifth Republic as part of the President's 'state power'.

His successor, the republican Jules Grévy, accepted parliamentary supremacy in his presidential message of 6 February 1879, amounting to an 'abdication' from the office of strong President which Thiers and MacMahon had sought to establish.[11] However, although he did not exercise his constitutional powers of appointment or dissolution, he was far from being the rubber-stamp President that is often portrayed. One should not confuse his liberal view that governments should govern as little as possible with presidential powerlessness. While parliament – which elected the President – was the sole legitimate authority capable of speaking in the people's name, this nevertheless allowed the President to exercise significant political influence. Grévy insisted – as had MacMahon – upon his right to share in the appointments of the Ministers of Foreign Affairs and War,[12] which partly explains why presidential influence in these fields remained particularly important up to the First World War. That this hard core of state power was regarded as the presidential preserve was facilitated by the fact that the offices of Prime Minister and of Foreign Minister were usually combined, so that in selecting the one he also selected the other. It was principally to prevent 'warmonger' Gambetta from involving France in war with Germany that Grévy blocked the great orator's appointment as Prime Minister. When the offices of Foreign and Prime Minister were not combined, the former often stayed in office as governments changed. Ribot served for half of Sadi Carnot's presidency and Delcassé for most of Loubet's. The preoccupation with mere survival, due to the pressure of domestic dissensions, meant that most Prime Ministers were content to leave much of foreign policy to the President.[13]

10. Quoted by Odile Rudelle, *La République Absolue, 1870–1889*, Paris, 1892, p. 56; cf. 55. See also Deslandres, pp. 503, 530–4.
11. Deslandres, p. 511; cf. 510 and Jacques Julliard, 'La Tentation du Prince-Président', *Pouvoirs*, no. 41 (May 1987 – special issue on 'Le Président') pp. 32–4.
12. Dansette, pp. 66–72. See also Bernard Lavergne, *Les deux Présidences de Jules Grévy, 1879–87. Mémoires de Bernard Lavergne*, Paris, 1966, pp. 67, 132, 337–8.
13. Massot, pp. 50–3 and Abel Combarieu, *Sept Ans à l'Elysée. Avec le Président Emile Loubet*, Paris, 1932, pp. vii–viii.

While the President's discretion in the choice of Prime Minister was limited to one who could command a parliamentary majority, this was much less of a constraint in practice than it would be in a country with a two-party system such as Britain. In France the 'parties' consisted of undisciplined parliamentary groups, each of whom followed in turn a number of rival leaders. Ambition to secure office could be used to play them off against each other, and the frequent disintegration of coalition governments meant that the President was often called upon to find the person capable of solving the ensuing 'crisis'. He could thus exclude some and favour others, exercising in the process a decisive indirect influence over the conduct of French politics. In the pre-First World War period, the emergence of Ferry, Méline, Waldeck-Rousseau, Clemenceau and Poincaré were particularly significant examples of the presidential power of selection.[14] As governments 'waltzed', the President symbolised the continuity of state power emerging above the shifting sands of partisan manoeuvres. However, although as Prime Minister and Foreign Minister in 1912 Poincaré was able to exclude President Fallières from much say in foreign policy, when as President he was himself confronted by Clemenceau as Prime Minister in 1917–19, he had to give way. So, partly as a consequence of the personalities concerned, there was a presidential retreat from the influence exerted by early Presidents of the Third Republic such as Grévy.

Presidential personality was a function of the selection process which produced men who were generally provincial lawyers, old, conservative and increasingly recruited from the Senate. Parliament deliberately avoided choosing someone who might challenge government by Assembly. This meant excluding self-assertive politicians like Jules Ferry who wished to reverse the trend towards Assembly dominance. At the cost of promoting the anti-parliamentary appeal to popular sovereignty of a General Boulanger, Clemenceau – who was in 1920 to be a victim of the same reluctance to choose a strong President – was supposed to have promoted the 'stop Ferry' candidature of Sadi Carnot in 1887 with the cynical comment: '*Votons pour le plus bête.*' His actual words were 'He is not impressive but he bears a republican name.'[15] Not merely was he a grandson of the First Republic hero Lazare Carnot and the son of Hippolyte Carnot, a minister during the Second Republic and an opposition leader in the fight against the Second Empire; he could be relied upon not to challenge parliamentary supremacy.

14. Massot, pp. 48–9.
15. Rudelle, *La République Absolue*, op. cit., pp. 192–3; cf. 188–91 and Dansette, pp. 86–7, 330, 413.

However, Carnot was not simply a republican dynast in place of a monarchical dynast. He proved a very effective crisis President, taking a leading role in the formation and functioning of the Tirard government that successfully dealt with the Boulangist threat. He insisted, for example, that there would be no meetings of Cabinet Council (excluding the President). Carnot also played an effective role in the 'defence' of parliamentary democracy against the Boulangist threat by his presidential visit to seventy-three towns in all parts of provincial France.[16] This precedent became an established practice, continuing even after the parliamentary Republic ceased to be threatened. Carnot's immediate successor in 1894 barely lasted six months in office, resigning in protest at the failure of ministers – especially Foreign Minister Hanotaux – to keep him properly informed. Casimir-Périer refused to be reduced to a ceremonial role. He declared in his farewell message of January 1895 that he could not accept 'the impotence to which I have condemned myself' by accepting an office whose 'moral responsibilities' far exceeded its powers.[17]

The symbolic presidential role of ceremonial republican monarch that Casimir-Périer spurned was welcomed by his more modest successors, with presidency of the Senate significantly becoming the best stepping-stone to the presidency of the Republic, as with Loubet (1899–1906) and Fallières (1906–13). The presidential function became identified more with promoting national reconciliation and then personifying a new-found relative unity than with playing an active role in the domestic policy-making process. Thus Loubet, who disliked Combes' aggressively anti-clerical policy, was forced to reply to an irate Pope Pius X that he could not prevent it. In response to the Pope's remonstrations, Loubet explained in December 1903 'the role assigned to him by the French Constitution. The President must remain within the limits of his constitutional irresponsibility as far as the government's measures are concerned and avoid all personal acts. He can only offer advice to his ministers and I have not failed in that duty.'[18] However, Combes was not interested in foreign affairs, saying in the Council of Ministers: 'Leave that matter alone, it is the concern of the President of the Republic and the Minister of Foreign Affairs.'[19] So, although the more stable governments of the fifteen years preceding the First World War did restrict presidential room for political manoeuvre in

16. Dansette, p. 97.
17. Massot, p. 40; cf. 41, 60–1 and Dansette, pp. 115–16.
18. Quoted in Dansette, p. 150.
19. *Ibid.*, p. 151.

selecting Prime Ministers, Loubet developed very close ties with Delcassé, to whom must go (with the British Foreign Secretary Lord Lansdowne) much of the credit for promoting the Franco-British *Entente Cordiale*, although King Edward VII and Loubet deserve to share in it. Yet when Delcassé's policy seemed to threaten war with Germany in June 1905, Loubet was not able to save him, after a vote in the Council of Ministers left Delcassé in a minority of one.[20]

Loubet was the first President of the Third Republic to retire normally at the end of his term of office. Thiers, MacMahon and Grévy had been forced to resign, and Casimir-Périer had chosen to resign. Carnot and Faure had died in office, the latter in more pleasant circumstances than the former in that he was not assassinated but expired in the arms of his mistress. At his first Council of Ministers, Fallières reassured the government that 'no more during my presidency than during that of my predecessors, will there be an Elysée policy in opposition to that of the government.'[21] This was formally reflected in the fact that the Third Republic President was not chairman of the Council of Ministers, the French title of the Prime Minister being President of the Council (of Ministers). It was the latter, not the President, who set the agenda, steered the discussion and where necessary called for a vote. The President gave his opinion and formally approved the government's decisions, whether he liked them or not, although from time to time even a Loubet or a Fallières would sometimes refuse to sign a decree.[22] So the President of the Republic was not a mere figurehead. As well as rejecting the appointment of Delcassé as Foreign Minister in a Caillaux government, Fallières gave Clemenceau, Briand, Caillaux and Poincaré their first prime ministerships. He complained about being kept inadequately informed about foreign policy but said before the First World War that he would appoint Clemenceau as Prime Minister should hostilities break out. On handing over to Poincaré in 1913, Fallières' parting summing-up of the presidential office was: 'The job is not bad but there is no promotion.'[23]

Following his election, Poincaré confessed to his friend Maurice Paléologue, Secretary-General of the Foreign Ministry, that he had spent a sleepless night thinking of 'the terrible responsibility that will weigh on me, while the principle of constitutional irresponsibility condemns me to seven years of silence and inaction'. Since Poincaré

20. *Ibid.*, pp. 155–8 and Combarieu, pp. viii–ix, 93, 169–70, 247–8, 257–9, 314–17, 333.
21. Dansette, p. 168.
22. Massot, p. 44; cf. Dansette, pp. 149–68.
23. Quoted in Dansette, p. 172; cf. 169–71.

was preoccupied with the need to prepare France for war with Germany, his frustration was based upon his orthodox, Third Republic interpretation of the constitutional role of arbitrator to mean 'ensuring respect successively for the views of others and abdicating one's own ideas'.[24] However, his determination in practice to influence the conduct of the First World War led him to exclude Clemenceau from the premiership for as long as possible. Despite the President's attempt to acquire popularity, notably by frequent visits to the army, power was effectively concentrated in the Prime Minister's hands. Clemenceau bluntly told Poincaré: 'I am popular and you are not.'[25] Poincaré made a stand over the terms of the Versailles Peace Treaty, threatening to resign and send a message to parliament setting out his objections. Nevertheless, in the end, he played the game by the Grévy rules and accepted that as President he lacked the democratic legitimacy to force his views on the Prime Minister. The same rules ensured that in 1920 parliament voted for Deschanel – who had never even been a minister – in preference to the 'Father of Victory', Clemenceau.

However, the challenge to the parliament-centred Republic's determination to reduce the presidency to an impersonal and non-responsible institutional role quickly came from Alexandre Millerand, who succeeded Deschanel in 1920. Not yet openly seeking a revision of the Constitution, Millerand declared when invited to be a presidential candidate that in his view the President should be the proponent of a clear policy applied in close collaboration with his ministers.[26] Once in office he proceeded to by-pass ministers by going direct to the senior civil servants and expounded his own policies, interfering particularly in matters of foreign policy. He forced Briand's resignation as Prime Minister over the application of the Versailles Treaty, and pushed Poincaré into occupation of the Ruhr in 1923, but was not successful in compelling him to sacrifice the British alliance in the pursuit of Franco-German economic unification.

Matters came to a head in the 1924 general election, with Millerand not only identifying himself with the continuation of a tough foreign policy but as the leader of the Right-wing parties. Their defeat placed the President in an impossible position. He was reminded of his attacks thirty years before on Casimir-Périer for having a personal presidential policy, and like MacMahon he was

24. Both quotations from Dansette, p. 179.
25. *Ibid.*, p. 189; cf. 182–6. For a hostile view of President Poincaré in January 1915, see Abel Ferry, *Carnets Secrets*, Paris, 1957, pp. 45–6.
26. Dansette, chapter 12.

faced with the unenviable choice of submission or resignation.
Millerand first tried to persuade three Left-wing leaders to form a
government. Following their refusals, he turned to Poincaré who
also refused. The attempt by a Right-wing former minister to form
a government failed after a presidential message was met with the
snub that, as in 1877, the Chamber of Deputies would 'have no deal-
ings with a government whose composition is a negation of Parliament's rights.'[27] Millerand was compelled to accept total defeat and
resigned. His successor Doumergue also interfered frequently but
more discreetly both in the formation of governments and in their
policy debates. However, in 1931 he consoled the defeated Briand
with becoming modesty: 'No great man has ever been able to become
President of the Republic.'[28]

This statement was certainly true of the Third Republic, concerned as it was to escape the authoritarian fate of the First and
Second Republics. Ironically, it was the inadequacy of its President
in 1940 that was to play a decisive part in the fall of a regime which
had accustomed its head of state to abdication. Albert Lebrun,
last President of the Third Republic, usually adopted an orthodox
abstentionist stance *vis-à-vis* Prime Ministers, although he refused
to sign some decrees, usually nominations or revocations. Nevertheless, he first tried to dissuade Léon Blum from taking office in
1936. He was later instrumental in preventing the Popular Front
government from sending arms to its sister-government in Spain
by delaying the decision until the Foreign Minister returned from
London to use the argument of opposition by France's ally, the
British government.

Lebrun's decisive failure of judgement and nerve came in 1940
when Prime Minister Paul Reynaud resigned because the majority
of his Cabinet favoured asking Nazi Germany for armistice terms.
Although Lebrun personally favoured retreating to North Africa to
continue the fight, he called on Marshal Pétain to form the government, against the advice of the Presidents of both chambers of
parliament, knowing him to be in favour of an armistice on any
terms. What seems to have motivated him was the pressure of public
opinion, wanting to end the disastrous war at all costs and seeking
shelter under the faded glory of Pétain, as well as the knowledge
that the Marshal had a ministerial team ready to take office. As de
Gaulle wrote subsequently of Lebrun, 'Fundamentally, he lacked
two things as head of state: he was not a leader and there was no

27. Massot, p. 42; cf. Dansette, pp. 225–36.
28. Quoted by Dansette, p. 251; cf. 247–50.

state.'[29] While making allowances for de Gaulle's desire to urge the need to recreate the authority of the French state, his judgement on the inadequacy of Third Republic Presidents, especially in the hour of crisis, stands as an epitaph of a regime that led from the convention of presidential abstention to national abdication. Lebrun went to Vichy instead of North Africa and signed the bill giving Pétain the power to draw up a new constitution. On 10 July 1940 Pétain proclaimed himself 'Head of the French State', and the office of President of the Republic was abolished.[30]

Vichy never formalised the draft constitutions it spawned, although a ten-year presidency was envisaged. The possibility of strengthening the President when democracy was restored – with which leaders like Léon Blum toyed – was severely inhibited by reaction against the autocratic position of Marshal Pétain during the Vichy regime and General de Gaulle's *de facto* dictatorship when he led the external Resistance. He could not prolong it during the provisional government which was in power following the Liberation. As de Gaulle recalled his 1945 standpoint: 'According to me it is essential that the state has a head, a leader, in whom the nation can identify, over and above the changing circumstances, the person in charge of what is essential and the guarantor of its destiny. It is also essential that the executive does not derive from parliament.'[31]

De Gaulle's own constitutional ideas were not presented until his 1946 Bayeux speech, in reaction against the Resistance constitution-makers, led by Socialists such as André Philip. They looked for their inspiration to British parliamentary government. Executive power would be confined to a Prime Minister, relying upon a stable parliamentary majority based upon an alliance of disciplined political parties. The President, elected by the National Assembly, would be restricted to a British-style monarchical function. He would not be chairman of the Council of Ministers and would not even have the traditional power of granting pardons. Such was the 'vast operation to castrate presidential power', inspired by the reinvigorated fear of Bonapartism, which was undertaken by the republican party leaders who created the Fourth Republic.[32] This

29. Charles de Gaulle, *Mémoires de Guerre*, III, Paris, 1959, pp. 23; cf. 22 and Dansette, pp. 280-3.
30. Dansette, pp. 284-8. See also Jean Lacouture, *De Gaulle: The Rebel, 1890-1944*, London, 1990, pp. 206-7.
31. *Mémoires de Guerre*, III, p. 240.
32. Jean Lacouture, *De Gaulle. Le Politique*, II. *1944-1959*, Paris, 1985, 1990 paper edn, p. 227; cf. 223, 226, 266, 275. More generally, see Andrew Shennan, *Rethinking France: Plans for Renewal, 1940-1946*, Oxford, 1989, pp. 111-18, 139.

preoccupation was to persist in the intransigent resistance by Pierre Mendès-France to de Gaulle's Fifth Republic, against which he pitted his vision of *A Modern French Republic*, published in 1962 but looking back to the aspirations of the 1940s.

Recalling the excitement of 1945-6, Michel Debré asked the rhetorical question: 'Who does not have a draft constitution in his pocket?'[33] Because of his pivotal role in the process of drafting the 1958 Constitution, it is important to grasp that from his Resistance and Liberation schemes Debré was wedded to strengthening both the presidential and parliamentary components of executive power. He was determined to combine a 'republican monarch' chosen by an electoral college with a Prime Minister accountable to parliament in accordance with the British parliamentary system which he – like so many of his contemporaries – regarded as the model to which France should attempt to approximate. His 1945 remarks on the need for a 'republican monarch' (whom he envisaged as elected for a twelve-year term, 'the average life of hereditary monarchs') if France were to achieve political stability, anticipate de Gaulle's ideas on the subject, until the 1962 reform of the system for presidential elections. 'A true head of state cannot simply be elected by parliamentary assemblies, because experience demonstrates that they only choose one of their own members and never from among the best. He also cannot be elected by universal suffrage, because in a parliamentary system there will certainly be conflict between an Assembly and a President both elected by the people. So the way is clear: one is obliged to establish a special college' to elect the President, who would become the 'keystone' of the nation's political institutions.[34]

However, whereas Debré remained loyal to his conception of an adapted British parliamentary system, rejecting both presidentialism and government by Assembly, de Gaulle was adamantly opposed to the inordinate place of political parties in such a system. He regarded himself as the mediator between the people and France, a task for which parliamentary party leaders were unfit. The Third Republic had proved that true national leaders like Ferry, Waldeck-Rousseau and Clemenceau would not be permitted by party leaders to become President. The Second World War had allowed him to exercise power in an improvised personal manner.

33. Michel Debré, *Trois Républiques pour une France. Mémoires*, I. *Combattre*, Paris, 1984, p. 392.
34. These quotations come from the book Debré published with Emmanuel Monick (future Governor of the Bank of France) under their *noms de guerre* Jacquier-Bruère, *Refaire la France*, Paris, 1945, p. 122; cf. pp. 120-4. See also Shennan, pp. 118-24. The idea of a presidential electoral college had been suggested by Millerand in 1924.

During his Fourth Republic 'exile' from power, he recalled nostalgically: 'I was France, the State, the Government. I spoke for France. I was the independence and sovereignty of France. That was why, in fact, everyone obeyed me.'[35] To institutionalise and impart democratic legitimacy to presidential authority, he would ultimately demand that the people not merely ratify the constitution but themselves elect the President. In 1945-6, the task of devising new institutions was left to a Constitutent Assembly, de Gaulle momentously not following Debré's suggestion that he should propose a constitution to the French people.

Having resigned in protest at the resurrection of a regime that would repeat the errors of the Third Republic, de Gaulle – who had meanwhile been coached in constitutional law by René Cassin and René Capitant as well as interacting with Michel Debré – expounded in 1946 speeches at Bayeux and Epinal his conception of how a nation-state should be governed. Lacouture says of de Gaulle's 'Bayeux tapestry' that it took him two months to prepare, twelve years to contemplate and ten years to apply. Asserting the pre-eminence of state authority, this was to be embodied in the 'head of State, above parties, elected by a college including but much broader than parliament . . . from whom executive power would derive. The head of State's task is to harmonise the general interest as far as selecting people is concerned with the predominant political tendency that emerges from parliament. His mission is to appoint ministers, starting of course with the prime minister. The head of State promulgates laws and issues decrees . . . He is chairman of the governmental councils . . . He serves as arbiter over contingent political circumstances . . . If the country should be in peril, he has the duty of guaranteeing national independence.'[36] His speech was treated as a 'Bonapartist' declaration of war on the parliamentary and party-centred Republic. Léon Blum described it as demonstrating the 'temperamental incompatibility' between de Gaulle and democracy, and correctly predicted that it implied election of the President by universal suffrage, while Jacques Duclos waspishly referred to de Gaulle as Charles XI.[37]

35. Press conference of 7 April 1954, *Discours et Messages*, II, Paris, 1970, p. 617. For de Gaulle's hostile views on political parties, see Lacouture, *De Gaulle*, II, pp. 204, 224, 235, 239.
36. De Gaulle, *Discours et Messages*, II, p. 10. See also Lacouture, *De Gaulle*, II, pp. 269-73. On Debré's interaction with de Gaulle on constitutional matters from May 1945 to June 1946, see Jacques Boitreaud's testimony in Bernard Tricot *et al.*, *De Gaulle et le Service de l'Etat*, Paris, 1977, p. 100.
37. Lacouture, *De Gaulle*, II, pp. 41, 271-2, 551-2; cf. Léon Blum in *Le Populaire*, 21 June 1946. See also Lacouture, *De Gaulle. Le Souverain, 1959-1970*, III, Paris, 1986, 1990 paper edn p. 572.

The Party-centred Fourth Republic

Although the first draft constitution stopped short of abolishing the office of President, its holder would have been reduced to a cypher. This was one reason why it was rejected at the constitutional referendum. In the redrafted constitution which was approved, the principles were brought into line with the practice of the Third Republic. The President lost the formal power to summon and adjourn parliament, take legislative initiatives and negotiate treaties. The right to dissolve the Assembly was restricted. The President only selected the Prime Minister, who formed his government after receiving an investiture vote from the Assembly. While the President chaired the Council of Ministers, its agenda was prepared for the Prime Minister by the Secretary-General of the government. The latter prepared the minutes (none were kept during the Third Republic) subject to the control of the President, who quickly decided to reduce a full report stating the rival views to a simple list of decisions reached. The President acquired the new functions of Chairman of the High Council of the French Union and the Supreme Council of the Judiciary. However, the clear intention of the constitution-makers was to restore the situation under the Third Republic as Poincaré sourly described it: 'The President of the Republic presides and does not govern, that is the A, B, C of the parliamentary regime.' Or again, 'The Constitution states: article 1, The President can do anything he pleases. Article 2, He cannot decide anything without the authorisation of the Cabinet.'[38]

The first President of the Fourth Republic, Vincent Auriol, was to make much more of his role, becoming the most influential political personality in French public life.[39] He followed the classic Third Republic route of deputy, minister and President of the National Assembly. In a book written during the Second World War, he had criticised the Third Republic presidency, suggesting that the office of Prime Minister be abolished and executive power be concentrated in a strong President. He was to be elected by the Assembly at the start of the legislature (both serving for three years) with automatic dissolution of the Assembly in the event of serious disagreement.[40] However, he rejected de Gaulle's Bayeux-style

38. Quoted in Dansette, pp. 323–4; cf. 293–5 and Massot, pp. 45–6.
39. See the testimony of Philip Williams, *Crisis and Compromise. Politics in the Fourth Republic*, London, 1964, 3rd edn, pp. 197–201; Dansette, p. 301 and René Rémond, Preface to Vincent Auriol, *Journal du Septennat, 1947–54*, Paris, 1970, I, p. ix.
40. Vincent Auriol, *Hier . . . Demain*, Paris, 1945.

presidentialism as 'monocracy' in the manner of Napoleon III and MacMahon.

Unlike the Third Republic, parties now presented presidential candidates, a demonstration of the party-centred nature of the regime which was anathema to de Gaulle. Auriol's election on the first ballot by his own Socialist Party and the Communists was to an office that resembled the Third Republic presidency rather than the one he had personally favoured, but this did not prevent him from acquiring a much more important role in the working of the Fourth Republic than had been envisaged. In 1951 he was to describe his function as that of impartially exercising a 'moral magistracy . . . the advisory, warning, conciliatory power that should be that of the head of state' above the party battle,[41] as envisaged in Bagehot's conception of the monarch in *The English Constitution*.

It had been hoped that the Fourth Republic would be able to avoid the chronic government instability of its predecessors: ninety-eight administrations in sixty-five years. This was not to be the case, and Pierre Nora, in introducing Auriol's diary, comments on 'the central place occupied by the [government] crisis rituals, sinister in their litany, that he had to resolve, the Elysée constituting, in this sort of Cancer Institute of the Fourth Republic, the central laboratory in which political scientists can find the best of micro-scopes.'[42] Thus, after having been an 'active adviser' of his first Premier, Ramadier, meeting him before each Council of Ministers (still the current practice) and planning with him the tactics leading to the exclusion of the Communist ministers from the government, Auriol fought hard to keep him in office. He spent much time in preventing the Mollet-led SFIO from voting against a Socialist-led government it was failing to control through its Socialist ministers. The President finally yielded to Ramadier's pleas and party pressure. These old friends parted with tears, the outgoing Premier declaring to the President: 'You have been a father to me.'[43]

Having selected Robert Schuman as Premier, Auriol told him that he wanted no part in the choice of ministers but advised him not to take on any other portfolio himself. Nevertheless the President was involved in the tortuous negotiations concerning the selection

41. Speech of 15 November 1951 quoted in Dansette, p. 300. On the 'Bayeux Con-
    stitution' presidency, see Auriol, *Journal*, I, p. 33, remark dated 21 Jan. 1947.
    On the role of the Fourth Republic President, *ibid.*, I, p. 59.
42. *Ibid.*, p. xix; cf. 66, 311, 397–8, 405–7, 430–7.
43. *Ibid.*, p. 565; cf. 523–37, 561–5. When Mitterrand and Mauroy parted in 1984
    they both wept. Franz-Olivier Giesbert, *Le Président*, Paris, 1990, p. 214.

of the members of the Schuman government.[44] Part of the problem, as Auriol wrote in his diary, was that because 'there are 140 ex-ministers, the others ask themselves why they have not become or are not ministers.'[45] He continued the practice inaugurated by Félix Faure of consulting widely after the fall of each government. He made repeated attempts to prevent Premiers from resigning when they had not been constitutionally defeated, otherwise 'It is a party and not a parliamentary regime.'[46] Bidault at last having been defeated in 1950 by a constitutional majority, Auriol was furious when in 1951 Pleven resigned without having been overthrown according to the letter of the Constitution. As he confided to his diary: 'I wanted a vote, so that I could bring pressure to bear on parliament by threatening a dissolution.'[47]

Auriol tried to ensure that most controversial issues were settled before the Council of Ministers met. In 1947 he expressed annoyance at the number of unresolved disputes with which it had to deal. 'The Council of Ministers should confirm the agreements between the ministers concerned, arbitrated by the Premier.' 'In my opinion, the Council of Ministers should only deal with foreign policy matters and issues of principle. Details and more specialised matters should be worked out in Cabinet Council under the Premier's chairmanship. The Council of Ministers should only be concerned in cases of conflict that I have to arbitrate and for decisions that will become draft decrees or bills.'[48] As we shall see, this presidential function of 'arbitration' and guidance was to take on a markedly different character when exercised by de Gaulle.

Auriol made it quite clear that, unlike Lebrun in 1940, he would protect the Fourth Republic from threats against its survival from the Communists and the Gaullists by all means at his disposal: 'If I am an arbitrator between the parties, I am also a defender of the Republic, and impartiality does not require me to hand the Republic over to its enemies. Arbitrator between the republican parties that respect the Constitution: yes. Resolute enemy of those who wish to threaten our institutions: yes.'[49] As the Communist threat receded,

44. Auriol, *Journal*, pp. 578–84.
45. Auriol, *Mon Septennat, 1947–1954*, Paris, 1970, p. 583. This is the abridged version of his diary.
46. *Ibid.*, p. 223; cf. 157, 217.
47. *Ibid.*, p. 329; cf. 331. Lacouture, *De Gaulle*, II, p. 448 note, quotes Premier René Mayer as saying that 'The best time in the life of a government is when, after being defeated, it "deals with day-to-day business" without the fear of being overthrown.'
48. *Journal*, pp. 104, 335. On Auriol's insistence upon receiving all the Foreign Ministry telegrams, see *Mon Septennat*, pp. 289, 574.
49. *Mon Septennat*, p. 161, entry dated 10 Sept. 1948.

that from de Gaulle increased, partly owing to the lack of a stable majority in the National Assembly. Auriol refused suggestions in 1951 that he call on de Gaulle to form a government – 'another President will do so' – because he would not govern according to the Constitution, and 'I will not hand over the Republic to peril and the unknown . . .'[50] After the fall of a Pleven government, Auriol declared in an offensive analogy that he would not play the role of Hindenburg to the Fourth Republic by calling on de Gaulle, who would change the regime which it was Auriol's duty to preserve.[51] Instead, he used Pinay's appointment to the premiership in 1952 to split the Gaullist RPF parliamentary party, and when the Mayer premiership in 1953 completed this task, Auriol wrote in his diary: 'The RPF is broken and integrated into the [political] system. It was inevitable and I knew that my attitude and decisions would lead to this result.'[52] Nevertheless, he refused to stand again for the presidency, having lost confidence in the 'system' which he would have to defend. 'I fear that there will soon be a crisis which it will not be possible to resolve. My views have been in contradiction with the policy I have defended and this is difficult to sustain.'[53]

The semi-paralysis of the party-centred political system was spectacularly exemplified by the December 1953 election of Auriol's successor by the Congress of both chambers at Versailles. It required a damaging thirteen ballots before the obscure Senator René Coty was elected. He satisfied one of the characteristics which de Gaulle had attributed to a President in 1946. 'What, above all, is the purpose of a head of State? Certainly not to intervene constantly in the country's affairs. On the contrary, his role should be discreet and in appearance self-effacing: to take the initiative if necessary, keep things moving – but self-effacing.'[54] Well, Coty did not only appear self-effacing; he was self-effacing in the Third Republic tradition. No one would accuse de Gaulle of possessing this trait. Yet dramatic circumstances were to bring these two men together.

Like such authentic republicans as Pierre Mendès-France, Coty had discreetly contacted de Gaulle in 1956, but nothing came of such approaches until the May 1958 crisis that allowed de Gaulle to return to power on his own terms. Pompidou reports de Gaulle as saying about his eventual recall: 'I rely upon catastrophe rather than on

50. *Ibid.*, pp. 381, 385, entry dated 25 Sept. 1951.
51. *Ibid.*, p. 403; cf. 382, 402.
52. *Ibid.*, p. 504, entry dated 7 Jan. 1953.
53. *Ibid.*, p. 565, entry dated 8 Oct. 1953; cf. 519, 543.
54. Quoted by Jean Lacouture, *De Gaulle*, II, p. 283, from Claude Mauriac's report of his conversations with de Gaulle in *Aimer de Gaulle*, Paris, 1978, p. 339.

elections.'[55] Under the imminent threat of invasion of the mainland
by troops from Algeria, President Coty sent a message to parliament
on 29 May. He recalled de Gaulle's glorious role during the Second
World War, when 'having achieved national unanimity around him,
he rejected dictatorship to establish the Republic.' Coty called upon
de Gaulle to establish 'a government of national salvation' aimed at
achieving 'a fundamental reform of our institutions' and threatened
that if parliament did not accept this solution from its *'supreme
arbitrator'*, he would resign.[56] Faced with this unprecedented ulti-
matum and under the threat of military dictatorship, most of the
party leaders in parliament reluctantly yielded and, as de Gaulle put
it, 'the facts were accomplished.'[57]

   As Premier for seven months, while the new constitution was
prepared and elections held to parliament and the presidency, de
Gaulle did not bother to inform Coty about much of what he was
doing, particularly in foreign policy matters. On 8 January 1959, the
Constitution of the Fifth Republic having been approved by referendum, the newly-elected President took over from Coty, who may be
said to have chosen his successor although de Gaulle did not regard
Coty as his predecessor. Before the outgoing President accomplished the ultimate self-effacing formalities to cries of 'Thank you,
Coty' from the crowd, he said to de Gaulle: 'The first of the French
is now the first in France.' The new President declared that his intention was not to 'preside over [France's] sleep' but to mobilise popular
support for state-led action under his guidance.[58]

The Fifth Republic President: from Shakespearean Sovereign to Partisan Statesman

At the start of the Fifth Republic, the Constitution appeared to give
priority to the President's role as non-partisan arbitrator, above the
party battle, over that of committed leader of a party or coalition.
Yet, during the four presidencies we survey in this book, there have
been changes of emphasis within what is an equivocal, dualist
office. Although the direction of change has not been linear, it

55. Georges Pompidou, *Pour Rétablir une Vérité*, Paris, 1982, p. 73.
56. Quoted in Massot, p. 64; cf. 62–5. More generally, see Francis de Baecque, *René Coty, tel qu'en lui-même*, Paris, 1991.
57. Charles de Gaulle, *Mémoires d'Espoir*, p. 28.
58. Reported by de Gaulle, *ibid.*, p. 41; cf. 42. On all aspects of de Gaulle's career, see the November 1990 conference papers published by the Institut Charles de Gaulle, *De Gaulle en son siécle*, of which six massive volumes have appeared, Paris, 1991–2.

Table 1.1.   THE PRESIDENT AS LEADER OF THE MAJORITY
OR ABOVE PARTY (%)

	de Gaulle	*Pompidou*	*Giscard d'Estaing*	*Mitterrand*
Leader of the Majority	29	55	71	66
Above party	62	28	17	24
No opinion	9	17	12	10

Source: SOFRES, 'De Gaulle en son Siècle', Feb. 1990, p. 15.

has resulted in an increasing partisanisation of the office, which
threatens the President's capacity to embody a supra-partisan state
function.

A century after his birth and twenty years after his death, de
Gaulle's standing with French public opinion as a dead republican
hero was measured. In the 1990 opinion poll referred to in Table 1.1
he emerged as second only to Charlemagne as the most important
person in French history. Although de Gaulle's wartime role was his
salient characteristic, 88 per cent approved of his institution of the
direct election of the President, higher even than his 18 June 1940
appeal in favour of resistance (84 per cent). Although, virtually
across all parties, more people regarded de Gaulle as a Right-winger
than as someone who was above ideological disputes, he was
undoubtedly considered to be the most non-partisan of the four
Presidents. As Table 1.1 shows, only de Gaulle, by a majority of
over 2 : 1, was regarded as above party. Giscard, even more than
Pompidou, emerged as a highly partisan figure, with his explicit
presidential programme and public directives to the Prime Minister,
while by 1990 Mitterrand had somewhat readjusted his image,
without beginning to approach de Gaulle's Jove-like elevation above
the party battle.

De Gaulle himself drew a clear distinction between presidential
elections, in which he scrupulously avoided party links, and parliamentary elections when he was willing to support his partisans
explicitly. Pompidou, who as Prime Minister had assumed the
de facto leadership of the parliamentary majority and oversight
of party management, continued to take a very close interest in
party affairs after his election to the presidency in 1969. Lacking
de Gaulle's historic legitimacy, Pompidou leaned upon majority
partisan support as his sole claim to presidential power. Giscard was
elected in 1974, thanks particularly to the defection of Chirac
from the Gaullist candidacy of Chaban-Delmas. Although he later
created the Right-Centre *Union pour la Démocratie Française*
confederation, Giscard did not command the support of a reliable
parliamentary majority for long once Chirac ceased to be Prime

Minister in 1976. So he did not succeed in fulfilling either the role
of supra-partisan or that of effective leader of the majority coalition, which partly accounts for his failure to win re-election in 1981.

Mitterrand has the distinction of having stood in all the direct
elections to the presidency except that of 1969. In 1965, he could
plausibly claim that he was a candidate 'neither of a party nor of a
coalition'.[59] This was not true after he became First Secretary of
the Socialist Party in 1971. When he was elected President at the
third attempt in 1981, he was clearly the Socialist candidate on
the first ballot and that of the Left on the second ballot. From the
mid-1980s, Mitterrand shifted the emphasis, within his dualist role,
to the function of supra-partisan, national leader. This was made
particularly necessary by the 1986–8 period of *cohabitation* with a
hostile Prime Minister and parliamentary majority. The change of
emphasis nevertheless persisted in part after his 1988 re-election
against a hyper-partisan Chirac and the return of a relative Socialist
majority at the subsequent Assembly election. The stress upon presidential detachment from day-to-day politics was underlined by the
appointment of his former rival Michel Rocard as Prime Minister
and by Mitterrand's concentration on foreign and defence policy
during the 1990–1 period of the Gulf crisis and war. Nevertheless,
of all four Presidents, Mitterrand has been the least inclined to mask
his political affiliation. So, the polarisation between monarchical
and partisan presidential functions, if not usually explicit, has been
clearer than ever before.

While de Gaulle confided in a letter to his son written in 1961
that the unprecedented regime he had established and sought to
perpetuate was a 'popular monarchy',[60] there was a purely personal
aspect that derived from the heroic role he had played during the
Second World War. Unlike the venerable monarchical state of the
Kings, based upon traditional authority, and the ephemeral imperial authority of the Bonapartes, which could not survive military
defeat, it was out of military defeat that de Gaulle built a republican authority that incorporated France's warring legacies. He
recalled that it was without benefit of 'hereditary right, without
plebiscite, without election, answering the imperative but mute
appeal of France alone, that I was previously led to take command
of its defence, its unity and its destiny.'[61] De Gaulle would have
preferred the designation 'Head of State' rather than President

59. François Mitterrand, *Politique. Textes et Discours, 1938–1981*, 1981, Paris,
    Marabout edn 1984, p. 281.
60. Charles de Gaulle, *Lettres, Notes et Carnets*, IX, Paris, 1986, p. 94.
61. *Mémoires d'Espoir*, p. 289.

of the Republic,[62] and remained throughout his years in office happier with his temporary military title of General. Obsessed by the view that the democratic republic had decapitated and depersonalised political power, de Gaulle was determined to recapitate it. This meant that the personal authority of the ruler had to be legitimised by popular support, hence the primordial importance de Gaulle attached to the referendum and popular election of the President, especially as far as his successors were concerned. He proudly declared that he had given the Fifth Republic 'for origin, basis and mainspring the direct agreement of the people and its guide'.[63]

Through the way he fashioned the practical operation of France's new institutions, de Gaulle set a pattern that was subsequently modified rather than fundamentally changed. Although the anti-partisan statesman's stance he adopted led him to maintain more of a reality and less of a pretence of impartiality than were possible for his successors, he made it abundantly clear from the start that the Fifth Republic President would be in command. By contrast with the formal powers of the Fourth Republic Presidents, 'henceforth, the head of State is really at the head of affairs, really responsible for France and the Republic. He really chooses the government and presides at its meetings, he really makes civil, military and judicial appointments, he is really the head of the armed forces. In brief, every important decision and all authority derives from him. He can at will dissolve the National Assembly, propose any law on the organisation of the public authorities to be decided by the people by referendum, that in case of serious internal or external crisis, he can take whatever measures are required by the circumstances'; whereas the Prime Minister, 'only deriving from the President, whose role is capital, can naturally only act on serious matters after receiving his directives'.[64]

Michel Debré, whose key role in the constitution-making we examine in the next chapter, was appointed by de Gaulle as the first Prime Minister of the Fifth Republic with the words: 'You made the Constitution, now it is up to you to apply it.'[65] Debré subsequently made it clear that they did not see eye to eye on their respective roles, because whereas he wished to operate a genuine duality of executive

---

62. Debré reports that de Gaulle yielded to objections, led by Guy Mollet, because of the guilt by association with Vichy. See Debré's *Mémoires*, II, Paris, 1988, p. 374.
63. *Mémoires d'Espoir, L'Effort*, p. 352. On the notion of the President as guide, see *Discours et Messages*, III, pp. 64, 269, 275 and Georges Burdeau, *Traité de Science Politique*, X, 2nd edn, 1976, pp. 52–65.
64. *Mémoires d'Espoir, Le Renouveau*, pp. 37–8.
65. Debré, *Mémoires*, III, p. 12.

power, de Gaulle emphasised its unity, with the Prime Minister in a subordinate capacity. Having had to take command during the desperate struggle to settle the Algerian problem, in which Debré was overruled in all matters relating to an act of decolonisation with which he was in disagreement, de Gaulle aspired to decide in all matters. Debré recalled: 'In 1959, the General had accepted a parliamentary form of government. Two years later, the "presidentialisation" of the regime took shape . . . the General was tending personally to command . . . he was maturing in his mind the constitutional doctrine that he would strikingly assert in his 14 January 1964 press conference.'[66] While the tone was more regally absolutist than the reality, de Gaulle asserted that 'the indivisible authority of the state is wholly confided to the President by the people, who elected him, and that there is no other authority, be it ministerial, civil, military or judicial, which is not conferred or maintained by him. Finally, he adapts his own supreme sphere of action to those whose execution he delegates to others. Nevertheless, normally, it is essential to preserve the distinction between the function and sphere of action of the head of state and that of the Prime Minister.'[67] Despite the qualification in the last sentence, what former parliamentarian Debré found unpalatable in the subordination of Prime Minister to President, the more pliable Pompidou – at least initially – accepted without question.

De Gaulle appreciated Pompidou's sound judgement and dispassionate discretion, so that although he was appointed to his staff thanks to the *Normalien* old boy network after the Second World War, he quickly won his confidence. 'At 34, without any political past, without any Resistance record, this former schoolteacher was installed at the heart of the state machine, a modest collaborator but still a collaborator of the leader of Free France.'[68] Elevating prudence to the supreme virtue, never himself taking risks, he profited from those of others, so that after a period in the Rothschild Bank, he became Director of de Gaulle's *cabinet* in 1958 after others had helped the General back to power. His capacity as a fixer made him an efficiently unobtrusive instrument of the presidential will. Refusing the office of Finance Minister, he returned to the Rothschild Bank until summoned in 1962 to replace Debré as Prime Minister.

66. *Ibid.*, p. 447; cf. 409, 448.
67. Charles de Gaulle, *Discours et Messages*, IV, p. 168.
68. Eric Roussel, *Georges Pompidou*, Paris, 1984, p. 61; cf. 58 and testimony of René Brouillet and Olivier Guichard in *Georges Pompidou. Hier et Aujourd'hui*, Neuilly sur Seine, 1990, pp. 19–32. For de Gaulle's portrait of Pompidou – regarded by its subject as a posthumous 'execution' – see *Mémoires d'Espoir*, pp. 363–4.

Emerging from the backroom patronage politics at which he had excelled, this political unknown had to be shown how to find his way around the Assembly. Owing all to de Gaulle, he accepted without demur the increasing presidential intervention which Debré had resented as a deviation from the letter of the Constitution. Thus he accepted de Gaulle's directive not to hold formal meetings of ministers other than in the Council of Ministers,[69] although he sometimes informally entertained them to lunch. Pompidou, however, provided de Gaulle with the solid party majority that he had hitherto lacked, in the process replacing heroic Gaullism with partisan Gaullism. He thereby prepared the way for the transformation of the Gaullist phenomenon into the stepping-stone for his own assumption of power.[70] Having learned from the RPF era how to manipulate a party from outside its ranks, Pompidou as Prime Minister and President steadily increased his control over the successive incarnations of partisan Gaullism. For in the 1973 general election campaign Pompidou controlled everything through his choice as UDR Secretary-General, Alain Peyrefitte, personally selecting not merely the candidates and the programme but even the slogans and the posters. As such, he demonstrated that he was a consummate political tactician in the service of his role as a surreptitiously partisan statesman.

The only Prime Minister thus far to become President, Pompidou believed that holding the premiership destined him for the presidency. As he confessed in 1967, 'In my heart, I know I am condemned to politics, whether as President of the Republic or Opposition deputy. As far as preparing myself to be President is concerned, I have been doing it after a fashion from dawn to dusk' since becoming Prime Minister.[71] Bitterly disappointed when de Gaulle chose to stand at the 1965 presidential election, his ambitions were merely postponed. The years 1968-9 proved to be decisive for Pompidou. In May 1968, he made up for de Gaulle's failure to deal effectively with the crisis, having learned the lessons of his own failure in the case of the 1963 miners' strike. When all about him seemed to take leave of their senses, Pompidou handled the unpredictable situation calmly. He dissuaded de Gaulle from calling a referendum, substituting a general election that proved to be a

---

69. See testimony of Roger Belin, Secretary-General of the government from 1958-64, in *Georges Pompidou*, pp. 99-100; cf. 97-8, 111.
70. Jean Charlot, *Le phénomène gaulliste*, 1970, especially pp. 14, 37; cf, Roussel, pp. 77-80, 213-16, 229-30, 418-20, 479, 483.
71. Pompidou interview of 11 Sept. 1967, quoted by Pierre Viannson-Ponté, *Histoire de la République gaullienne*, Paris, 1971, II, p. 363; cf. 364. See also Alain Peyrefitte's testimony in *Georges Pompidou*, pp. 288-9.

political masterstroke. It earned Pompidou both the gratitude of
the partisan majority and dismissal from power because he now
existed in his own political right.[72] De Gaulle appears to have
planned to retire at eighty and to have told Pompidou of this intention in January 1969, before Pompidou's visit to Rome at which
he declared that he would be a candidate to succeed de Gaulle.[73]
Coming during the run-up to the referendum defeat that led to the
President's resignation, this declaration has been widely regarded as
having contributed – however unintentionally – to that result.

The 1969 presidential election proved decisive, not merely in
securing the transition from heroic to humdrum Gaullism; it also
ensured the survival of the Fifth Republic. The contrast was stark
between the Fourth Republic style of Alain Poher, squandering
twelve crucial days in negotiating with the opposition parties (and
in the process losing the support of Giscard), and Pompidou's
personal candidacy, followed by the support of the UDR and other
parties. As Duverger put it at the time: 'What are really at stake in
the battle between M. Pompidou and M. Poher are the institutions
[of the Fifth Republic]. Both would carry out almost the same policy
but they would exercise the presidential function in different ways,
almost leading to two opposed regimes.'[74] While Poher, without a
parliamentary majority, seemed reconciled to the prospect of
cohabitation, willing to act in a minimalist, non-partisan manner,
Pompidou made clear that he would accentuate the maximalist
presidential style, and his victory was a momentous vindication of
this standpoint.

In the ten-month interval between ceasing to be Prime Minister
and being elected President, Pompidou wrote a short book which
contains some premonitory remarks about the relationship between
the holders of these two offices. Because government 'business goes
first to Matignon, which constantly intervenes to guide and choose,
so that there is a danger of "dyarchy" emerging', this should be
avoided at all costs, decision belonging to one person alone, the
President. After de Gaulle, is there not a danger of 'a gradual
shift of real power to the Prime Minister? Such a development
would be disastrous. From the day when the real holder of power
is the man responsible to the National Assembly, a return to government by Assembly would be unavoidable, despite precautions and

72. Roussel, pp. 247–84.
73. Testimony of General Alain de Boissieu in *Georges Pompidou*, p. 181; cf.
    testimony of Jacques Foccart, *op. cit.*, pp. 173–5.
74. *Le Monde*, 20 May 1969. More generally, see Françoise Decaumont, *La
    Présidence de Georges Pompidou. Essai sur le Régime Présidentialiste Français*,
    Paris, 1979, pp. 34, 46–51.

appearances.' To preclude this danger, Presidents must choose as their Prime Ministers people 'who are closely linked to them, not only politically but intellectually and personally, from whom they would never have cause to fear . . . competition. I am convinced that future Presidents will be led to intervene constantly and permanently in the direction of the State and maintain by day-to-day action the supremacy that they will not automatically have on personal grounds. In short, I believe that we have no alternative to a covert but rapid return to government by Assembly other than the accentuation of the presidential character of our institutions.'[75] We have no further to seek than this statement for the subsequent clash between Pompidou and his first choice as Prime Minister, chosen because he was complementary to the President rather than because their views coincided.

Chaban-Delmas was all that Pompidou was not, but most notably a link with heroic Gaullism. He tried to treat the President as an equal, stealing the limelight with his 'New Society' programme in a keynote speech which was drafted by Simon Nora and only finished two hours before being delivered in the Assembly, so that Pompidou was faced with a *fait accompli*. Quite apart from disliking its 'Left-Centre' tone, the taciturn Pompidou as a former Prime Minister thought he knew better than the exuberant Chaban-Delmas what should be done. Although it was undoubtedly the case that the presidential adviser Pierre Juillet worked assiduously to undermine the Prime Minister, helped inside the parliamentary party by Chaban's successor Pierre Messmer,[76] nevertheless the incompatibility of Pompidou and Chaban was much more fundamental than these machinations alone would indicate. Like Pompidou in 1968, Chaban was dismissed for threatening the President's supremacy and seeking to force his hand,[77] a lesson learnt for example by Michel Rocard. Such conflicts have led to the substitution of independent-minded politicians by Prime Ministers more willing to accept and carry out the President's policies: Pompidou for Debré, and Couve de Murville for Pompidou, by de Gaulle; Messmer for Chaban by Pompidou; Barre for Chirac by Giscard; and Fabius for Mauroy, and Cresson for Rocard, by Mitterrand. In May 1972 matters came to a head when Chaban-Delmas secured an Assembly vote of confidence by 268 to 96 on the general policy of the government. Pompidou warned him: 'Be careful, you have infringed upon

75. Georges Pompidou, *Le Noeud Gordien*, Paris, 1974, pp. 63–5.
76. Roussel, pp. 350–4, 395–400, 418–20. For an excellent study of this instructive episode see Samy Cohen, *Les Conseillers du Président*, Paris, 1980, chapter 7, *passim*.
77. Decaumont, pp. 110–18.

my constitutional powers'[78], and dismissed him from office shortly afterwards for seeking to substitute the Assembly's confidence for that of the President.

The colourless, uninspiring and unimaginative Pierre Messmer having (at Juillet's instigation) been appointed Prime Minister, power shifted even more completely to the ailing President and his entourage, Pompidou and Juillet not merely choosing most of his ministers but the director and members of his personal staff. When Pompidou reshuffled the Messmer government in February 1974, the Prime Minister declared: 'The President of the Republic gave me his directives on the composition of a new government.'[79] Decision-making shifted from the interministerial committees chaired by the Prime Minister (at which Pompidou had required the presence of a member of his staff) to the interministerial councils chaired by the President.[80] Pompidou placed particular emphasis upon industrial policy, which was reflected not only in the number of interministerial councils devoted to it but also in the centrality of the industrial theme of numerous speeches, visits abroad and lunches or dinners at home, amounting (as a leading industrialist put it) to 'absolutely unfailing support'.[81] Because industrial policy had widespread implications, it was a factor in extending detailed presidential intervention into many public policies.

The 1972 French referendum on British entry to the European Community (EC), a key feature of his European policy, failed to provide Pompidou with the renewed popular support he sought, the President having prudently not linked his fate to the result, so Pompidou sought to reinforce presidential legitimacy by reducing the duration of the President's term of office from seven to five years. Whereas de Gaulle had wanted to separate presidential and parliamentary elections so that the President could remain above the party battle, Pompidou saw the need to keep the President and parliamentary majority in step. However, whereas Mitterrand was then seeking a reduction in the President's term of office together with a *reduction* in his powers, Pompidou saw it as a corollary of the *increase* in his powers. In the event, the constitutional amendment appeared unlikely to secure a three-fifths majority of both chambers sitting together in Versailles, and Pompidou's plans thus

78. Roussel, p. 465; cf. 463–8.
79. Quoted in Dansette, p. 406. See more generally Roussel, pp. 470–2, 480 and Decaumont, pp. 190–7.
80. Decaumont, pp. 165–8.
81. Testimony of Pierre Jouven, ex-President Director General of Péchiney, in *Georges Pompidou*, p. 240. See *ibid.*, Bernard Esambert on industrial policy, pp. 226–7, 238–9.

remained unrealised when he died in 1974. After some hesitation, Giscard decided to preserve the seven-year presidential term.[82]

Pompidou and Giscard had come into sharp conflict as Prime Minister and Finance Minister over the 1963 Economic Stabilisation Plan imposed by de Gaulle, Pompidou eventually getting rid of Giscard – a potential presidential rival – in 1966. The two Auvergnats were sharply contrasted in terms of their social backgrounds: Pompidou the *petit bourgeois*, Giscard the *grand bourgeois*; Pompidou the literary *Normalien*, Giscard the *Polytechnique* and *Ecole Nationale d'Administration* techno-bureaucrat. Giscard reluctantly rallied to Pompidou in 1969, being rewarded with a return to the Finance Ministry. Giscard triumphed at the 1974 presidential election thanks to the betrayal of the Gaullist Chaban-Delmas by Pompidou's protégé Jacques Chirac, described as 'one of the most perfidious and most effective destructions of a politician recorded in history'.[83] Ironically Giscard, who had played an important part in de Gaulle's defeat in 1969 by criticising his 'solitary exercise of power', was himself to become a monocrat overnight on assuming presidential office. (As the same process would be observed in the case of Mitterrand, the nature of the office rather than personality predispositions would seem to be crucial to the transformation.) However, while Giscard sought to domineer, he lacked the support of a majority party in the Assembly that would allow him to impose his will. He was therefore condemned to adopt the role of the pseudo-consensual statesman, presupposing a non-existent predominant socio-political centrism. He was compelled to practise a tender-minded appeasement of Chirac, his former accomplice and future rival.[84]

Both of these features are evident in his 1976 book *Démocratie Française*, which was the simplistic ideological launching-pad for the loose Giscardian confederation of his own Republican Party, the CDS residue of Christian Democrats, and the conservative wing of the old Radical Party, which combined in 1978 to form the Union for French Democracy, the UDF. Such driving force as it had came from Giscard's *Perspectives et Réalités* clubs, but apart from selecting common candidates the UDF lacked the organisation and

82. Dansette, pp. 403–4 and Decaumont, pp. 25–8, 61, 76–90, 199–216, 462–8.
83. Dansette, p. 409. More generally, see Pierre Rouanet, *Le Cas Chaban*, Paris, 1974 and Jacques Chaban-Delmas, *L'Ardeur*, Paris, 1975. On the Pompidou-Giscard conflicts, see Roussel, pp. 167–72, 201.
84. On Giscard's 'sociological centrism', see Valéry Giscard d'Estaing, *Towards a New Democracy*, 1976, English transl. 1977, London, pp. 45–7. On the conflicts with Chirac, see Françoise Giroud, *La Comédie du Pouvoir*, Paris, 1977, pp. 34, 41–2, 49–50, 94, 98–9, 128, 187–9, 210.

discipline capable of dominating the post-Gaullist RPR that Chirac had created as the vehicle for his 1981 presidential candidature. The most humiliating demonstration of Giscard's partisan weakness occurred with the 1977 election of Chirac as the Mayor of Paris, Giscard having restored the office which had been abolished after the overthrow of the Commune in 1871. What he had hoped would become his power-base instead became that of his main Right-wing rival. The pathetic pretence that moderation and mutual tolerance would suffice were exposed as wishful thinking. That Giscard did not learn the lessons of his past experience is clear from a post-presidential book, which has been brutally but accurately described as 'institutionalising the experience of his own impotence'.[85] Giscard never demonstrated the party management skills of Pompidou and Mitterrand or even showed a grasp of their necessity.

Giscard deserves the credit for some important advances that were not partisan in character such as reducing the voting age to eighteen, increasing women's rights, expanding the role of the Constitutional Council and improving decision-making within the EC. Nevertheless, Giscard found it more difficult than either his predecessors or his successor to reconcile his dual role as the neutral President of all the French people and the partisan President of a winning coalition. Faced with the prospect of a Left-wing victory at the 1978 Assembly elections, Giscard made a revealing speech, proclaiming: 'The President of the Republic is not a partisan, he is not a party leader . . . He is both an arbitrator and the person responsible' for the nation's fate. 'As arbitrator, I shall express myself with moderation . . . As the person responsible, I shall speak to you of the correct choice.' Having attacked the Left's Common Programme, he went on: 'If you choose it, it will be applied. Do not believe that the President has the constitutional means of preventing its application.'[86] While he did not have to do so – thanks to the split on the Left deliberately engineered by the Communist Party, rather than to his own exertions – Giscard subsequently failed to overcome the threat from Chirac, so that at his third attempt François Mitterrand won the presidential election in 1981 and parts of the Left's Common Programme were implemented.

As the most overtly partisan President of the four, François Mitterrand was least inclined to hypocrisy and equivocation over the

---

85. Olivier Duhamel, 'La Nouvelle République de M. Giscard d'Estaing', *Le Monde*, 11 April 1984. This is the second of three articles on Giscard's *Deux Français sur Trois*, Paris, 1984, which inter alia proposed reducing the presidential term to six years.
86. Speech at Verdun-sur-le-Doubs, 27 Jan. 1978, appended to Giscard's memoir *Le Pouvoir et la Vie*, I, Paris, 1988, pocket edn, pp. 402–3.

dual role of the office, especially before he was elected President. Thus, while pointing out the contradiction – 'One cannot be both the referee and the captain of one of the teams' – implicit in Giscard's Verdun-sur-le-Doubs speech, a 'right choice' meaning that the alternative was the 'wrong choice', Mitterrand gave a realistic description of the situation. 'The President of the Republic is improperly but in fact the head of the executive and has always been the leader of the majority . . . The President of the Republic, whatever he says and whatever he does, is a committed man . . . He attempts to combine the role of presidential President that he is in reality and the role of arbiter-President that he pretends to be.'[87] Grévy had occupied in the 1880s the office of President he had voted against (both in 1848 and 1875); Mitterrand went further. He expanded rather than restricted the role of the President in the 1980s. Olivier Duhamel has shown that as early as his first presidential campaign of 1965, the polemicist of *The Permanent Coup d'Etat* had implicitly accepted all the powers of the Fifth Republic President other than those of article 16. His acceptance of the President's political supremacy 'could not be explicitly formulated, since those of his supporters who wished to believe the opposite had to be allowed to continue to do so.'[88] This tactical skill in employing the election campaign to concentrate upon the misuse of presidential power by appealing to the letter of the Constitution allowed Mitterrand to steer the Left towards a *de facto* acceptance of the new institutions, including the direct election of the President, which had initially been castigated as promoting 'personal power'. His seven options and twenty-eight propositions of 1965 anticipated his 110 propositions of 1981 and his much vaguer 'Letter to the French' of 1988 which ensured that it was his programme which mattered, not those of the parties that supported him. In this sense, the 1974 debate with Giscard over whether or not they had made a 'contract' with the electors was secondary.[89] It was the link between presidential candidate and the voters rather than with the parties that was of decisive importance.

Mitterrand's parliamentary debate with Pompidou in 1964 on the relative powers of the President and the Prime Minister helped to establish Pompidou as de Gaulle's *dauphin* and Mitterrand as the Left's challenger even before the 1965 election. Pompidou's description of Mitterrand – 'neither a man of the Left nor a man of the

87. Quoted from Olivier Duhamel, *La Gauche et la Ve République*, Paris, 1980, p. 455.
88. *Ibid.*, p. 258; cf. 254–60, 280.
89. *Ibid.*, p. 281 reporting a Radio Luxembourg Giscard-Mitterrand debate on 2 May 1974.

Right, an adventurer' – contains a kernel of truth.[90] In the manner of Henry IV, Mitterrand thought the presidency was worth a Socialist mass. His pragmatic attitude is revealed by a remark made in 1972 that helps to explain the ease with which he adapted to the presidential office he at last attained in 1981. 'Experience has taught me that institutions are good or bad according to the person or people who apply them.'[91] His grasp of the partisan realities was demonstrated by promptly carrying out a 1965 pledge to follow up his presidential victory by dissolving the National Assembly, so that he would acquire the support of a parliamentary majority.

Both de Gaulle and Mitterrand have had the capacity to attract the indestructible loyalty of a group of supporters, more like feudal barons than liberal democratic leaders. Mitterrand took pains in the 1970s and early 1980s to disguise this with republican rhetoric and Socialist shibboleths, but in the faction battles for control of the Socialist Party, reliance upon the fealty of his partisans has always been an essential feature of his manner of winning and wielding power. The programmatic urge to offer five fundamental choices in 1974 after his seven fundamental choices and twenty-eight propositions of 1965 and before the 110 propositions of 1981 were the tactical packaging for party, press and public consumption of a profoundly private and pragmatic personality. For example, having noticed that the Communist presidential candidate George Marchais had proposed a 131-point plan in November 1980, Mitterrand asked Michel Charasse at short notice to produce 'something similar in about a hundred propositions. Take the Common Programme, the Socialist Project, make a complete catalogue and we shall select afterwards.'[92] Out of an initial list of 270, the 110 campaign propositions were worked out between Mitterrand and Charasse. Most of them were implemented after 1981. We are a long way here from de Gaulle's refusal even to campaign for the first round of the 1965 presidential election.

Despite the many things they have had in common, it is essential to grasp that 'mitterrandism is born of anti-gaullism'.[93] The Fifth

90. Remark to Georges Suffert, quoted in Roussel, p. 184. For extracts from the important Mitterrand-Pompidou debate in 1964, see Martin Harrison, *French Politics*, Lexington, Mass., 1969, pp. 68–76.
91. Duhamel, p. 468 note, quoting Mitterrand's *La Rose et le Poing*, Paris, 1973, p. 134.
92. Reported in Pierre Favier and Michel Martin-Roland, *La Décennie Mitterrand, I: Les Ruptures (1981–84)*, Paris, 1990, p. 108.
93. Alain Duhamel, *De Gaulle-Mitterrand. La marque et la trace*, Paris, 1991, p. 37; cf. chapter 1, *passim*. On de Gaulle's hostility to Mitterrand, see Catherine Nay, *Le Noir et le Rouge ou l'histoire d'une ambition*, 1984, pocket edn, p. 157; cf. 153–4, 158–9, 175.

Republic has been moulded by the practice of its main challenger, second only to that of its founder. Unlike Pompidou and Giscard, who could be absorbed in the routine of day-to-day decision-making, de Gaulle and Mitterrand seemed to require big challenges to give of their imperious best, the former in an epic, the latter in a lyrical style. Superlative orators and wordsmiths both, de Gaulle's painstakingly crafted prose contrasted with Mitterrand's more fitful improvisations, but they were both capable of the illuminating evocation, the inspiring appeal or the devastating *coup de grâce*, drawing upon the resources of a vast literary and historical culture. Both were rebels, but whereas de Gaulle was identified with a refusal to accept national servitude, Mitterrand embodied the rejection of citizen servitude. In the event, despite the personal incompatibility of these champions of a traditional, non-capitalist France, they used a reconstituted presidential authority to modernise their country so that its historic role as a world power could, as far as possible, be preserved, at the cost of eliminating much that they valued.

Reflecting upon his first seven-year term in 1988, Mitterrand sought to show that he had deliberately reduced the extent and intensity of presidential intervention which had grown during the Fifth Republic, bringing practice more into line with the Constitution. 'The President of the Republic, who did not do everything, could do everything. So it is not surprising that the regime, which remained in principle parliamentary, suffered from imbalance. I knew when I arrived at the Elysée that the search for this balance would be one of my most important tasks. I gradually reduced the daily flood of matters which should not have invaded the President's office. It was only the start of a restoration of order that still seems to me to be necessary.'[94] His aim was to overcome the institutionalised ambiguity of the President's role by steering a middle way between 'the function of arbitrator and the function of authority . . . Neither the rubber-stamp President of the Fourth Republic, nor the all-commanding President of the Fifth Republic, but a President who chooses the road for the nation to follow, in matters in which its security, its place in the world, its freedoms, its continuity are at stake.'[95]

This is very close to de Gaulle's conception of presidential *guidance*, but Mitterrand was unable to restore the rather Olympian style it implied immediately. De Gaulle had been involved more intimately in daily decision-making than he had anticipated because

94. Mitterrand interviewed by Olivier Duhamel, 'Sur les Institutions' in *Pouvoirs*, no. 45 (April 1988), p. 131; cf. p. 62 quoting a Mitterrand broadcast of 9 Dec. 1986 on Europe 1.
95. *Ibid.*, p. 137.

of the Algerian war, which remained unresolved until 1962. The Socialists had been out of office for more than twenty years, so it was only after they had acquired experience of ministerial office during the government of 1984–6 headed by his protégé Laurent Fabius that Mitterrand was able to adopt his intended presidential style, rather than during the Mauroy government of 1981–4. Of the 1986–8 period, Mitterrand tartly remarked that 'M. Chirac often thought he was snatching from me powers that I had already reallocated.'[96] Partly as a perpetuation of this evolution, the appointment as Prime Minister of Michel Rocard – Mitterrand's erstwhile rival and possible successor – involved an uneasy coexistence, punctuated by presidential interventions and admonitions. The least that can be said of Rocard's resignation in May 1991 was that, like its Fifth Republic predecessors, it did not conform with Mitterrand's assertion that 'the Prime Minister, who applies the policy of the parliamentary majority, can only be dismissed by it.'[97] At least Mitterrand appears not to have demanded of his Prime Ministers an unsigned letter of resignation as de Gaulle did of Pompidou, and Pompidou of Messmer, and which Chirac proffered in 1974 to Giscard without it being requested.[98] Even before the appointment of the Cresson government in 1991, Mitterrand had conspicuously taken personal control of all matters involved in the Gulf war, and this – in conjunction with the Socialist Party's conspicuous incapacity to prepare for the electoral battles to come – led Mitterrand to take a much more active part in detailed decision-making than he would ostensibly have preferred.

Whether he is reticently anti-partisan like de Gaulle, covertly partisan like Pompidou, pseudo-consensual like Giscard or overtly partisan like Mitterrand, the presidential statesman seems impelled to act like a republican sovereign. In the next chapter we recount how the practical problem of converting the permanently subversive constituent power of the nation into the sole legitimate basis of political authority has been resolved. The sheer difficulty of this achievement accounts for the obsessive urge to tinker with its institutions that characterises the French political class in the intervals between its electoral struggles for power, indicative of a congenital reluctance to accept that the centrepiece of their institutions should

96. *Ibid.*, p. 132.
97. *Ibid.*, p. 136. On the difficult relations between Mitterrand and Rocard, see Jean-Pierre Liégeois and Jean-Pierre Bédéï, *Le Feu et l'Eau*, Paris, 1990 and Thierry Pfister's three articles on 'Le couple impossible' in *Le Figaro*, 17–19 April 1991.
98. On this 1974 episode, see Valéry Giscard d'Estaing, *Le Pouvoir et la Vie*, II, Paris, 1991, p. 30.

be the instrument of reform rather than its object. Mitterrand's own ambivalence is reflected in his post-1981 remarks: 'The institutions were not designed with me in mind but they suit me' and 'The institutions? With anyone else but me they are dangerous. They were before me and they will be once again after me.'[99] While allowance must be made for his self-serving rhetoric, Mitterrand's characterisations of the role of the Fifth Republic President are not merely the consequences of political calculation. They remind us that 'the institutions' can work in more ways than one and that each President plays a pivotal role in determining how they will work.

99. 'Un entretien avec M. François Mitterrand', *Le Monde*, 2 July 1981 and quotation in Nay, p. 408.

2

THE PRESIDENT AND THE CONSTITUTION: ITS SPIRIT, ARTICLES AND PRACTICE

Jack Hayward

With the foundation of the Fifth Republic, 'after having tried out over a century and a half all possible systems, we have adopted a Constitution pregnant with almost every system.'[1] While such a sweeping judgement rightly draws attention to the highly complex and flexible nature of France's political system, by contrast with its past preference for simple and rigid systems, it does not focus attention sufficiently on the peculiar character of the hybrid constitutional amalgam it incorporates.

The Revolution's abrupt substitution of the nation for royal sovereignty as the sovereign constituent power enduringly destabilised French governments. The failure to establish a British-style constitutional monarchy (itself the product of a revolutionary process that was mastered) meant ninety years of regime instability. The Third Republic provided such stability at the cost of reducing state power to a minimum and preserving the socio-economic *status quo*. To break this state-denying stalemate required the cataclysm of military defeat in 1940 and de Gaulle's achievement of a fusion between the monarchist tradition of state authority and the Revolutionary tradition of democratic nationalism. '. . . It was left to a man brought up to respect monarchy to sustain and finally restore a republican regime for which, as such, he felt neither respect nor spontaneous enthusiasm but which appeared to him to be the only modern form of unity.'[2] The state-building Frankish monarchy of the early Middle Ages was formally elective, but this fiction masked a combination of force and heredity with the consent of the grandees and the consecration of the bishops. Hugues Capet's seizure of the throne in 987 was accompanied by election, but thereafter the hereditary principle replaced election – until the replacement of

1. Olivier Duhamel, 'L'hypothèse de la contradiction des majorités en France' in Maurice Duverger (ed.), *Les Régimes Semi-Présidentiels*, Paris, 1986, p. 271.
2. Jean-Paul Cointet, 'De Gaulle et la République ou la double reconnaissance, 1940–44' in P. Isoart and C. Bidegaray (eds), *Des Républiques Françaises*, Paris, 1988, p. 693; cf. 686.

monarchy by a republican head of state. The crucial intervening change was the separation of the King's law from the kingdom's law, with the restriction of the monarch's authority first by custom and then by the emergence of the notion of fundamental laws, such as those of monarchical succession. The inability to attain a British combination of custom and statutory constitutional law led to the attempt to formalise and prescribe rules that were broken when they would not bend. 'The constitution-making fever – the constitutional superstition – is certainly a disease from which France has suffered more than any other country', writes a French authority, 'so the rather contemptuous scepticism of the British towards learned constitutional architects is not without some substance.'[3]

France having followed the Sieyès rather than the Maistre approach to constitution-making (the faith in explicit rules rather than implicit tradition), the Third Republic came closest to the British style, without a preliminary declaration of rights and confined to a piecemeal set of constitutional laws. While intransigent republicans like Louis Blanc attacked, in 1875, the establishment of a monarch-like President – unaccountable to parliaments which he was able to dissolve, and exercising the power to pardon[4] – such a 'threat' quickly receded as the focus for a reconstituted state power. Instead, France was supposedly and successively governed by 'the Dukes, the *notables*, the lawyers, the teachers, the [partisan] committees, the [parliamentary] comrades and the [Gaullist] *compagnons*'[5] before being governed by the higher civil servants of the *Ecole Nationale d'Administration* (ENA). It is no accident that the latter, which was to be the instrument *par excellence* of state power, was the creation of Michel Debré, future architect of de Gaulle's Fifth Republic Constitution. The school for public servants was an indispensable part of reviving a French state that would impart republican patriotism to a reinvigorated structure of authority. By the time that de Gaulle had returned to power in 1958, the trained cadre of public officials on whom he would rely to restore the power of the French state was ready for action. However, they required a constitutional framework within which to act and this Debré was expeditiously to provide. As Paul Reynaud declared in welcoming

3. Paul Bastid, *L'idée de constitution*, Paris, 1985, p. 186; cf. 21, 51, 60, 140-1, 173. See also the early chapters of Léo Hamon and Guy Lobrichon (eds), *L'Élection du Chef de l'Etat en France de Hugues Capet à Nos Jours*, Paris, 1988. On the Sieyès and Maistre views of the Constitution, see Jack Hayward, *After the French Revolution*, London, 1991, chapter 1, pp. 18-20; chapter 2, pp. 36-8; and chapter 3, pp. 48-9.
4. *Journal Officiel*, 22 July 1875, p. 4505.
5. René Jean Dupuy in Isoart and Bidegaray, p. 736.

de Gaulle to the Constitutional Consultative Committee: 'The government has accomplished in a few weeks what took our British friends several centuries.'[6]

The Spirit of the Constitution: the State Imperative

It is to the credit of Georges Burdeau that he grasped from the outset, and was able to theorise, the main innovation constituted by 'the wholly unprecedented regime' of the Fifth Republic: the re-establishment of state prerogative power, embodied in the President of the Republic. Unlike de Gaulle who, having returned in 1958 not 'to save the regime but to save the state', regarded state power as antithetical to party power, Burdeau regarded them as complementary. State power had to be combined with 'popular power which is now inseparable from the existence of parties. Between the power of the state and of the people it does not choose: it consecrates both of them. It seeks to reconcile authority with democracy: the authority indispensable if democracy is not to dissolve in factional rivalry and the blindness of interests; no less indispensable democracy, if authority is to remain legitimate.'[7] Burdeau predicted that the Constitution's 'future is bound up with the possibility of its adopted concept of power becoming rooted in the French political mind.'[8] Its substantial success in doing so will concern us in what follows.

However, Burdeau's dualist conception of state and popular power needs to be modified by making explicit that his 'state power' amounts primarily to presidential prerogative power and the resources it can mobilise. It is part of a wider phenomenon of executive power, which will involve us notably in a discussion of the relationship between the President and the government. De Gaulle's achievement was to borrow from the monarchists the notion of a strong executive, to meet the weakness in the republican conception of politics that Charles de Rémusat had pointed out in 1848: 'the constitution of the executive power. As that is precisely what distinguishes it from monarchy, it follows that it is characterised by an enigmatic void: it specifically lacks what is commonly called a government.'[9] Burdeau confuses matters by declaring that his 'one

6. *Documents pour servir à l'Histoire de l'Élaboration de la Constitution du 4 Octobre 1958*, II, Paris, 1988, p. 43.
7. George Burdeau, 'La conception du pouvoir selon la Constitution du 4 Octobre 1958', in *Revue Française de Science Politique*, IX/I (March 1959), p. 89; cf. 92, 99.
8. *Ibid.*, p. 88.
9. Charles de Rémusat, *Mémoires de ma vie*, IV, Paris, 1962, p. 251.

sovereign, two powers' represent dual aspects of the people: the President representing the Rousseauist 'general will' of the indivisible people, while parliament represents the pluralist variety of wills of a divided people. Although election of the President by universal suffrage undoubtedly gives the victor popular support, it is a divisive partisan election, and it cannot therefore fulfil the role Burdeau assigned to it. We need to revert to the idea of partisan power – of which legislative power is only an aspect – as a separate, competitive form of power from that of state power, which has a monopolistic, impersonal and semi-permanent apparatus. Finally, in 1958 it was not possible to anticipate the emergence of an autonomous judicial power in the shape of the Constitutional Council, whose function would be to defend the emerging *état de droit* that would prevent either the state or partisan powers from misusing their strength. It is precisely the emergence, in part, of this third power that has given a measure of balance in a system that threatened first to subordinate partisan power to state power and then to colonise state power by partisan power (see below, chapter 5). De Gaulle took some of the credit for 'the strengthening of the judicial power on which, in so many ways, the condition of man and the foundations of the state depend.'[10] However, the major developments have occurred since the Giscard presidency and thanks to his initiative.

The most extensive use of Burdeau's conception of a state prerogative power personified by the President of the Republic was made by Jean-Louis Quermonne in the 1980s. He argued that the Fifth Republic had established an autonomous and higher-order state power, over and above a parliamentary partisan power, while rejecting the idea of a third judicial power. He conceded that the notion of a regal state power corresponds best to the de Gaulle presidency, its limits becoming evident with the increasing role of partisan power, to which we have alluded. Its irreducible minimum was demonstrated by the years of *cohabitation*, in 1986–8, between a Socialist President and a Right-wing Prime Minister and parliamentary majority.[11]

10. Charles de Gaulle, *Mémoires d'Espoir*, Paris, 1970, 1980 paper edn, p. 303.
11. Jean-Louis Quermonne, 'Les ressources et les soutiens du pouvoir d'Etat exercé par le Président de la République' in J.-L. Seurin and J.-L. Martres (eds), *La Présidence en France et aux Etats-Unis*, Paris, 1986, p. 366. The earliest statement is in Quermonne's 'La notion de pouvoir d'Etat et le pouvoir présidentiel sous la Ve République' in *Mélanges Léo Hamon*, Paris, 1982, and the fullest argument is developed in Quermonne's *Le Gouvernement de la France sous la Ve République*, 1980, 3rd edn 1987, where he rejects the idea of a 'judicial power', pp. 415, 420–1. According to J. Massot, *L'Arbitre et le Capitaine*, Paris, 1987, p. 226 note, Giscard apparently coined the term *'cohabitation'* in an interview with *L'Express* of 14 January 1983.

We are prepared to go part of the way with this analysis, although it is exaggerated for the purpose of differentiating it from Duverger's stress on the partisan dimension.[12] From the outset of the Fifth Republic, Debré proclaimed in a 7 July 1958 speech entitled 'Remake a democracy, a state, a power' that its purpose was to found an effective political authority.[13] De Gaulle would have preferred the title 'Head of State' to the narrowly legalistic one of President. Although he yielded to the opposition, he deliberately referred to himself as Head of State in carefully prepared key statements, such as at his press conference in January 1964, in response to a planted question. He twice repeated that a constitution was 'a spirit, a text and a practice' and he was concerned to interpret the text in the light of its spirit and the way he had put it into practice. The spirit and the practice were that 'power was not at the disposal of partisans' but belonged solely to 'the Head of State . . . its source and holder . . . the President is obviously the only person that holds and delegates the authority of the State.'[14] We must briefly consider how far this extensive interpretation of the spirit of state power corresponds with reality, leaving till later a more detailed examination of how the specific powers accorded by various articles of the Constitution have been applied in practice by successive Presidents.

Rather than stressing either the President's privileged role in the fields of foreign, post-colonial and defence policy, in which the state deals with other states, Quermonne emphasises the President's control over the civil service machine – although he does mention his role as head of the armed forces.[15] De Gaulle undoubtedly attached great importance to the role of senior officials in the restoration of state power. This, first, took the form of appointing civil servants to key government posts. Eight out of fourteen ministers in his June 1958 government were senior officials, notably the Foreign Minister, the Defence Minister and the Minister of the

12. Jean-Louis Quermonne, 'Le cas français: le Président dominant la majorité' in Maurice Duverger (ed.), *Les Régimes Semi-Présidentiels*, pp. 183–207.
13. The collection of Debré's speeches took as its title *Refaire une Démocratie, un Etat, un Pouvoir*, Paris, 1958. In 'Le problème constitutionnel français', *Les Cahiers politiques*, April 1944, p. 10, Debré wrote that presidentialism had 'an immense advantage: it combines democracy with authority'.
14. De Gaulle's 31 January 1964 press conference in his *Discours et Messages*, IV, Paris, 1970, pp. 163–7; cf. *Mémoires d'Espoir*, pp. 37–40.
15. Quermonne in Seurin and Martres, p. 364 and *Le Gouvernement de la France*, pp. 490–1, 592–5. More generally, see Francis de Baecque and Jean-Louis Quermonne (eds), *Politique et Administration sous la Ve République*, Paris, 1980, 2nd edn 1982 and Jean-Louis Quermonne and Jean-Luc Bodiguel, *La Haute Fonction Publique sous la Ve République*, Paris, 1982, pp. 243–66.

Interior. From February 1960 to May 1968, de Gaulle had only one Foreign Minister (Couve de Murville) and one Defence Minister (Messmer). However, despite making the functions of minister and member of parliament constitutionally incompatible (article 23) and trying to ensure that ex-ministers would not retrieve their seats immediately, he was not able to prevent the reparliamentarisation of ministers, a process that demonstrated the intrusive force of partisan power.

Secondly, de Gaulle and his successors attached great importance to the nomination of the holders of top administrative posts, so that a dependent relationship developed between the President and senior officials. However, the tendency of both ministers and senior civil servants to come from the ENA and for party considerations to play an increasing role in the post-Gaullist period, leading to talk of a UDR-state and a PS-state, has meant that politico-administrative symbiosis at the summit of state power has been unable to exclude partisan penetration and even domination. The patronage power to make senior administrative appointments has played an important role in building a network of support for presidential leadership. The common practice has developed that 'if a member of his staff thinks that the person being prepared for a particular post will not be cooperative, he advises the President to block the appointment. In this way, the network into which the President's staff fits is continually enlarged.'[16] The spoils system under Mitterrand has taken the form of political appointments to his staff of people who are not former senior officials but party loyalists, some of whom have subsequently become ministers (see below, chapter 3). So the hopes placed by de Gaulle in the ENA – 'capital institution . . . which emerged fully armed from the brain of my adviser Michel Debré' and intended to become 'the basis of the new state'[17] – has not lived up to his expectations. The ambivalent character of the President's function – representing both state and partisan power – has been admitted by his successors. As Mitterrand put it: 'I am elected by the Left but I am the President of the French people.'[18]

State power also takes the non-constitutional form of traditional control over the audiovisual sector of mass communication – regarded as the 'voice of France' – and a large public economic

16. Ezra Suleiman, 'Presidential Government in France' in Richard Rose and Ezra Suleiman (eds), *Presidents and Primes Ministers*, p. 127; cf. 129–30.
17. Charles de Gaulle, *Mémoires de Guerre. Le Salut (1944–46)*, Paris, 1959, p. 277.
18. *Le Monde*, 6 April 1984; cf. Giscard's press conference of 17 Jan. 1977, quoted in Quermonne, *Le Gouvernement de la France*, p. 199.

sector ranging from public utilities, banks and insurance companies to major industrial enterprises. The evolution has been different in the period between the presidencies of de Gaulle and Mitterrand. De Gaulle – who had, in the immediate post-war period, initiated a major extension of the public economic sector through a programme of nationalisation – adamantly maintained a highly interventionist state control of radio and television. Radio had played a crucial part in his wartime role, but he also regarded control of audiovisual media as counterbalancing the predominance of the opposition parties in the press. However, he did not, as President from 1958, resume his earlier strengthening of public ownership as the instrument of state economic power.

By contrast, Mitterrand's presidency was characterised by a deliberate weakening of state control over the mass audiovisual media, with the emergence of an important private sector in radio and television, although the temptation to intervene in the selection of those who ran the media demonstrated the difficulty experienced in shaking off past habits (see below, chapter 7). There was a very substantial extension of the public economic sector in 1982, which allowed the nomination of a large number of heads of public enterprises who were intended to act as instruments of the Socialist-led state's economic policies. Partly reversed during the Chirac government by the 1986–7 programme of privatisation, the way in which it was conducted gave the state rather than the market the choice of the new controlling interests. President Mitterrand's retreat in 1988 to a neutral policy of neither systematically expanding nor contracting the public economic sector was part of a general tendency to soft-pedal partisan state interventionism, which circumscribed the President's scope for action.

1958: The President as Guide and Arbitrator

While de Gaulle had a Maistrian scepticism towards trying to constrain 'the nature of things' by man-made constitutions,[19] and a corresponding high-handed attitude when the letter of constitutional law clashed with political expediency, he was conscious of the urgent need to institutionalise the personal power of a reconstituted head of state. His self-appointed historic task was to be the 'Legislator' that Montesquieu and Rousseau had envisaged to found a new system of government. As he declared in his first broadcast to the nation after returning to power in 1958: 'Our whole future is blocked if France does not have a state able to guide it. It is the precondition

19. Charles de Gaulle, *Discours et Messages*, III, p. 246.

of everything.'[20] At his inauguration as President in January 1959, de Gaulle made it clear that he considered that the French people had 'once again given me the task of leading them towards their destiny'.[21] Having been rescued for a second time from national cataclysm – this time from civil war rather than a foreign one – the French people had overwhelmingly approved by referendum the Constitution whose detailed drafting the Legislator had delegated to Michel Debré.

Debré shared with de Gaulle a commitment to Péguy's assertion that 'The one and indivisible Republic is our French kingdom.'[22] Like de Gaulle, he thought that this synthesis of republic and monarchy meant reversing a Revolutionary democratic tradition that substituted the people's representatives for the people, transforming popular sovereignty into parliamentary sovereignty. In France, 'democracy had been established by brutal reaction against an arbitrary power, that of the king, Robespierre, the Bourbons, the Napoleons. The democratic tradition had been to smash one-man rule . . . The French Constitution seeks to resolve these problems: find a man, confer legitimacy upon him, guarantee him duration in power, avoid arbitrariness.'[23] In retrospect, de Gaulle took pride in having 'founded the new Republic by giving it for origin, basis and mainspring the direct agreement of the people and its guide.'[24] While it was not until the institution of the direct election of the President in 1962 that this somewhat telescoped description of his achievement became accurate, it was from the start the spirit in which the new Constitution was devised.

Describing his pivotal part in drafting the Constitution of the Fifth Republic, Debré asserted: 'No one dreamed of contesting my control over the preparation of the text and I had no wish to share it.'[25] With only eight weeks to undertake the task, Debré relied upon a working party largely drawn from Gaullist-inclined young members of the Council of State. His central purpose was to transfer the power to command from the legislature to the executive and in particular to the President. More inclined than de Gaulle to look to

20. *Ibid.*, p. 19, broadcast of 13 June 1958.
21. *Ibid.*, p. 72.
22. Michel Debré, *Mémoires*, II, Paris, 1988, p. 24.
23. Debré's testimony in Duverger (ed.), *Les Régimes Semi-Présidentiels*, p. 86.
24. Charles de Gaulle, *Mémoires d'Espoir*, p. 352; cf. Debré, *Mémoires*, II, pp. 370–1.
25. Debré, *Mémoires*, II, p. 348; cf. 351–4. A possible rival, René Capitant, was teaching at the time in Japan (*ibid.*). François Goguel, who was frequently consulted, was prevented from joining Debré's constitution working party because he was Secretary of the Second Chamber, the Council of the Republic.

Britain as a model, Debré persuaded him that as the President would chair the Council of Ministers, the 'President of the Council' should in future be called Prime Minister, who with the government would be accountable to the National Assembly, 'allowing the President to play fully his role of arbitrator' by leaving day-to-day politics to the government.[26] Debré recalled that in the early stages of the Constitution's preparation 'the General briefly spoke to me about the points in which he took a close interest. They concerned the President of the Republic and in particular his right to appeal to the people by referendum and to dissolve the National Assembly. The General spoke to me of the President of the Republic's mode of election. Universal suffrage was raised, only to be rejected. French citizenship was then so extensive that it was not possible to adopt that type of election.'[27] As we shall see, there were reasons that influenced this decision, other than the end of France's African empire and the decolonisation of Algeria.

Debré wryly remarks: '"Our Constitution" the General would sometimes say to me. "Your Constitution" he would also say to me when he found this or that disposition inconvenient or questionable.'[28] One such reproach was over the drafting of article 11. Debré recounts that 'For the General as for me, there is no shadow of a doubt. The referendum is a weapon of the President of the Republic', and Debré had wanted to allow him to call a referendum on 'any matter that is fundamental for the life of the nation'. This wide definition was restricted at the instance of the Constitutional Consultative Committee (CCC), but Debré insists that he deliberately included the phrase 'organisation of public authorities' which allowed de Gaulle subsequently to call a referendum in 1962 on the direct election of the President by the people.[29]

The CCC was created as a sop to parliament, which had been deprived of its traditional role of constituent assembly. Although it did create some subsequent difficulties for de Gaulle, the CCC played only a marginal role by comparison with Debré's working

---

26. Michel Debré's interview with his son Jean-Louis Debré, *Les Idées Constitutionnelles du General de Gaulle*, Paris, 1974, p. 163; cf. Debré, *Mémoires II*, p. 350. The office of Prime Minister was originally a British import from the France of Louis XIV, Richelieu being designated *Principal ministre d'Etat* by Letters Patent of 21 Nov. 1629, although 'in the King's entourage it is more usual to refer to the "Prime Minister".' (Alain Claisse, *Le Premier Ministre de la Ve République*, Paris, 1972, p. 12). So the French adoption of the term is a re-import of a title originally of French coinage.
27. Michel Debré in Jean-Louis Debré, p. 160; cf. *Documents pour servir à l'Histoire de l'Élaboration de la Constitution*, I, Paris, 1987, pp. 241-2.
28. Debré, *Mémoires*, II, p. 362.
29. *Ibid.*, pp. 375-6, 406-8.

party, whose activities were directed and supervised by an Inter-ministerial Constitutional Committee (ICC) under de Gaulle's chairmanship. It included four senior ministers (notably Guy Mollet and Pierre Pflimlin), the Ministers of Finance and of Justice (Debré), the Vice-President of the Council of State, the Secretary-General of the government, the Director of de Gaulle's staff (Georges Pompidou) and his adviser on constitutional matters, Raymond Janot, who represented him on the CCC.[30] Because the 1958 Constitution was not the product of a Constituent Assembly, it was considered that its authors could not prepare a new declaration of rights. They decided simply to reaffirm the 1789 Declaration and the Preamble to the 1946 Constitution.[31]

Janot testifies that 'the starting-point' of the ICC 'really was the section dealing with the President of the Republic, which for a long time was the first section' of the Constitution.[32] Debré presents, as a mark of the new regime's self-assurance, the fact that members of previously reigning families were not excluded from standing for election to the presidency. However, he also recalls the far-sighted de Gaulle saying to him that the French ex-royal family should be regarded as an alternative if the Republic should fail. 'Who knows if in a hundred or two hundred years, we shall not turn to monarchy . . . that is why we should respect the House of France.'[33] For the foreseeable future the republican monarchy he had instituted should preclude the need to have recourse to hereditary monarchy.

The ability to dismiss phantoms from the past proved less easy in the case of the election by universal suffrage of Louis-Napoleon

30. See Janot's testimony in *Georges Pompidou Hier et Aujourd'hui*, Neuilly-sur-Seine, 1990, pp. 40–3, 48. Janot describes how Pompidou introduced him – then Secretary-General of the Council of the State – to the General while de Gaulle was on his way to meet President Coty to discuss the handover of power. His advice on how to avoid both the 1940 delegation of constituent power to Pétain and the 1946 Constituent Assembly led to de Gaulle offering him the post of constitutional adviser on the spot (*ibid.*, pp. 38–9). When unexpected issues were raised on the CCC and Janot needed to know what de Gaulle thought, he consulted Pompidou (*ibid.*, p. 45).
31. *Documents*, I, p. 243.
32. Janot in *Georges Pompidou*, p. 59.
33. Debré, *Mémoires*, III, Paris, 1988 p. 40; cf. II, p. 377. De Gaulle mentions the importance he attached to visits from the Comte de Paris (*Mémoires d'Espoir*, p. 306), but when in 1965 it was thought that de Gaulle would not stand in the presidential election and the Pretender asked through a common friend whether the General would support his candidacy, de Gaulle dismissed the matter with the observation: 'He would not get 5 per cent . . .' Quoted by Jean Lacouture, 'De Gaulle, une certaine idée de la République' in Isoart and Bidegaray, p. 726. See also the testimony of Léon Noël, *La Traversée du désert*, Paris, 1973, p. 259.

as the first and only President of the Second Republic. It was undoubtedly a factor in postponing the adoption of direct popular election (alongside the large number of non-metropolitan people eligible to vote for the President of the French Community as well as France), a majority of the ICC being opposed to it.[34] So, despite the presentation of cogent arguments against a 'super-senator' President, on the grounds that the Second Republic fiasco was due to the majority of French people not being republican and that in modern France legitimacy necessitated a vote by universal suffrage, it was decided to use an electoral college dominated by local notables.[35] A seven-year term was accepted without discussion as a republican tradition. Although Debré would have preferred to restrict Presidents to a single term to avoid a subsequent reduction in its duration, he did not press the point since he did not wish to exclude de Gaulle from standing for election again.[36]

The 1958 Constitution-makers did not produce a clear choice between the two senses of the word *arbitre*: first, an arbitrator of disputes or referee, who remained politically neutral and impartial, and secondly an arbiter, whose direct involvement in taking controversial political decisions meant that he would have to be politically accountable. This hesitancy was due to the impossibility of reconciling de Gaulle's grandiose conception of the President's role, in which his judgement of what the circumstances required must always take priority over legalistic constraints, with the view of those – including Debré – who attached importance to constitutional constraints. The danger of arbitrary power, the tendency of the arbiter to substitute personal preference for legal requirements, was precisely what had led the liberal theorists of constitutional monarchy and the constitutional republic since Benjamin Constant to insist upon the need to have institutional safeguards to ensure that the rules were respected.[37] In the absence of a Supreme Court in

34. Janot in *Documents*, II, p. 68 and in *Georges Pompidou*, pp. 50–1. Massot (*L'Arbitre et le Capitaine*, p. 142) estimates the potential 'French' electorate in 1958 at 100 million.
35. See the interventions of Constitutional Law Professor François Luchaire, especially his note 'Nécessité de l'élection du chef de l'Etat au suffrage universel', in *Documents*, I, pp. 309–11; cf. 285 and Jean-Louis Debré, *Idées Constitutionnelles*, pp. 427–9.
36. Debré, *Mémoires*, II, p. 375.
37. Benjamin Constant, 'Principes de Politique of 1815', chapter 2 in *Oeuvres*, Paris, 1957. More generally on Constant, see Jack Hayward, *After the French Revolution*, chapter 5. Several writers have drawn attention to the partial links between Constant and the 1958 Constitution. For example, see René Capitant's 'L'aménagement du pouvoir exécutif et la question du chef de l'Etat' of 1964 included in his *Ecrits Constitutionnels*, Paris, 1982, p. 380, and Jean Gicquel, *Essai sur la pratique de la Ve République*, Paris, 1968, pp. 11 note, 21, 57, 69, 117, 259.

the American manner, this task belonged to the head of state. The difficulty of reconciling this liberal tradition – which for most of the Third and Fourth Republics had reduced the referee President to the more modest status of a linesman – with de Gaulle's desire that the President should always have the capacity to intervene at will, even if he generally avoided doing so in normal circumstances, led to confusing contradictions in the text of the Constitution. However, the flexibility offered by hybrid rules, capable of being interpreted to suit varying circumstances, has given the Fifth Republic institutions great adaptability, albeit at the cost of the predictability that unequivocal rules provide.

The text of the 1958 Constitution offers in several of its articles a clear implication that the President should not be held responsible for his actions, except in the case of high treason (article 68). Traditionally, this had been associated with the countersignature of the President's actions by accountable ministers who accept responsibility to parliament for them. Article 19 of the Constitution specifies which presidential acts are not countersigned by the Prime Minister and other ministers, but we shall see that in practice this indicator no longer distinguishes those actions for which the President is nominally responsible from those for which he is really responsible. The reason is that ministers, rather than protecting the President by taking the burden of accountability away from him, in fact share responsibility with him, being 'associated with presidential discussions'.[38] Although the powers of the President and the Prime Minister are distinct, they are not separate, so they have to act in collaboration, a collaboration which, as we shall see, has usually worked in favour of the pre-eminence of the President. The Prime Minister is the executant of decisions that may – though not always – be jointly arrived at but which the President finally settles, as long as he does not have to deal with a Prime Minister supported by a hostile Assembly majority (see below, chapter 4).

That the President should only communicate with parliament indirectly and his messages are not debated (article 18), and that criticism of the President should be a punishable offence, is characteristic of a non-accountable head of state. While de Gaulle insisted upon the rigour of the law being enforced in the cases of offences against the President, his successors have adopted a more permissive attitude, acknowledging by implication that, being politically active, they should not claim immunity from criticism. Thus President Mitterrand declared on television in 1981: 'You have the right to criticise me because I above all am committed to the policy

---

38. Françoise Decaumont, *La Présidence de Georges Pompidou*, Paris, 1979, p. 159; cf. Capitant, *Ecrits Constitutionnels*, pp. 382–90.

prepared by the Government. I am the person most responsible for French policy.'[39] Similarly, the fact that former President Giscard d'Estaing did not choose to serve as an *ex-officio* member of the Constitutional Council (article 56) to which he gave a new lease of life was due not only to his decision to resume an active political career but because he could not sit in neutral judgement on the legislation which his successful opponent in the presidential election was enacting.[40]

A key sentence in the key article 5 of the Constitution, by which de Gaulle tried to ensure that his successors would live up to his elevated conception of the presidential function, was: 'He ensures, through his arbitration, the regular working of the public authorities as well as the continuity of the State.' It corresponds to the passage in his Bayeux speech in which he attributed to the President the function of 'arbitrator above the political circumstances.' Two contexts in which the President would act as arbitrator can be distinguished. First, in normal political circumstances, the President decides who will be Prime Minister (article 8) and acts as chairman of the Council of Ministers (article 9). Secondly, in conditions of crisis and political conflict, or where a vital matter concerning the organisation of political institutions has to be resolved, the President can dissolve the National Assembly (article 12) or submit the issue to a referendum (article 11). Where the crisis takes the much more serious form of a threat to France's political regime, national independence or application of its international commitments, and the public authorities have ceased to work normally, the President ceases to arbitrate and acquires complete decision-making power, with a view to restoring power to the constitutional public authorities as soon as possible (article 16). We shall later consider how these functions have been discharged in practice. Let us meanwhile consider the illuminating discussion of the notion of 'arbitration' in the ICC and the CCC.

Alarmed by the attempt of former Fourth Republic parliamentary leaders to use the notion of 'arbitration' to exclude presidential political involvement, the President's constitutional adviser Raymond Janot drafted a confidential note on the subject for de Gaulle. On pain of reducing the President to someone who could not take sides on major issues, 'arbitration' should be defined as the personal power of the President to take decisions. '. . . It should be

---

39. Quoted in Massot, p. 145; cf. chapter 3 on the President's non-accountability, especially pp. 78–83.
40. Massot, pp. 90–1. De Gaulle did not sit in the Constitutional Council after ceasing to be President.

stated clearly that certain powers belong personally to the President of the Republic, with the consequence that these powers should not require countersignature. This is not a formal but a fundamental matter, of capital importance . . . France will only have a Government that governs (instead of being an agent of the Assembly) to the extent that, thanks to his personal powers, the President of the Republic, supported by the people, is the guarantor of governmental authority.'[41] Janot specified that the power to accept the Prime Minister's resignation, call a referendum and dissolve the Assembly should not require ministerial countersignature.

In the CCC discussions, Janot, quoting the future article 20 in support, emphasised the non-decision-making aspect of the President's 'arbitration function, which is different in character because the executive power is the Government'.[42] In reply to those who asked bluntly why 'the head of state, with his new powers, remains unaccountable', Janot repeated that 'The head of the executive power is the Prime Minister', the President only intervening in 'exceptional circumstances', his 'specific role being that of arbitrator'.[43] Janot denied that the Prime Minister was responsible to both President and Assembly and could be dismissed by the President. The CCC's chairman Paul Reynaud remaining unconvinced, de Gaulle gave what appeared to be a categoric assurance on this score. The President 'cannot dismiss the Prime Minister, otherwise the Prime Minister could not govern as he wishes . . . The Government is responsible to Parliament, it is not responsible to the Head of State, who is impartial, who does not and should not meddle in everyday politics. . . . He is an arbitrator . . . and that is one of the reasons why the Prime Minister and the Government should not be responsible to him . . . Otherwise the whole balance of our draft Constitution would be destroyed.'[44] This reply so impressed Reynaud that when the CCC discussed amending article 8 to state that the President could not dismiss a Prime Minister who enjoyed the confidence of the Assembly, he declared it to be unnecessary, 'especially as we have in the preparatory deliberations a categoric declaration from General de Gaulle'.[45] Reynaud also believed that a non-accountable President would not dare to dissolve the Assembly for fear, as in 1877, of having to 'submit or resign' on being disavowed at the general election.

41. *Documents*, I, pp. 257–8, note dated 16 June 1958; cf. 246–8 and II, p. 68.
42. *Ibid.*, II, p. 70; cf. 69.
43. *Ibid.*, pp. 80, 95; cf. 278.
44. *Ibid.*, p. 300.
45. *Ibid.*, p. 320.

He was to be proved wrong in 1962, and de Gaulle gloated over his discomfiture.[46]

1962: The President as Guide and Supreme Decision-Maker

De Gaulle claimed in retrospect: 'I have long believed that the only way to elect the President of the Republic is by the people.'[47] This would end the 1958 anomaly by which a President exercising extensive responsibilities did not have the legitimacy conferred by being the chosen of universal suffrage. Although his historic role rendered such electoral legitimacy superfluous in his own case, de Gaulle was anxious to ensure that after him the President would be empowered to play the role designed for him by the Constitution. This meant ensuring that the legitimising force of popular sovereignty was mobilised on his behalf, so that a lesser President would feel constrained to rise to the demands of his function. If it is true that de Gaulle had 'long believed' this to be necessary, why had the Legislator failed to establish the direct popular election of the President when he had a free hand?

It is in fact not clear when de Gaulle became convinced of the desirability of popular election, although it is much clearer when he was persuaded of its urgency. He explains that neither in 1946 nor in 1958 did he think it expedient to do 'everything at once', thereby upsetting an 'almost unanimous support' (in 1958 though not 1946) by raising the spectre of Louis-Napoleon.[48] We have already suggested that the matter is more complicated than this. Apart from the fact that until 1962 the presidential electorate would have been distorted by large numbers of non-metropolitan voters, both de Gaulle and Debré had a strong prejudice against adopting an American-type presidential election. In addition, parties would be likely to play an important role, and at that time the danger of a Communist candidate winning such an election was not dismissed as wholly implausible. As early as 1946, Léon Blum had suggested that de Gaulle would be logically driven to adopt presidential election by universal suffrage, but it required more than the expectation that the 1958 electoral college would be likely to yield Antoine Pinay as de Gaulle's successor to precipitate his decision in 1962.[49]

46. *Ibid.*, p. 76; cf. Charles de Gaulle, *Mémoires d'Espoir*, pp. 343, 346.
47. *Mémoires d'Espoir*, p. 326.
48. *Ibid.*, p. 327.
49. Jean Lacouture, *De Gaulle*, III. *Le Souverain, 1959–1970*, Paris, 1986, pp. 572–4. Pierre Messmer has also claimed that France's acquisition of nuclear weapons meant that the President needed popular legitimacy to authorise him to use them. See Duverger (ed.), *Les Régimes Semi-Présidentiels*, p. 96.

In April 1961, having just vanquished the 'generals' putsch', de Gaulle confided to a staff member his anxiety about his succession: 'In fact, I re-established monarchy in my favour, but after me there will be no one who will impose his authority on the country. I was elected without the need for a referendum [note the assimilation with a direct presidential election] but after me this will no longer be true. So it will be necessary to establish a presidential system to avoid returning to the struggles of the past. The President of the Republic must be elected by universal suffrage. Elected in this way, whatever his personal qualities, he will nevertheless have some semblance of authority and power when in office.'[50] A year later, the matter became more urgent. De Gaulle saw the narrow Assembly majority of the new Pompidou government (259 for, 247 against) and the resignation of five MRP ministers as indications that 'the clash between two republics' was about to begin: the protagonists of a return to a Fourth Republic-style presidency using the end of the Algerian war as an opportunity to eliminate the man who personified the Fifth Republic.[51] The ranging shot was fired by de Gaulle in a June 1962 broadcast, announcing that 'in due course' it would be necessary to ensure that 'the direct agreement between the people and the person who has the duty of leading it' would be guaranteed by the President being elected by universal suffrage.[52] However, it required a dramatic event to precipitate presidential hostilities, allowing the master-tactician to seize the initiative for a decisive onslaught.

On 22 August 1962 de Gaulle narrowly escaped death during an ambush by those determined to kill him for having granted independence to Algeria. A week later, he informed the Council of Ministers that he would propose amending the Constitution to 'ensure the continuity of the State', subsequently announcing that this would be done by referendum. On 20 September he explained on television to the French people that he needed their support to prevent a return to 'the sterile and derisory games of the past' by giving them the choice of who should be their President in future. He emphasised that 'the keystone of our political system is the institution of a President of the Republic chosen by the minds and feelings of the French people to be the head of State and France's guide.'[53] The previous day, at the Council of Ministers, all those present were asked to give their views on the subject. The only opponent, Minister of Education Pierre Sudreau, objected not only to the use of the

50. François Flohic, *Souvenirs d'outre-Gaulle*, Paris, 1979, p. 58.
51. *Mémoires d'Espoir*, p. 341; cf. 329–30.
52. *Discours et Messages*, III, pp. 422–3.
53. Quoted in *Mémoires d'Espoir*, pp. 331–2; cf. 333.

referendum procedure but to the danger that the popular election of the President would 'exacerbate the imbalance of power'.[54] He resigned from the government as battle was joined, de Gaulle and his supporters being confronted by the whole of the political class, from Communist Left to Conservative Right, via former Presidents Auriol and Coty.

In the name of 'national sovereignty', de Gaulle explained that he had chosen to amend the Constitution by 'the most democratic method, that of the referendum'.[55] This was not the view of the French political class. Their attitude had been expressed in the CCC (when article 11 on the President's power to call a referendum was being discussed) with revealing frankness by a Socialist deputy. 'That the referendum is the master of us all . . . is true, but allow me to keep to myself what we think of our master! . . . The reason that the representative system was organised from 1790 was because when it came to discussing and amending legislation, it was thought that representatives were best fitted to do so.'[56] This debate indeed goes back to the French Revolution. Although the 1791 Constitution had rejected recourse to a referendum, Danton proposed in September 1792 that the republican constitution in preparation should be approved by the people. Included as article 58 of the 1793 Constitution, the referendum was not held because the Constitution was immediately suspended on account of the war in which France was involved. Furthermore, a referendum on the Constitution did not amount to a 'Rousseauist' legislative referendum, to which article 11 has remote affinities.[57] De Gaulle could also appeal to article 3 of his Constitution, which declared that 'National sovereignty belongs to the people who exercise it through their representatives and through the referendum.' However, the President's conception of direct democracy was one in which the sovereign people provided or withdrew their support at the behest of the leader, to whom it delegated power.

54. Quoted by Lacouture in *De Gaulle*, III, p. 579; cf. 577–81. During preparatory work on the Constitution, this was also the view of Luchaire in opposition to Janot, who argued that the President should be able to propose amendments to the Constitution by referendum. *Documents*, I, p. 394. Janot said that the right to call a referendum 'belonged' to the President. *Documents*, II, p. 69; cf. 68.
55. Lacouture, *De Gaulle*, III, p. 581. De Gaulle's constitutional adviser Jacques Boitreaud, as well as other members of his staff, having suggested taking the slower road of article 89, de Gaulle replied that he was in a hurry. See the testimony of Bernard Tricot in Tricot *et al.*, *De Gaulle et le Service de l'Etat*, Paris, 1977, p. 147; cf. 146.
56. René Dejean on 8 August 1958 in *Documents*, II, p. 321; cf. 322–4.
57. Bastid, pp. 152, 164–6; Jean-Louis Debré, pp. 200–1.

Because the proposal that the people elect the President was popular, its opponents concentrated their fire on the procedure adopted, the use of article 11 rather than article 89, which specifically prescribed the procedure for revising the Constitution. At the Council of Ministers, de Gaulle went to the heart of the problem. 'If one accepts that the only possible way of amending the Constitution is article 89, one grants the Senate the exorbitant and incomparable privilege of blocking everything . . . If there is a mistake in the 1958 Constitution, this is it . . . It is not possible to accept the constitutional monopoly of an article 89 which, in practice, confers this monopoly on the Senate. It is not possible. It was not really intended by the 1958 constitution-makers, of which I am honoured to have belonged. If one accepts that the Constitution cannot be amended by article 11, one consequently accepts that all reform becomes impossible. The President of the Republic, guarantor of the State's interests, cannot accept it.'[58]

In the circumstances, it was not surprising that the President of the Senate took a leading part in the campaign against the 'deliberate violation of the Constitution', on which the Constitutional Council decided it was not competent to pronounce.[59] While de Gaulle was clearly right in half-admitting the mistake of giving the Senate a constitutional veto power, instead of seeking to attack that problem he proposed to ride roughshod over it. He asserted his right as the Legislator to interpret the Constitution without being bound by the rules he had erroneously instituted. The exasperation is evident in his statement: 'I am myself the main inspirer of the new institutions and it is beyond the limit to contradict me on what they mean.'[60] Told that he had been accused by Paul Reynaud of violating the Constitution, de Gaulle commented: 'Come, come! One does not rape one's wife.'[61]

Despite Pompidou's assurance in the Council of Ministers that 'Twenty-two years of Gaullism have wiped out the stain of Bonapartism',[62] his government was censured in the Assembly on 5 October 1962 by 280 out of 480 deputies. After a bitter campaign, de Gaulle not only won a decisive referendum success (62 per cent voted in favour) but a crushing victory when he dissolved the National Assembly and secured an absolute majority of deputies on whose support he could rely, including all the seats in Paris.

58. Lacouture, *De Gaulle*, III, p. 580.
59. *Ibid.*, p. 581; cf. 575–6, 582, 589–90.
60. *Mémoires d'Espoir*, p. 335; cf. 334–6.
61. Quoted in Pierre Viannsson-Ponté, *Histoire de la République Gaullienne*, II, Paris, 1971, p. 42.
62. *Ibid.*, p. 39.

De Gaulle had dropped his idea of replacing the President of the
Senate by the Prime Minister as the person temporarily in charge
if the President of the Republic were to resign or die; he did so
because of Pompidou's opposition, and dismissed the suggestion
of creating a Vice-President with the remark 'He would be my
widow.'[63] Otherwise, he had triumphed over those nostalgic for
a return to parliamentary sovereignty, while at the same time
securing a reliable Assembly majority. He had reinforced the
President and ensured that, as far as was humanly possible, he
had provided the French state with a head capable of 'guiding' it.
By 1965 he could boast that the direct election of the President
had led to 'the coming of the people . . . as the direct source of
the Head of State's power, to which when necessary the latter can
have recourse', as well as making 'the President of the Republic
alone the representative and trustee of the whole Nation, with the
duty to determine its conduct in essential matters and the means to
do so.'[64]

   The Left, which had been hostile to the expanded role of the
President, reinforced by popular legitimacy, could not stand out
against the revised articles 7 and 8 of the Constitution which
prescribed the new presidential electoral arrangements. The election
of 1965 saw Mitterrand embark on the long haul which showed –
despite the tactical reticence of some of his remarks – that he
had grasped that the Left's only hope of winning power would
be to accept the institutions of the Fifth Republic, subject to
some modest changes. Asked in 1988 whether article 11 could be
used to revise the Constitution, Mitterrand replied: 'The practice
established and approved by the people can henceforth be considered as one of the modes of revision, concurrently with article
89.'[65] After all, the Senate was far more likely to block Left-wing
constitutional amendments. Another lesson of the 1962 battle
was that the President could use the dissolution of the Assembly
to create the correspondence between the President, his popular
support and parliamentary support to facilitate the smooth working
of the Constitution. Mitterrand was to wield the dissolution weapon
with punishing effect in 1981 and 1988. It remains to examine
the implications of the new constitutional order for presidential
practice.

63. Quoted in Lacouture, *De Gaulle*, III, p. 578; cf. 576 and Debré, *Mémoires*, II,
    p. 406. On the powers of the interim President, confined to the role of a Fourth
    Republic President, see Massot, pp. 87-8.
64. *Discours et Messages*, IV, p. 389; cf. *Mémoires d'Espoir*, pp. 319-20, 353-7.
65. *Pouvoirs*, no. 45 (April 1988), p. 138.

The Constitution as the Point of Departure

The Protector President. Both before and after the relegitimisation of the President in 1962, it would generally be agreed that in his relationship with the Constitution, 'practice diverged from the text to the extent of unceremoniously ignoring it.'[66] However, after de Gaulle, while Presidents intervened more extensively in affairs of state, they have had more difficulty in living up to the ambitious terms in which article 5 sought to 'constitutionalise the spirit of the presidential function' by 'dictating to the President the objectives that should motivate his acts'.[67] Part of the problem is that it is difficult to give legal force to intangible and controversial concepts such as guardian, arbitration or guarantor. While the President is supposed to ensure respect for the Constitution, this task has partly been taken over by the Constitutional Council, including the defence of rights, which President Mitterrand has particularly emphasised. As far as arbitration is concerned, restricted to ensuring the regular working of government and 'the continuity of the state', it is difficult for a partisan President to act impartially in exercising powers such as that of dissolution. To assert that the President 'guarantees national independence' and the application of treaties does reinforce the President's role in defence and foreign policy, but he usually has to act in conjunction with the Prime Minister and other ministers. Nevertheless, as we shall see, while the 1986–8 period of *cohabitation* led to a return to 'a practice of the presidential function in accordance with the conception invented by the Constitution-makers',[68] it left the President's predominant role in these matters substantially intact.

The President's function as 'guarantor of judicial independence' (article 64) has at times become a subject of controversy. During the Fourth Republic, the Supreme Council of the Magistracy, responsible for a wide range of senior judicial appointments, met weekly under the President's chairmanship. De Gaulle claimed that the substitution of presidential appointment of all for the election of most members of the Supreme Council of the Judiciary in the Fourth Republic made it apolitical, but this would only be true insofar as the President himself could be assumed to be acting in a non-partisan manner. Acting as the head of the state's 'judicial power', he treated the views of the Minister of Justice and the nine members of the Council as 'advice on each general or particular subject. So

66. Philippe Ardant, 'L'article 5 et la fonction présidentielle' in a special issue on 'Le Président' of *Pouvoirs*, no. 41 (May 1987), p. 38.
67. *Ibid.*
68. *Ibid.*, p. 39; cf. 40–8.

that the views expressed are not in any way influenced by my own attitude, I only make my decisions when the meeting is over.'[69]

As part of his general policy of giving law primacy over the arbitrary will of the executive, Mitterrand as President has made a point of not interfering with recommendations on appointments and promotions in the Supreme Council. As the Constitutional Council has developed the idea of an independent judicial authority at the summit of the state, it has seemed natural to break the ties between the executive and the judiciary, of which reform of the Supreme Council of the Judiciary would be only a part. This is a theme which is usually developed in opposition and neglected in government. Nevertheless, as part of the strengthening of the *état de droit* in France, and stimulated by an increasingly restive judiciary, it is likely that progress will be made in securing greater judicial independence in practice.

Michel Debré, addressing his Council of State colleagues on the new Constitution in 1958, declared: 'The creation of the Constitutional Council expresses the will to subordinate law, that is the decision of parliament, to the higher rule of the Constitution.'[70] What he and his colleagues did not anticipate was that as most laws were in fact the government's legislation, it was the President and the executive generally whose will would be subordinated to that of an independent Constitutional Council (CC). Raymond Janot confessed that the Constitution-makers had not foreseen how the CC would expand what was intended to be 'an extremely limited mission . . . It seemed amazing to us that nine distinguished and intelligent gentlemen, just because they were distinguished and intelligent, could block the results of the popular will, expressed by an elected assembly. It seemed extraordinary to us. That was why when the question was put to me as government commissioner . . . Should the CC not be prevented from referring to a preamble [those of 1789 and 1946]? I said no, it is not necessary, it goes without saying. Well, I was later proved wrong and definitively so, since according to the Constitution the Constitutional Council cannot be mistaken. It has refuted what was said at the time, which then accurately reflected the views of the government. . . .'[71]

What was intended as a watchdog on executive supremacy over

69. Charles de Gaulle, *Mémoires d'Espoir*, p. 302; cf. 303. See also Patrice Verrier, *Les Services de la présidence de la République*, Paris, 1971, p. 47 and Massot, pp. 270–2.
70. Quoted by Didier Maus, 'De la IVe à la Ve République: ruptures et continuités' in Isoart and Bidegaray (eds), p. 492.
71. Janot in *Georges Pompidou*, p. 51.

parliament has, thanks to the CC's own actions and Giscard's reform in 1974 allowing sixty members of parliament to refer legislation to the CC, become a restraint on the executive which is required to act in conformity with the values enshrined in the Constitution and its preambles. The Socialists have been confined within the liberal limits of the 1789 Declaration, and the Right has been restrained within the Socialist limits of the 1946 Preamble.[72] It is precisely because the President cannot wholly be relied upon to 'arbitrate' impartially in defence of the Constitution that it has been both necessary and acceptable for the CC partially to fulfil this role, at least where new legislation is concerned.

Turning to the President's power in times of national crisis, of which the controversial manifestation is article 16 of the Constitution, it can be regarded as the most forceful expression of the Burdeau-Quermonne conception of the President's 'state power'.[73] 'Personally written by General de Gaulle, article 16 bears from beginning to end the mark of his memories, his fears and his will.'[74] He presented his argument vigorously in the CCC, after Paul Reynaud had challenged Janot's 'historic argument' that President Lebrun lacked the power and legitimacy to act in 1940 to defend the republican form of government and national independence. At Marshal Pétain's trial after the war, Lebrun testified that he had 'arbitrated' in his favour both because a majority of ministers favoured an armistice and because of the catastrophic military defeat and civilian distress. Pressed by Reynaud to confine article 16 specifically to circumstances of foreign or civil war, de Gaulle sidestepped this issue by referring to the 1940 drama. He had been obliged to assume the role of personifying national and republican legitimacy 'because no one else could play this role, which should normally have been played by the head of State'. In 1958 President Coty had managed to secure de Gaulle's return to power to deal with the Algerian crisis acting within the Fourth Republic Constitution but he might have been forced 'to take initiatives without the right to do so . . . In 99 cases out of a 100, in such circumstances, the man at the head of the State would not be inclined by his age, temperament or the circumstances to take such initiatives. The Constitution must oblige him to do so. The Constitution must give him the duty and then he will carry it out.'[75]

---

72. Olivier Duhamel quoted in Alain Duhamel, *De Gaulle-Mitterrand. La marque et la trace*, Paris, 1991, p. 56.
73. Quermonne, *Le Gouvernement de la France*, p. 197; cf. 196–8.
74. Claisse, p. 114.
75. See the CCC discussion on 8 Aug. 1958 in *Documents*, p. 301; cf. 68, 74, 302.

Resistance against article 16 was partly motivated by the unsavoury precedents of Charles X invoking article 14 of the Constitutional Charter, which precipitated the 1830 Revolution, and the Vichy Constitutional (Number Two) Act, which granted the head of state the power to act alone in circumstances of external tension or internal crisis.[76] Article 16 sets two preconditions for conferring the sweeping power on the President to do whatever is required by the circumstances. There has to be a 'serious and immediate threat' to the nation's political institutions and independence, the integrity of its territory and the application of its international commitments, as well as an 'interruption in the normal working of the constitutional public authorities'. (Although the CCC had wanted the Constitutional Council to have a veto over whether these conditions were met, de Gaulle was able to restrict its role to giving advice, which could be ignored.[77]) Immediately after the 'barricades crisis' in Algiers in January 1960 de Gaulle wished to invoke article 16, but he was dissuaded from doing so by his Prime Minister Debré. However, on 23 April 1961, and perpetuated long *after the failure* of the 'generals' putsch' in Algeria, de Gaulle – this time with Debré's agreement – did invoke article 16. Although he was closely associated with the preparation and application of the decisions in the period up to 29 September 1961, Debré recalls: 'It was with evident pleasure that the General signed them without countersignature.'[78] The use of article 16 had the merest symbolic part in ending the military uprising, and its duration was clearly motivated by de Gaulle's desire to demonstrate how right he was to include it in the Constitution, giving it *ex post facto* legitimacy.

President and Government. Turning from exceptional to normal constitutional practice, the relations between President and Prime Minister have been described as a 'subtle alternation between vigilant surveillance and a fake detachment'.[79] Whatever the warmth of his initial sentiments, which may vary from the paternal to the instrumental, experience suggests that, irrespective of the persons concerned, 'the French Constitution engenders an institutional organisation that ineluctably undermines the relations of mutual confidence between the President of the Republic and the

---

76. Jean-Louis Debré, pp. 207–9.
77. *Documents*, II, pp. 326–7, 341, 559.
78. Debré, *Mémoires*, III, p. 287; cf. 239 and Etienne Burin des Roziers, 'Les relations du travail avec le Premier Ministre' in Bernard Tricot *et al.*, *De Gaulle et les Services de l'Etat*, p. 363. More generally, see Massot, pp. 272–5.
79. Samy Cohen in Seurin and Martres, p. 217.

Prime Minister.'[80] This is because they are condemned to work together, a fact which is the constant factor, rather than because of a permanent subordination of all Prime Ministers, an increasing shift of power towards the President or variations within the duration of any particular presidency. Thus, while the experienced parliamentarian and constitutional architect Michel Debré tried to be a head of government according to the letter of the Constitution (article 21), while Pompidou and even more Couve de Murville, as non-parliamentarians, accommodated themselves readily to its President-centred spirit, all three Prime Ministers acted within the framework of an executive based upon the integration rather than the separation of functions under presidential leadership (see below, chapter 4). The quartet at the decision-making summit was constituted by the President and the Secretary-General of his Office, the Prime Minister and the Director of his *cabinet*. The function of these two key officials was to ensure that when their masters discussed important matters, they could arrive at a decision based upon common assumptions.[81]

However, practical considerations – if only the need to form a government rapidly – encouraged substantial presidential delegation of choice of ministers (article 8) to the Prime Minister. Although subsequent Presidents were more interventionist, under de Gaulle it was the Prime Minister 'who took matters in hand and brought them to a rapid conclusion after a few short visits to the Elysée and numerous consultations with the President of the Republic through the Secretary-General. He sometimes even imposed his own viewpoint, General de Gaulle being inclined, in the end, to accept the advice of the person who would have the daily task of carrying on the business of government with all the ministers.'[82] Debré recalls that when he formed his first government, de Gaulle simply asked him to keep the existing Ministers of Foreign Affairs and Defence, as well as appointing André Malraux Minister of Culture (see below, chapter 7).

The shift from Michel Debré to the anonymous adviser and confidant Georges Pompidou and finally to the evasively tactful and unswervingly reliable diplomat Maurice Couve de Murville, produced, during the same presidency, greater presidentialisation. Even if the President wishes to interfere in everything, he does not have

---

80. Charles Debbasch in *ibid.*, p. 204.
81. Boitreaud and especially Burin des Roziers in Tricot, pp. 81–2, 361–9. See also Massot in Duverger (ed.), *Les Régimes Semi-Présidentiels*, pp. 283–4.
82. This is the testimony of the Secretary-General of the President's Office, from 1962–7, Burin des Roziers, in Tricot, pp. 367–8; cf. Claisse, pp. 74–6 and Debré, *Mémoires*, III, pp. 12–19.

the capacity to do so. He has about 1 per cent of the budget and 1 per cent of the staff of an American President, so although he can play a key role generally in policy-making, he cannot do so in policy implementation. 'A Prime Minister who is hostile towards a decision of the head of State can block its application under the critical but powerless eye of the presidential staff.'[83]

Dissolution power. The power to dissolve the Assembly was part of the royal prerogative during the Restoration and was exercised at the discretion of the monarch. The experience of the Third and Fourth Republics had not only curtailed the dissolution power of the President; on the two occasions when it was used, 1877 and 1955, it had resulted in defeat for the government. Article 12 of the Constitution of the Fifth Republic restored the President's personal prerogative of dissolution, with the restriction that he could not use it twice in the same year. Although it can now be employed in the British manner, simply to suit the partisan convenience of the President's supporters, past practice has acted as a constraint. It has only been used four times: twice by de Gaulle and twice by Mitterrand. De Gaulle used it in 1962 because of the Assembly censure of the Pompidou government, which was really an attack on him, and again in 1968, when Pompidou persuaded him (after threatening resignation) that it would be a more success-ful way of restoring his authority than a referendum. In 1977 Giscard threatened that if the RPR refused a vote of confidence in the Barre government he would dissolve the Assembly, which proved in the event unnecessary. Mitterrand also successfully dissolved twice, in 1981 and 1988, after winning presidential elec-tions, only to be faced with a hostile party majority in the National Assembly. Although in 1988 the Socialists only secured a relative majority, this experience confirms the success of relying upon a presidential coat-tail effect. When asked if he would dissolve the Assembly elected in 1986 rather than cohabit with it, he replied: 'Dissolution is only worthwhile after a presidential election, never before one.'[84]

83. Samy Cohen, 'Les hommes de l'Elysée', *Pouvoirs*, no. XX (Feb. 1982), p. 88. See also Burin des Roziers in Gilbert Pilleul (ed.), *'L'Entourage' et de Gaulle*, Paris, 1979, p. 225 and Boitreaud in Tricot *et al.*, pp. 93–7. On the bitter battles bet-ween the Giscard and Chirac staffs, see Ezra Suleiman in Rose and Suleiman (eds), pp. 116–20. More generally see Samy Cohen, *Les Conseillers du Président*, Paris, 1980, Massot, chapter 5, and chapter 3 of the present work by Anne Stevens.

84. Massot, p. 268; cf. 266–7. See also Claisse, pp. 110–14.

Collective deliberation and presidential decision. The Council of Ministers dates back to 1814, when it was chaired by the King. Not wishing to use the British term Prime Minister, because of its association with the fact that he was increasingly replacing the monarch as the effective head of the executive, the title President of the Council of Ministers was adopted on the pretext that he acted as chairman in the King's absence.[85] Hence the designation was both cumbersome and inaccurate, obscuring the role of an active head of state, a legacy bequeathed by the Restoration to the Fifth Republic. While President Auriol was kept informed of the agenda through contacts between the Secretary-General of his staff and the Secretary-General of the government, he did not have the final say. Since 1959 the agenda has been jointly prepared by the two Secretaries, referred to the President and his staff for comments, and finally settled by the President, being circulated a day before the meeting. Although the President is no longer constitutional custodian of the minutes, these are prepared jointly by the two Secretaries – a silent presence at the Council of Ministers – and kept in the presidential archives.[86]

Meetings lasted much longer under the Fourth Republic – one going on for fourteen hours on 27 August 1948 – and usually longer during Pompidou's presidency (over three hours) than under de Gaulle (two and a half hours). De Gaulle's more expeditious style is conveyed by a revealing comment he made to the President's Secretary-General of 1967–9, Bernard Tricot: 'What is essential is that the decision is taken and the fact accomplished. One should not wait for everyone to be agreed.'[87] De Gaulle fixed Wednesday morning as the time for the weekly meeting, although the room changed to accommodate the larger number of ministers attending from the Pompidou presidency. Article 9 simply stating that the Council of Ministers is chaired by the President, the ritual follows the practice adopted by de Gaulle. After a preliminary meeting with the Prime Minister to settle any last-minute problems and the conclusions they wish to reach, the President enters with him and shakes hands with each minister (a characteristic French practice repeated at the end of the meeting). The President sits opposite the Prime Minister, the others seated according to their official status. The Prime Minister generally makes the penultimate contribution

85. Claisse, pp. 18–19.
86. Verrier, pp. 15, 44–5 and Jacques Fournier, *Le Travail Gouvernemental*, Paris, 1987, pp. 56–9.
87. Tricot, 'Le processus de prise des décisions' in Tricot *et al.*, p. 119; cf. *Discours et Messages*, IV, p. 228. See also Claisse, p. 121 and Eric Roussel, *Georges Pompidou*, Paris, 1984, pp. 428–30. On the Council of Ministers in the Giscard presidency, see Françoise Giroud, *La Comédie du Pouvoir*, Paris, 1977, pp. 21–30.

and the President expresses his views and the conclusion is reached, although Mitterrand usually left it to the Prime Minister to sum up except on foreign and defence policy issues. De Gaulle would sometimes prefer to think the matter over and would then simply inform the Prime Minister, having finally taken the decision alone. When the Council of Ministers' list of decisions stated 'The Council decided', he reformulated it to read: 'The President of the Republic decided in Council . . .'[88] This was not a matter of arrogance but a punctilious concern to reaffirm the primacy of presidential authority. After the President approves the list of decisions, copies are sent to each minister.

Although it is the one time each week when all the ministers meet collectively since de Gaulle put a stop to the Fourth Republic practice of the Cabinet Council (which Debré had perpetuated on a monthly basis and de Gaulle 'accepted with bad grace' until he appointed Pompidou), it is not really the place where collective decision-making takes place.[89] This is done in cabinet committees or in more informal ways, sometimes being replaced by the President's personal decision. The resignation of five ministers, led by Pierre Pflimlin, in protest against de Gaulle's denunciation of European federalism at a 1962 press conference was procedurally justified on the ground that the President should not have announced an important policy position without prior discussion in the Council of Ministers. However, this forlorn attempt to prolong Fourth Republic practice exemplified how the role of collective decision-making had been curtailed under the Fifth Republic.

The secondary if significant role that the Council of Ministers can play in taking important decisions is illustrated by de Gaulle's refusal to devalue the franc in 1968. With France losing $400 million daily, devaluation seemed inevitable – the Finance Ministry was in favour and the press reported it as unavoidable – until a minister, Jean-Marcel Jeanneney, intervened. As de Gaulle said pathetically: 'When it is a diplomatic matter I know which ambassadors to talk to; when it is a defence matter I know my generals, but in economic matters to whom can I turn?'[90] Despite being told by Prime

---

88. Claude Dulong, *La Vie Quotidienne à l'Elysée au temps de Charles de Gaulle*, Paris, 1974, p. 85; cf. 118–28, 121, 135 and *Mémoires d'Espoir*, pp. 291–2. See also Fournier, p. 58 and Pierre Mauroy, *C'est ici le chemin*, Paris, 1982, p. 38.
89. Debré, *Mémoires*, III, p. 29. Pompidou got around the interdiction by sometimes inviting his ministers to lunch (Dulong, p. 142 note).
90. Jeanneney testimony in Pilleul, p. 326; cf. 323–30. For Alain Prate's less colourful version, see his account in Tricot *et al.*, pp. 177–83 and Prate, *Les batailles économiques de Général de Gaulle*, Paris, 1978, pp. 269–73. Prate was then de Gaulle's economic adviser and opposed to devaluation.

Minister Couve de Murville that the decision to devalue had been taken, Jeanneney secured from fellow-economist and French EC Commissioner Raymond Barre the vital information that an EC loan to France was not dependent upon devaluation. Jeanneney explained to de Gaulle how to avoid devaluation – which he considered an 'utter absurdity' but did not know how to prevent. On the occasions when he went round the table at the Council of Ministers, de Gaulle normally started from the left of the Prime Minister but not this time. Jeanneney was asked to speak immediately after the neutral remarks of the Finance Minister and helped to rally resistance against devaluation, de Gaulle taking his decision after the meeting and announcing his refusal to devalue the next day on television. Less than a year later, in August 1969, de Gaulle's successor as President decided to devalue the franc after all. Pompidou took the decision with Finance Minister Giscard; Prime Minister Chaban-Delmas was merely informed.[91] These examples show that the Council of Ministers is a forum at which the President can consult ministers or formally register decisions taken elsewhere rather than collectively deciding anything.

The use of *conseils restreints* or interministerial councils by the President goes back to Auriol, who anticipated Fifth Republic practice, particularly after 1950, in dealing with important foreign or colonial policy matters. The Prime Minister and Foreign Minister were regularly present, with other ministers invited when relevant.[92] President Coty did not continue this practice, but de Gaulle revived it to deal initially with Algerian policy on which he was not in agreement with Prime Minister Debré. For his part Debré held numerous interministerial committee meetings – ninety-six in 1959, 103 in 1960, 171 in 1961 and fifty-six in January to April 1962 – and resented a silent member of the President's staff attending. Pompidou by contrast welcomed this indirect presidential presence as a way of coordinating decision-making. If there was no presidential reaction within two days to the decisions taken, the Prime Minister felt he could proceed.[93] When he became President, Pompidou increased the number and range of matters covered by presidential interministerial councils compared to prime ministerial interministerial committees. A further increase took place when Giscard became President, owing to the need to short-circuit Prime Minister Chirac. They declined during the Mitterrand presidency.[94] These interministerial councils allowed the President to

91. Roussel, pp. 344–5.
92. Verrier, p. 16.
93. Debré, *Mémoires*, III, pp. 28–9, 37–9 and Dulong, p. 138–43.
94. Massot, pp. 133–5 and Roussel, pp. 431–2.

take an active part in examining how to carry out certain policy decisions in conjunction with selected ministers and senior officials, rather than relying upon the advice of his own staff. The Secretary-General of the President's Office prepared the list of decisions, sometimes after laborious negotiations with the Prime Minister and other ministers present.[95]

Legislation and delegated legislation. On average each year about 120 laws and ten times that number of decrees are passed (although only about sixty of these go through the Council of Ministers). Article 10 of the Constitution requires the President to promulgate the laws. He does not have the old royal veto; however, he can send a law back to parliament for reconsideration. Although his predecessors never used this power, Mitterrand used it twice, in 1983 to allow a matter to be dropped (holding a World Exhibition in Paris in 1989) and in 1985 to allow a law to be modified in the light of a decision by the Constitutional Council (on New Caledonia).[96] The President's role in matters of delegated legislation under article 13 has caused more controversy. De Gaulle established the convention at the start of the Fifth Republic that the President signed all decrees, including those that do not have to be approved by the Council of Ministers. The period of *cohabitation* led to conflict with the Chirac government in the matter of Mitterrand's refusal to sign three ordinances in 1986: on privatisation, constituency boundaries and working hours, all highly sensitive political issues. The government was compelled in each case to have a parliamentary debate, with the delay in its legislative programme and greater publicity that ensued, together with the possibility of referring the legislation to the Constitutional Council. When passed, Mitterrand duly promulgated these laws.[97] He did not avail himself of the power under article 61 to refer legislation to the Constitutional Council, since he was able to rely on Socialist members of parliament to do so.

Appointing to top positions. Article 13 also involves the President (with the Prime Minister) in making a wide range of senior public appointments, which are a crucial aspect of his 'state power'. Although these discretionary appointments are a far smaller proportion of the total than those made by the US President, who does not

95. Tricot, 'Les conseils restreints' in Pilleul, pp. 167–72 and Bernard Chantebout on the decision to withdraw from NATO's military organisation, *ibid.*, pp. 228–37. See also Boitreaud in Tricot *et al.*, p. 90 and Roussel, pp. 431–2.
96. Massot, pp. 99–102.
97. *Ibid.*, pp. 293–8 and Fournier, pp. 61–7.

have to secure anyone else's countersignature, they have given rise to the claim that partisan choices have led successively to a UDR (Pompidou), UDF (Giscard) and PS (Mitterrand) state *nomenklatura*. About 5,000 appointments are made annually, of which about 500 concern key state actors.[98] It is these that are of particular importance, increased in number by the heads of enterprises nationalised under Mitterrand. Audiovisual appointments have been a particular presidential preoccupation. Although since 1982 they are supposed to be the responsibility of independent authorities, presidential influence is still brought to bear (see below, chapter 7). Because both President and Prime Minister must agree on the discretionary appointments made by the Council of Ministers, disagreements have to be resolved beforehand, whether they are Right-wing versus Left-wing choices in 1986–8 or between members of cohabiting *tendances* of the Socialist Party, before and after the years of *cohabitation*. From the Gaullist *compagnons* to the Mitterrand *Conventionnels*, a spoils system at the summit of the French state has characterised the difficulty of separating the policy-making state officials from the head of state.

A personal foreign and defence policy. Articles 14, 52 and 54 of the Constitution provide a fragile basis for the dominant role of the President in matters of foreign policy (see below, chapter 6). De Gaulle set a pattern which his successors have all followed, and it is therefore worthwhile to recount his contrast between the roles of presidential statesman and Foreign Office diplomat. Speaking to just such a person, he declared: 'The statesman's . . . mission is to lay down a precise political line that the country must follow if it is to defend its national interests and accomplish its destiny. On the contrary, the diplomat tends to modify this line to achieve agreement with the person with whom he is negotiating. You are loyal to your vocation in proposing this compromise today. I must be able to refuse it because my role is to prevent you from deviating, in any way, from the political line that I have defined in the interest of the State.'[99] This did not prevent de Gaulle from developing a very close understanding with Couve de Murville, France's foreign policy being largely decided between them for a decade without the Prime Minister having much say, although he and the Defence Minister did know in advance of the decision to leave NATO's integrated military organisation in 1966. It is significant that both Pompidou and

98. Fournier, pp. 68–71, and Massot, pp. 290–3.
99. Testimony of Raymond Offroy in Tricot *et al.*, p. 21.

Giscard selected their former Secretary-General of the President's
Office as Foreign Minister.

In addition to giving French ambassadors their instructions
before they take up their posts abroad, the President receives
foreign ambassadors. This can lead to delicate negotiations, such as
those between de Gaulle and the British ambassador Christopher
Soames on EC admission, which badly misfired.[100] The European
Community has involved French Presidents in exploiting all the
resources of their office. Thus in 1976 Giscard referred to the Constitutional Council the decision to elect the EC Assembly by universal suffrage, to counteract the hostility of the RPR wing of his
majority. He was successful, but the Council insisted that this was
conditional upon there being no transfer of sovereignty or infringe-
ment of the Republic's indivisibility! In 1985 Mitterrand, wishing to
make it more difficult for a future Right-wing Assembly to restore
capital punishment, referred the European Convention of Human
Rights to the Constitutional Council which declared that it was com-
patible with France's sovereignty.[101] Summit meetings presented a
problem during the period of *cohabitation*, with Chirac seeking to
intrude upon Mitterrand's privileged diplomatic sphere of action.
Although this competition did expose France to some international
ridicule, the President saw off his competitor without too much
difficulty.

Faced with a similar attempt to invade his control over defence
policy as head of the armed forces (article 15) by Chirac's appeal
to his constitutional responsibility for national defence (article 21),
Mitterrand asserted in 1986: 'It is the head of State who has ultimate responsibility for the employment of our arms and thereby
the decision on which the country's fate depends . . . The final
decision belongs to a single person', the President.[102] Mitterrand
rejected several Chirac nominations as Minister of Defence in
1986 before accepting Giraud, because of their need to work closely
together. Even before nuclear weapons (over which the President
has personal control) set the seal on his domination, de Gaulle's
role in restoring mastery over the army was an essential part of
the process by which the presidency shifted from arbitration to
guidance. Just as Debré played a negligible part in the long-drawn-
out Algerian war, so Rocard had little say in the lightning Gulf war,
in which French policy was personally controlled by Mitterrand
throughout.

100. See the account in Lacouture, *De Gaulle*, III, pp. 552–5.
101. Massot, pp. 254–5.
102. Quoted *ibid.*, p. 282; cf. 280–4 and Fournier, pp. 73–5.

Post-colonial Africa: a presidential preserve. Articles 77–87 of the Constitution are a melancholy relic of de Gaulle's intention to sustain post-colonial links with France's African empire in the form of a Community. These nominally independent states were ill prepared for independence and still dependent upon France militarily, economically, politically and culturally, and de Gaulle established a Secretariat for African Affairs under the control of Jacques Foccart to give France a continuing capacity to manipulate their dictators. Under the presidencies of de Gaulle and Pompidou, Franco-African affairs entirely by-passed both the Prime Minister and the Foreign Minister, with parliament totally prevented from having any oversight of this private presidential hunting-ground. Although Giscard brought the 'Foccart "anomaly"' to an end in 1974, he still retained substantial personal control over Franco-African affairs, and his ties with Bokassa, the sanguinary dictator of the Central African Republic, in particular became a major political embarrassment.[103] Mitterrand has continued to treat Franco-African affairs as part of his reserved sector, with one of his sons acting as a family link with the Presidents who run so many of these caricatures of the Fifth Republic as their personal fiefdoms. Such are the continuities that persist as Presidents change.

The Pardoner. The President (article 17) exercises the traditional right of pardon (formalised in the sixteenth century) as well as the more recent right to amnesty, i.e. to annul not merely the punishment but the initial condemnation. Now that the death penalty has been abolished (by Mitterrand in 1981), attention is focussed on the Fourteenth of July, which it has become customary to celebrate by pardoning large numbers of mainly minor offences. However, the Ministry of Justice makes a preliminary selection from the appeals, so that for example between 1976 and 1979 only 2,000 out of 33,000 appeals lodged were passed on to the President. In the 1980s, the number pardoned each year averaged less than 1,000 cases.[104] From the start of the Fifth Republic it has been customary for governments to ask parliament to pass a law after the presidential election to amnesty certain offences. In addition, Giscard restored the traditional republican practice of a school holiday on the day the new President is installed in office. All of this generates a feeling

---

103. Samy Cohen, *Les Conseillers du Président*, chapter 8 *passim* and 'Les Conseillers de l'Elysée' in Seurin and Martres, pp. 209–11. For Giscard's account of his relations with Bokassa, see Valéry Giscard d'Estaing, *Le Pouvoir et la Vie*, II, Paris, 1991, part VII, *passim*.
104. Massot, p. 95 and Joelle Jeanjean, 'Le droit de grâce' in *Pouvoirs*, no. 41, pp. 151–5.

that the nation can enjoy a temporary holiday from the rules which normally constrain its behaviour, associated with the moment at which the state's republican monarchy changes hands.

The mass communicator. While article 18 of the Constitution accords the President the traditional right to communicate with parliament by message, it is his command over the media of mass communication (to which the Constitution does not refer) that became crucially important during the Fifth Republic. The 'Queen's Speech' or the American President's 'State of the Union' address, delivered in person, offers the head of state an opportunity to set out a legislative programme as an expression of his leadership role. Presidential messages in France cannot be delivered in person, which marks a deliberate desire to confine the President to a largely ceremonial role. Starting with Marshal MacMahon in 1873, the message sent to his parliamentary electors on assuming office was an acknowledgement of parliamentary sovereignty. Messages were also sent at the outbreak of the First and Second World Wars and on presidential resignations – by Thiers in 1873, MacMahon in 1879, Grévy in 1887, Casimir-Périer in 1895 and Millerand in 1924 – although de Gaulle in 1969 made a point of sending his resignation to the Prime Minister, while Coty in 1959 sent no resignation at all. As de Gaulle bluntly put it in his memoirs, parliament having 'ceased to be the source of policy and the government', he contented himself with 'notifying important initiatives that I take on my own without reference to it'.[105] He did sent a message to parliament when he invoked article 16 in 1961 (an act of presidential power rather than of allegiance, to put it mildly), but he preferred to address himself to the nation.

Vilified by Vichy propagandists as the *Général micro* for the masterly use he made of the BBC during the Second World War, radio was the crucial instrument by which de Gaulle acquired historic legitimacy with his 18 June 1940 broadcast. However, it was during his presidency – which saw the number of TV sets in France increase from 800,000 to 11 million – that the most potent use was made of the medium, especially at times of national crisis. His superlative talents were deployed with decisive effect on 23 April 1961, not just on the nation at large but particularly on the

105. *Mémoires d'Espoir*, p. 297. See also Decaumont, pp. 131–4. On Woodrow Wilson's revival of the use of the presidential message to Congress, see David Mervin, 'The President and Congress' in Malcolm Shaw (ed.), *Roosevelt to Reagan: The Development of the Modern Presidency*, London, 1987, p. 86. De Gaulle sent five messages to parliament, Pompidou three and Giscard only one. During his first term Mitterrand sent three messages.

conscripts in Algeria, so that it has been called the *victoire des transistors*. Again, on 30 May 1968, he chose his old medium, radio, which had played an important part in spreading the current disorder, to rally his supporters in a situation over which he had previously lost control and which once more might possibly have degenerated into civil war had it been mishandled.[106]

His successors as audiovisual monarchs relaxed control over the public media, using them less to dramatise events with theatrical showmanship than to reassure in a low-profile manner (see below, chapter 7). Giscard used TV most often and least successfully. His pathetic attempts at making an emotional appeal to overcome his technocratic style failed to win over 'two out of three' French electors, while losing him many of his own initial supporters. Mitterrand had the painful task of adapting his platform style, which was unsuited to the TV medium, as well as shifting from the adversarial rhetoric of Socialist ideology to unanimist Gaullian discourse. He did this with application, helped by the loss of much of his power during 1986-8, which allowed him to cultivate an Olympian style that he perfected and preserved after he retrieved his previous power.[107]

Just as he pretended to improvise his broadcasts by memorising his speeches, de Gaulle's press conferences were carefully stage-managed to produce the desired effects, with planted questions to elicit carefully prepared answers. They took the form of a monologue thinly disguised as a dialogue. His successors have held fewer press conferences and attracted far fewer journalists, de Gaulle having an international standing which enabled him to draw an audience of up to 1,000 to his 'ritual ceremony'.[108] However, de Gaulle was also concerned to appear to the French people in person on carefully organised provincial tours, preferring the role of a general addressing his troops rather than that of a parliamentary leader debating with the people's representatives. Plunging into the crowd to shake hands – the democratic version of 'touching' for the 'royal evil' – de Gaulle imparted a major extension to the practice of the Third Republic Presidents. As he came to the end of his first term, he took pride in having 'visited 2,500 *communes*, including the main ones, replied in their town halls to the welcome of almost 400

106. *Mémoires d'Espoir*, pp. 307-8. See also Lacouture, *De Gaulle*, III, pp. 166-8, 673, 718-9 and Alain Duhamel, pp. 120, 133-5.
107. Jean-Marie Cotteret, 'Les stratégies de communications des Présidents de la République' in *Pouvoirs*, no. 41, pp. 116-21. For a list of all presidential TV/radio broadcasts from 1958 to 1986, see *ibid.*, pp. 122-32.
108. *Mémoires d'Espoir*, pp. 308-10; cf. Dulong, pp. 170, 179-81 and Lacouture, *De Gaulle*, III, pp. 19. 21-2, 28-9.

municipal councils and 100,000 notables, spoken to the assembled
population from platforms in 600 places, discussed with countless
people and shaken innumerable hands'.[109]

The difficulty of grasping the President's day-to-day impact upon
the country's political life is reflected in two other 'routine' features
of his activity. Presidents give private audiences to large numbers
of people. De Gaulle accorded 746 in 1964 alone. Pompidou also
received large numbers of visitors. Thus in 1972, out of a total of
611, he granted audiences 255 times to ministers, received fifty-four
foreign heads of state and ministers, forty-three French and twenty-
two foreign ambassadors, twenty-five generals and senior officials,
twenty-four members of parliament, fourteen businessmen and
seven trade unionists.[110] In 1975 Giscard granted only 340 audiences, an indication of his introverted personality, for which he paid
a severe political penalty. Mitterrand received more politicians than
his predecessors, as well as more non-political 'outsiders', especially
writers.

The massive presidential mail is another feature of modern democratic society. At times of crisis, such as January 1960 in Algeria,
the President received a record 210,000 letters in a single week. By
1990, the volume of presidential mail attained an average of a thousand letters per working day, enough to keep a staff of ninety people
fully employed, a third of them concerned with writing replies.
Having suffered a small but significant fall during the 1986–7
cohabitation years, the number of letters climbed again thereafter.
In 1990, 262,000 citizens wrote to the President, excluding the pres-
sure-group mail which raised the total to 470,000 missives. Many
of the private letters are requests for assistance from people in
distress or seeking privileged treatment, the President being naively
regarded as an absolute ruler capable of putting everything right
or granting favours at will. Most of the suppliants are answered
quickly, the relevant ministry, agency or Prefect being alerted
to deal with a complaint where relevant. Those who express opinions attract special attention, their views being evaluated by the
head of the President's mail service, who prepares a four-page
monthly report for him. Such feedback (2.35 million letters during
Mitterrand's first ten years) makes an excellent supplement to
opinion poll information as a way of keeping the President in touch
with public opinion because his capacity to respond to the people's

---

109. At a press conference on 9 Sept. 1965, *Discours et Messages*, IV, p. 391. See also
    Mémoires d'Espoir, pp. 310–12. More generally, see Dulong, pp. 68, 151–60.
110. Roussel, *Pompidou*, p. 482.

views is a fundamental component of his political authority.[111] No one has since attained Emile Zola's success in 1898, with his public letter to the President of the Republic, *J'Accuse*, which turned the tide in the Dreyfus affair.

Statesman or Partisan: a false dichotomy

It would be unwise to take entirely at face value de Gaulle's dictum that constitutional law is 'first a constraint that one hates, then a habit that one accepts and finally a tradition that one reveres' as far as the Fifth Republic is concerned.[112] Sticklers for legalistic rectitude present the matter differently. The historian Adrien Dansette, at the end of his history of the French presidency, roundly declares: 'The constitution of the Fifth Republic has not been applied. That of the Third was not applied either. In both cases, what prevailed was constitutional practice based on the text, respecting most of it - especially the least important parts - and ignoring others, especially the most fundamental.'[113] A constitutional lawyer has put the matter even more forthrightly: 'All the Presidents of the Fifth Republic have in effect violated the Constitution of which they were supposed to be the guardians. They have conceived their role with less concern for the constraints of the text than for what the state of political forces rendered possible . . .'[114] Although it is true that 'The British point of reference, tirelessly invoked by M. Debré in 1959, has not survived him',[115] the partisan challenge to state power could not subsequently be shrugged off.

In article 4 of the Constitution, the existence of political parties was formally acknowledged for the first time in one of the many solemn documents with which French history has been littered. Inserted at the suggestion of the CCC, parties were to be confined to the modest role of 'contributing to the expression of the suffrage'. Determined to avoid the re-emergence of the 'party regime', de Gaulle never openly admitted that the working of the French political system necessitated a partisan parliamentary majority supporting the President and 'his' government (see below, chapter 5). Insofar as there could be a leader of the 'presidential majority' other than the President himself, he was someone chosen by the President,

111. Eric Dupin, 'M. le Président, je vous fais une lettre', *Libération*, 12 March 1991, pp. 10–11. I am grateful to Jean-Luc Parodi for drawing my attention to this informative article.
112. Charles de Gaulle, *Lettres, Notes et Carnets*, vol. 11, Paris, 1980, p. 214.
113. Adrien Dansette, *Histoire des Présidents de la République*, Paris, 1953, p. 413.
114. Philippe Ardant in *Pouvoirs*, no. 41, pp. 51–2.
115. Pierre Avril in Seurin and Martres, p. 237.

not by the presidential Assembly majority. However, the first direct election by universal suffrage in 1965 brought home to de Gaulle that political parties were encroaching remorselessly upon presidential supremacy. Desacralised between the two ballots – an unexpected indignity inflicted upon him by the voters – de Gaulle warned of the consequence of electing his rival Mitterrand. 'If, instead of a head of State devised to prevent the Republic succumbing to the discretion of the parties, one puts a head of State who is merely an emanation of the parties, then, I reiterate, one would have achieved nothing, and everything that has been written in the Constitution will change nothing at all, there will be a return to party government.'[116] A President based upon a restored state power or the restoration of a President based upon partisan power: such was the choice. Is France condemned to this dichotomy at the summit: either a statesman or a partisan? Has an analytical distinction been transmuted into an exclusive separation of substance?

De Gaulle's fear has been theorised by those who have taken the view that 'founded against the party regime, the Fifth Republic is the first partisan regime that France has hitherto experienced.'[117] Maurice Duverger has been the leading exponent of the crucial importance of the relationship between the President with autonomous constitutional power and the presence or absence of a stable and supportive Assembly majority, with the emphasis upon the latter, partisan feature. If the President and the Assembly share the same partisan loyalties and the President is accepted as leader, then he has undisputed power. If they are of opposed partisan loyalties, the Prime Minister is the real head of the executive power and the President is confined to his constitutional prerogatives. If there is no stable Assembly majority, the Fifth Republic would approximate 'more closely to the letter of the Constitution. The Paris republican monarch might be a Protean king, changing in appearance and power according to the balance of parliamentary strength.' Writing in 1974, Duverger concluded: 'Today's all powerful President of the Republic could tomorrow be weak . . .'[118] He also anticipated both the 1986–8 and post-1988 situations. Without a loyal Assembly majority, 'the President of the Republic would exercise a tribune function, helping the Opposition to criticise the Majority in power

---

116. Charles de Gaulle, *Discours et Messages*, IV, pp. 433–4.
117. François Borella, *Les Partis Politiques dans l'Europe des Neuf*, Paris, 1979, p. 107.
118. Maurice Duverger, *La Monarchie Républicaine ou comment les démocraties se donnent des rois*, Paris, 1974, p. 188; cf. 13, 216; Duverger, 'Le concept de régime semi-présidentiel' in Duverger (ed.), *Les Régimes Semi-Présidentiels*, pp. 15–17; Duverger, *Bréviaire de la Cohabitation*, Paris, 1986, p. 8.

and preparing the conditions for a new *volte-face* by the electors.'[119] If the President's supporters almost had a majority or could rely on alternative majorities, he would remain powerful . . . as Mitterrand demonstrated after 1988.

There is an interesting convergence between the views of one of the Constitution's architects and one of its leading opponents. Looking back at the end of 1989 on the working of the Fifth Republic, Raymond Janot frankly confessed that 'the scenarios that have occurred are not at all what we imagined.' The extension of presidential power that occurred was due to the habits formed during the early years, owing to the Algerian war. 'The Constitution has only worked according to our hypotheses since there has been a limited majority in parliament, a majority that is not absolute, because we could not conceive of anything else, we had never known anything else.'[120] Mitterrand, in the electoral campaign following his 1988 dissolution of the Assembly, had suggested that he would prefer only a relative Socialist majority, allowing him to come closer to the letter of the Constitution. In the period of uneasy *cohabitation* with a Right-wing Assembly and government, Mitterrand remarked: 'During the first five years of my presidency, I lived – not in spirit but in fact – almost like my three predecessors . . . the practice established since General de Gaulle meant that everything reverted to the President of the Republic. I wrote books at the time to complain about this and I continue to think that the President disposed of too much power, in fact though not in law, in day-to-day practice. During the first five years of my presidency, I gradually adapted this practice, so that I was not as taken aback as you seem to believe when the majority changed.'[121] Political circumstances and political intentions would thus seem to have combined to produce a partial corrective to the hyper-presidentialist propensities of the Fifth Republic, although Mitterrand somewhat exaggerated the voluntary change in practice which he brought about.

Clearly, Burdeau went too far in claiming that the 'President is either apolitical or he is nothing. He is nothing, because he would cease to be the original component which the political system of the Fifth Republic has introduced into French political life.'[122] He gets into difficulties by arguing that presidential power depends upon the extent to which he is able to avoid being identified with the

119. Duverger, *Monarchie Républicaine*, p. 221; cf. 229–32.
120. Janot's testimony in *Georges Pompidou*, pp. 46, 48.
121. Mitterrand interview on Europe 1 of 9 Dec. 1986, included in an appendix by Philippe Ardant in *Pouvoirs*, no. 41, p. 62.
122. Georges Burdeau, *Traité de Science Politique*, vol. X: *La Révolte des Colonies*, 3rd edn, Paris, 1986, p. 440; cf. 445.

parliamentary majority, which provides him with 'the means, not the authority' to govern.[123] His authority depends upon his presidential majority of the popular vote, so that 'the whole art of presidential policy is to calculate how far he can go without losing his parliamentary support . . . he can coerce it by showing that another majority supports presidential policy: the composite and informal majority constituted by the collection of French people which the President has been able to please.'[124] Authority without the means to make it effective is remarkably like an Emperor without his clothes. Nevertheless, Burdeau is right to stress that as long as the President retains public support – which requires him to remain constantly in touch with public opinion – he retains the political initiative and can compel his political rivals to ask 'What will the President do?'[125] His ultimate strength is the (illusory) popular identification of the President as the only person capable of satisfying every wish. In that sense he is a supra-partisan sovereign.

It is tempting to identify each of the four Presidents with a particular type of relationship with the party system, although this is not possible. De Gaulle sought to maintain a rigid separation between presidential and partisan power, but was forced to rely in practice on acquiring and maintaining the support of an Assembly majority. Pompidou, like Mitterrand between 1981 and 1986 and again after 1988, identified presidential with partisan power, to prevent the emergence of a rival who combined the positions of Prime Minister and party leader. Giscard from 1976 till 1981 and Mitterrand from 1986 till 1988 had to manage a situation in which there was no partisan coincidence between the President and the Assembly majority. On both occasions Jacques Chirac played a key role, but whereas under Giscard the RPR usually supported the government, albeit reluctantly, under Mitterrand Chirac was actually Prime Minister, so that the President was forced to rely upon his 'state power' alone.

France has had to draw upon the strength of its state *mystique* as a corrective to the weaknesses of its partisan *politique*. This makes it especially important to have a flexible political system (Pompidou approvingly called it a 'mongrel' one) that can produce varying combinations of state and partisan power under the aegis of presidential authority.[126] Rather than an 'imperial president'

123. *Ibid.*, p. 447; cf. 440–2.
124. *Ibid.*, p. 448; cf. 446, 453–4.
125. *Ibid.*, p. 455; cf. 456–9.
126. Georges Pompidou, *Le Noeud Gordien*, pp. 66–7. The distinctions drawn here follow closely but are not identical with those made by Jean-Louis Quermonne in 'Le Président de la République et le système des partis', *Pouvoirs*, no. 41, pp. 98–112.

(Arthur Schlesinger's description of the US President),[127] France has forged a partisan statesman with a democratic authority that cannot be reduced to his constitutional or partisan powers. He draws upon both these sources of power as circumstances permit to sustain an authority that is based upon popular support. To acquire this democratic authority, he must show at the presidential election that his appeal transcends the limits of his own party. To attract this supra-partisan support, he must distance himself from his partisans so that he can plausibly personify the public interest.[128] Only then is a presidential candidate regarded as fit to impersonate the state and be elevated to France's supreme office.

127. Arthur M. Schlesinger, *The Imperial Presidency*, Boston, Mass., 1974 and Ezra Suleiman in Rose and Suleiman, pp. 103–5.
128. See René Rémond, 'La Cinquième République. Les partis et l'election présiden-tielle', p. 167 and Jean-Louis Quermonne, 'Le profil des candidats et la fonction présidentielle', p. 205, in Hamon and Lobrichon (eds), *L'Election du Chef de l'Etat en France.*

3

THE PRESIDENT AND HIS STAFF

Anne Stevens

The Elysée is not the White House.[1] Both are handsome buildings which serve as the official residence for a President who is not merely a head of state but also a head of government.[2] Each building has given its name as a generic term for the institution which it shelters.[3] But the similarities are superficial. The Presidents of the United States of America have found that the task of government, given the concentration of functions within the White House, has demanded a staff of increasing size and expanding functions. By the mid-1970s, it has been reckoned,[4] the Executive Office of the President, which incorporated some nine agencies, employed more than 5,000 staff, some 560 of them in the White House Office. This is the agency within the Executive Office of the President 'that houses the President's immediate personal staff, such as his top policy advisers, political managers, speech-writers, public relations specialists, congressional liaison aides, press secretary and those responsible for his schedule'.[5]

In many respects the main functions of the White House staff –

1. This phrase also heads Jean Massot's analysis of the French presidential staff beginning on p. 113 of Jean Massot, *L'Arbitre et le Capitaine*, Paris, 1987.
2. Of the four Presidents of the Fifth Republic only General de Gaulle actually lived in the building. It is perhaps worth noting that the palace was begun in 1718 by a noble speculator, the Comte d'Evreux. After a varied history, during which it was, among other things, the property of Mme de Pompadour, let out as individual apartments, and the place where Napoleon signed his abdication after Waterloo, it first became, in 1848 under Louis-Napoleon, the official residence of the head of state. As Emperor he inhabited the Tuileries, but from 1875 the Elysée, which had escaped the fires of the Commune, again became the residence of the President.
3. '*L'Elysée*' generally now embraces not only the palace itself, but also the offices at 2, 4 and 14 rue de l'Elysée and on the Quai Branly which house parts of the presidential staff and services, including a crêche for the children of the staff. The term is the one used by the press and by commentators generally. Within the administration the more colloquial nickname is '*le château*'. Michel Schifres and Michel Sarazin, *L'Elysée de Mitterrand. Secrets de la maison du prince*, Paris, 1985, pp. 45 and 83, and Jean Massot, *L'Arbitre*, p. 125.
4. John Hart, 'The President and his Staff' in Malcolm Shaw (ed.), *Roosevelt to Reagan: The development of the modern presidency*, London, 1987, p. 168.
5. *Ibid.*, p. 160.

those of coordinating the policy-making activities of the government, of controlling access to the President, of organising his[6]
necessarily limited time and creating and maintaining public and
media support for him – are shared by the staff of the Elysée.
Moreover both in France and in the United States the President's
personal programme and choices usually (though in France not
invariably) determine the policy orientation of the government.
The two Presidents, however, operate within very different constitutional, political and organisational contexts. For example, the
intensive liaison with elected political representatives to which an
important part of the staff resources of the White House is devoted
occurs in France through very different mechanisms. Moreover
the existence and role of the Prime Minister in France have a direct
influence upon the nature and functions of the Elysée. Not only
is the Elysée staff less than one-tenth the size of its counterpart in
the White House Office, but it also does not have the overriding
political authority upon members of the government which the
White House staff exercises. The powers of the French presidential
staff are a symptom, not a cause, of the role of the President. The
power and influence of the Elysée directly reflect the nature of the
role that the President himself is able and chooses to play.

Historical Background

Under the Fourth Republic the President fulfilled the normal ceremonial functions of a head of state. A presidential household was
required in order to enable him to fulfil his representational and
other duties. The President's personal advisory and administrative
staff, as distinct from the household, was very small. At the beginning of the Third Republic the President was assisted by a single
Secretary-General recruited from the army. By the turn of the century a civilian Secretary-General had also been appointed.[7] Under
the Fourth Republic the President's personal staff amounted to
some ten officials – a military staff of four, a civilian Secretary-
General with three or four assistants, and a *directeur de cabinet*
concerned both with the running of the household services and with

6. Throughout this chapter the President is referred to as 'he'. All the Presidents
   of the French Republic have been male, and distinctions between the incumbents
   and the more abstract notion of the office-holder, for which gender-neutral
   forms of expression might be more suitable, would be clumsy. There have been
   female candidates in presidential elections and a female Prime Minister. No one
   can rule out the possibility of a female President.
7. Massot, *La Présidence de la République en France*, 2nd edn, Paris, 1986, p. 168.

the organisation of the President's timetable and activities.

The President exercised the chairmanship of the National Council of Defence and of the Supreme Council of the Judiciary, through which he exercised the prerogative of pardon. He also became President of the French Union of colonies and protectorates. The Judicial Council and French Union Secretariats were the only executive parts of the presidental office.[8] Auriol took with him into the first presidency of the Fourth Republic some of the advisers who had been assisting him in his previous role as President of the National Assembly. He chose a relatively young staff – the civilian Secretary-General, his deputy (Auriol's son Paul) and the *directeur de cabinet* were all aged under thirty-five in 1947. All three stayed *en poste* throughout his seven-year term of office. In addition to the official members of the staff, however, the President could, and did, call upon other advisers. Verrier notes that Raymond Janot, subsequently the Secretary-General of the *Conseil d'Etat*, was his adviser on legal matters.[9] Janot subsequently fulfilled this role in de Gaulle's *cabinet* at the Hôtel Matignon[10] and was (see previous chapter) very closely involved in the drafting of the Constitution of the Fifth Republic.

When Réné Coty followed Auriol into the presidency in 1954, he retained a staff of much the same size as his predecessor's.[11] The organisation was modified; in addition to a Secretary-General and a *directeur de cabinet*, Coty appointed a *directeur du secrétariat général* and three *chargés de mission*, one of whom, the head of the Elysée's financial service, had served under Auriol, as had one of the *aides-de-camp*. It was perhaps a sign of changing times that one of the *chargés de mission* was designated as the head of the information service.[12]

The structure and organisation of the presidential staff reflected the nature of the tasks of the presidential office as the Presidents conceived them. Auriol, especially, saw a distinctive role for himself. He tried to ensure that his staff worked in close collaboration with the General Secretariat of the government in determining the Council of Ministers' business. He was prepared, as Tunisia moved towards independence, to entrust a mission to Tunisia to his own civilian Secretary-General. Nevertheless, the real limits to the role

8. See Vincent Auriol, *Journal du Septennat*, VII, Paris, 1971, p. 581.
9. Patrice Verrier, *Les Services de la Présidence de la République*, Paris, 1971, p. 15.
10. *L'Entourage et de Gaulle* (G. Pilleul, ed), Paris, 1979, p. 80.
11. See the testimony of Francis de Baecque, Director of the Secretariat of Coty's staff, in *René Coty, tel qu'en lui-même*, Paris, 1991.
12. Verrier, *Services*, pp. 16–17 and 77–8.

of the President and the extent to which it was a position of influence rather than power[13] determined the small size and very limited advisory capacity of the Fourth Republic presidential staff.

The radical change in the nature of the presidency that was introduced by the Constitution of the Fifth Republic and developed as de Gaulle's practice defined the scope and limits of presidential power was immediately symbolised by the creation of a much more substantial supporting staff around the President. On his appointment as Prime Minister in June 1958, de Gaulle had taken with him to the Prime Minister's office in the Hôtel Matignon the team that had begun to gather around him as his return to power became ever more probable. De Gaulle made it clear that he personally intended to take in hand the three major problems with which, as he saw it, the country was confronted: Algeria, the economy, and reform of the state.[14] During the period from June 1958 to January 1959, policy on all these matters was largely made within the Prime Minister's office, which became – quite exceptionally – central to the working of the government.

At Matignon, however, de Gaulle's *cabinet* did not differ very sharply from those of previous Prime Ministers in either its structure or its composition. Where it did diverge was in the sense of the magnitude and the urgency of the tasks with which it was confronted, and in the scope and legitimacy which it enjoyed in their accomplishment.[15] In this context it is unsurprising that Georges Pompidou, as *directeur de cabinet*, fulfilled a particularly crucial role. It was partly his acute and accurate perception that such a role would not be available even to the Secretary-General of the presidency if faced with a Prime Minister that caused Pompidou to decline to continue to serve on de Gaulle's staff after the General became President.[16]

The presidency of the Fifth Republic nevertheless required a much more extensive supporting staff. In 1959 the size of de Gaulle's civilian staff grew immediately to nineteen members, and by 1964 it had reached twenty-four members. His military staff also grew from four officers to eleven and was renamed, ceasing to be described as a 'household' – the *maison militaire* under a military Secretary-General – and becoming instead the *état-major particulier*, under a chief of staff (see below, chapter 6). The instant change in the shape and functions of that staff was one of the

13. Francis de Baecque, *Qui Gouverne la France?*, Paris, 1976, pp. 46–7.
14. Broadcast of 27 June 1958.
15. *L'Entourage*, p. 83.
16. Pierre Rouanet, *Georges Pompidou*, Paris, 1969, p. 68.

sharpest and most immediate symbols of the new role and interpretation of the presidency brought about by the Fifth Republic.

Personnel

The presidential staff after 1958 constituted a new institution. It had
some features in common with its antecedents, but the new role of
the presidency gave the staff unprecedented scope for action. Any
new institution is likely to be influenced by the people it contains;
by their backgrounds, expectations and general characteristics.
Who constitute the presidential staff, how are they recruited and
what type of career pattern are they likely to follow?

The size of the presidential staff, as distinct from the household, has varied since 1958. Under de Gaulle and Pompidou it
averaged forty-five members, including both civilian and military
staff. Under Giscard the numbers initially seemed somewhat
reduced; before Pompidou's death the *Journal Officiel* listed
twenty-seven civilian staff (not including the somewhat separate
Secretariat for African and Madagascan affairs, discussed later)
while after Giscard's election the list was reduced to eighteen. This
represented a real if somewhat exaggerated reduction, since the new
list left out some of those concerned with the more routine tasks. By
1979 the number of staff had grown again, reaching twenty-four
civilians.[17]

Under Mitterrand the size of the staff has grown compared with
that established by de Gaulle and Pompidou, but not markedly.
Strict comparability is not straightforward; for example, while it is
clear that the President's two personal secretaries are an important
part of his immediate entourage, they should perhaps not be classi-
fied strictly as members of a presidential staff. Samy Cohen[18]
states that de Gaulle never had more than twenty-three civilian and
thirteen military staff, Pompidou had a maximum of forty civilians
and six military staff, and Giscard's staff at its largest, early in 1981,
consisted of twenty-four civilians and seven military members.
Mitterrand's staff increased during his first ten years in office, rising
from some twenty-seven to just under forty civilians and seven
military members. These numbers are not large for the staff of the
person who has sometimes been described as potentially the most
powerful individual in the Western democratic world. They point to

17. S. Cohen, 'Le Secrétariat général de la Présidence de la République' in Francis
de Baecque and Jean-Louis Quermonne, *Administration et Politique sous la
Cinquième République*, Paris, 1981, p. 110.
18. S. Cohen, 'Les Conseillers de l'Elysée face aux hommes de la Maison Blanche.
Specificité du cas français' in J.-L. Seurin (ed.), *La Présidence de la République
en France et aux Etats-Unis*, Paris, 1986, p. 209.

some of the characteristics and limitations of the French concept of the presidential office.

There has been a fluctuating turnover of personnel within the presidential staff. Under de Gaulle staff members remained on average for only just over three years.[19] A total of seventy people served under him, while forty-four served under Pompidou during his five-year presidency. Giscard preferred to work with those whom he knew and trusted, so despite some renewal after the 1978 general election, many of his staff remained throughout his seven years. Under Mitterrand the rate of turnover increased again. During his first three and a half years in office twelve staff members left the Elysée.[20] Nevertheless, a few key people remained in their posts for considerable periods. Mitterrand's special adviser Jacques Attali remained from the election in 1981 until he became head of the European Bank for Reconstruction and Development in April 1991, and Jean-Louis Bianco stayed at the Elysée continuously for ten years, first as a specialist adviser and then from 1982 as Secretary-General, until he became a minister in May 1991. There was an interesting pattern in one or two careers, involving departure from the Elysée at the time of the general election of 1986 and return after the presidential victory in 1988.[21]

Many of those who make up this staff come from official backgrounds. The reasons for this are certainly akin to the reasons which explain why between 75 and 90 per cent of the staff of ministerial private offices under the Fifth Republic have been officials. First, the occupancy of a senior official post is regarded in France as a guarantee of intelligence and intellectual competence. Secondly, many of the tasks which the presidential staff fulfil involve very close contacts indeed with a wide range of ministries and administrative services. In these circumstances a profound knowledge of the system and an existing network of contacts within it are useful attributes to bring to the post. Equally important are the budgetary considerations. The Elysée's resources for the payment of its staff can only meet the cost of six administrative staff.[22] All the others are paid out of the budgets of other organisations from which they are

---

19. *L'Entourage*, p. 98.
20. M. Schifres and M. Sarazin, p. 323.
21. Two members of staff spent the intervening period at the *Conseil d'Etat*: Christian Sautter, who was deputy Secretary-General in 1982–5 and again from 1988 until the end of 1990, and Hubert Védrine, one of the team who accompanied Mitterrand from the Socialist Party organisation to the Elysée in 1981, where he stayed until January 1986, returning in 1988 and taking over from Jean-Louis Bianco as Secretary-General in May 1991.
22. Massot, *L'Arbitre,* p. 127.

seconded. For government departments this poses few problems. In other cases, public enterprises have paid the salaries.

It was estimated that 90 per cent of de Gaulle's staff were senior officials.[23] 'The rule was almost always to pick – as specialist advisers – senior officials who had specialised in the main areas of activity within their sector . . .'[24] Under Pompidou the proportion was only 73 per cent but it rose again to 89 per cent under Giscard. Under Mitterrand the percentage declined sharply in a movement comparable to, but much more marked than, that observed in the personal staffs of government ministers after 1981. Of Mitterrand's initial team at the Elysée in 1981 only some 40 per cent were senior officials[25] and this proportion has not greatly increased.[26]

Many of the Elysée staff have been aged between thirty-five and forty-five. Under de Gaulle, specialist adviser recruits were 'neither nearing the highest point of their careers, nor very young officials . . .',[27] and under all the first three Presidents the average age of the staff at recruitment was between forty and forty-one.[28] Under Mitterrand the staff initially recruited in 1981 fell broadly into two groups: a number of very long-standing friends and associates, all aged over fifty, and a group in mid-career, none of whom was much over forty. By the end of his first term the first group had largely left the Elysée and a number of somewhat younger staff had joined. In 1990 two advisers were appointed at an age markedly younger than had been the norm: Isabelle Thomas, who had been one of the leaders of the student movement in 1986 and a member of Mitterrand's campaign team in 1988, and Anne Lauvergeon, who at the end of the year became deputy Secretary-General.

The appointment of these two staff members highlights a striking contrast between the presidential staffs of the 1980s and of the 1960s. De Gaulle would have no women on his staff. He thought them a source of complications, since, he maintained, they brought personal, emotional and sentimental factors into the cold hard business of dealing with the country's affairs.[29] Pompidou, however,

23. Cohen, 'Le Secrétariat', p. 112.
24. *L'Entourage*, p. 88.
25. Monique Dagnaud and Dominique Mehl, *L'Elite Rose*, Paris, 1982, p. 243.
26. Schifres and Sarazin, *L'Elysée*, p. 147.
27. *L'Entourage*, p. 88.
28. Cohen, 'Le Secrétariat', p. 113.
29. Bernard Tricot, interview in *L'Express*, 31 Oct 1977, quoted in *L'Entourage*, p. 97. When Tricot, as Secretary-General, asked de Gaulle to take a woman on to the staff the President refused with some awkwardness, saying 'Women, you know, that's a different matter . . .' Bernard Tricot, oral communication to the June 1991 workshop at the Maison Française, Oxford, to discuss draft chapters for this book.

brought with him to the Elysée a former colleague from the Rothschild Bank, Anne-Marie Dupuy, who became his *chef de cabinet*. Altogether five women served on his staff.[30] Under Giscard the number of women fell again but on Mitterrand's staff the number grew steadily, from five in 1981 to eleven at the end of his first term (1988). In 1991 about half the staff were women.

Recruitment

Personal loyalty to the President has been one of the factors that has brought staff members into the presidential entourage. This characteristic was marked under the first President of the Fifth Republic, de Gaulle, who was constituting a new team to tackle a new conception of the presidency. This was also true under Mitterrand, whose accession to the presidency marked a pronounced political shift after more than twenty years of government by the Centre-Right.

In 1959 de Gaulle relied heavily upon men who had known him for many years and remained loyal to him throughout his period of political exile. Half his initial entourage had been with him at Matignon.[31] As his presidency continued, however, especially after the resolution of the Algerian problem, the number of staff members who were personally known to de Gaulle before recruitment diminished. Thereafter the choice of staff members was based usually upon their competence, their possession of a professional background appropriate to the post, and their willingness to work within the framework of de Gaulle's ideas. In many cases new staff members were known to existing staff members.

When Pompidou became President, Jacques Foccart retained responsibility for African and Madagascan affairs,[32] otherwise the civilian presidential staff was completely renewed. Again, the President brought with him staff members who had worked with him before; all the senior members of his office and five of his six original specialist advisers had been on his staff when he had been

30. Pompidou's staff included Mme Marie-France Garaud, to whom a certain degree of notoriety became attached, stemming from her supposed political influence, in tandem with Pierre Juillet, both over Pompidou and subsequently over Jacques Chirac as Prime Minister and then Mayor of Paris. She was a presidential candidate in 1981.

31. *L'Entourage*, p. 93. De Gaulle's first Secretary-General at the Elysée was Geoffroy de Courcel, a diplomat who had accompanied him on the flight to London in June 1940. His successor, Etienne Burin des Roziers, had also been on de Gaulle's war-time staff.

32. On Foccart's role, see S. Cohen, *Les Conseillers du Président*, Paris, 1980, chapter 8.

Prime Minister.[33] Again, as the presidency progressed, the element
of prior acquaintance became less important. Of the twenty-seven
new appointments under Pompidou none had previously worked
for him, although one was his niece.[34] With Giscard, the personal
staff from his period as Minister of Finance, many of whom also
worked in his presidential election campaign, were an important
resource for the recruitment of his presidential staff.

On his election in 1981, Mitterrand in some respects more closely
resembled de Gaulle in June 1958 than he did either of his two immediate predecessors. He had held no ministerial office since 1958.
His initial team, just like those of his predecessors, included a high
proportion of people who were well known to him and with whom
he had worked previously. This meant that he looked particularly
to a number of long-standing personal friends, to the staff of the
Socialist Party, and to his campaign team. Of the thirty-four civilian
staff members appointed early in the presidency, only eleven were
senior civil servants.

If loyalty and previous service to the President are two of the
criteria which have determined the choice of presidential staff, they
are certainly not the only ones. Ability, personality and experience
in an appropriate area have also been important. The role of identifying suitable people has often fallen primarily to the Secretary-
General,[35] but recommendation by common acquaintances also
plays a role. Certain 'networks' have been identified in the case of
recruitment to Mitterrand's staff, but it is clear these are neither
narrow nor exclusive. One staff member was recruited when she
came to the attention of the Elysée for the quality of the analysis
that she produced of the mass demonstrations of 1984 which led to
the withdrawal of the Savary education bill. The appointment of
Christian Prouteau from the Gendarmerie to the presidential staff
to form a unit directly concerned with ensuring the security of
the President, and subsequently to concern himself more generally
with anti-terrorism, was another such choice. It also illustrated
Mitterrand's loyalty to his staff once appointed. The scandal which
surrounded the alleged planting of evidence on Irish citizens with
possible IRA connections resulted in 1987 in Prouteau's indictment

33. William G. Andrews, *Presidential Government in Gaullist France*, Albany, NY,
    1982, p. 75.
34. *Ibid.*, p. 76.
35. See Schifres and Sarazin, *L'Elysée*, p. 144. 'Having been elected President of the
    Republic on 15 June 1969 . . . Pompidou one morning called together a number
    of his staff. . . . "You will be Secretary-General," he said to me. "As for the
    others, you sort that out!"' Michel Jobert, *Mémoires d'Avenir*, Paris, 1974,
    p. 155.

on charges of intimidating witnesses. However, it did not lead to his immediate removal from the presidential staff, which he finally left in November 1988.

The Elysée in itself does not provide a career structure for staff members. There are few senior posts, although promotion within the structure is not impossible. In general, presidential staff have gone to posts elsewhere, within the senior civil service or as ministers.[36] The network of patronage which the Elysée enjoys is part of the much wider system of patronage relating to top French administrative, public and private sector posts which fashions the career moves and the professional relationships of the tightly interlocking French élite.[37]

The French President, however, is not only the head of the state, and (except under *cohabitation*) the effective head of the government; he is also a political leader. Since 1962, he has needed a political campaign to put him into the Elysée in the first place, and re-election also requires a political campaign. His office is inevitably a strongly political office as well as an executive one. In the earlier years of the Fifth Republic, de Gaulle frowned upon political or ministerial ambition among his staff.[38] Very few of his or Pompidou's staffs competed in elections while they were actually on the staff, or moved on directly into ministerial posts.[39]

From the start of the Giscard presidency the political connections of the Elysée staff became much more marked, and it has become an increasingly important source of ministers. The key position of the Secretary-General at the intersection of political and administrative concerns no doubt explains why one of the incumbents of that office under Giscard, and the two men who between them filled that post for the first ten years of the Mitterrand presidency, have gone on directly to major ministerial posts. Both Giscard and Mitterrand brought on to their staff people who had already

36. Edouard Balladur took over from Michel Jobert as Secretary-General under Pompidou. Jean-Louis Bianco replaced Pierre Bérégovoy in 1982 and was in turn replaced by Hubert Védrine in 1991.
37. See for example E. Suleiman, *Elites in French Society*, Princeton, NJ, 1978, and J. Howorth and P. G. Cerny, *Elites in France*, London, 1981.
38. Bernard Tricot, oral communication, Maison Française, Oxford, June 1991.
39. Only three members of de Gaulle's staff stood for election as Members of Parliament, two of them successfully. Olivier Guichard was the only staff member subsequently to become a Minister. See Andrews, *Presidential Government*, p. 79. Of Pompidou's staff, only Michel Jobert was appointed a minister directly from his Elysée post, although much later Edouard Balladur became Minister of Finance in the Chirac government of 1986–8, having initially returned to the *Conseil d'Etat*. Bérégovoy became Finance Minister (1984–6 and 1988–92) before becoming Prime Minister.

held ministerial office, while under Giscard, and even more under Mitterrand, presidential staff members have fought election campaigns. The trend appears to be increasing. Five members of the Elysée staff were candidates in the general election of 1988, being placed on leave during the campaign. Two were successful, one of them subsequently becoming a minister in the 1991 Cresson government. Altogether, seven of the forty-six ministers in that government had at some time served within the Elysée staff.

The Structure of the Presidential Staff

In developing a new role for the presidential staff, de Gaulle gave this expanded institution a clear structure. The staff were divided into the military staff, the Secretariat-General – which was to be concerned, de Gaulle said, with the presidency's relationship with the state – and the *cabinet*, concerned not only with the practical details of the President's activities but also with 'relationships with the nation'. In practice this meant that the *cabinet* was responsible for dealing with the presidential mail, presidential travel, relationships with the press, protocol, the day-to-day management of the President's diary, and the running of the Elysée household.[40] The Secretariat for African and Madagascan affairs was a separate entity, but its head, Jacques Foccart, and his deputy functioned also as members of the presidential staff. From 1963 Foccart was the link between the President and the Gaullist party and the other political components of the presidential majority.

De Gaulle's organisation of the Elysée was essentially pyramidal and hierarchical. The heads of the main sections were assisted by specialist advisers (*conseillers techniques*), and they in turn might be seconded by assistant advisers (*chargés de mission*). At the end of his presidency the Secretary-General had under him four *conseillers techniques* to whom in turn ten *chargés de mission* reported.[41]

Under Pompidou the structure of the presidential staff changed slightly. He retained the division into Secretariat-General, *cabinet*, Secretariat for African and Madagascan affairs and military staff, but placed the military staff and the *cabinet* under the authority of the Secretary-General, who became from that time on clearly the head of the presidential staff. He also instituted the position of deputy Secretary-General. The organisational structure of the staff under Pompidou became less hierarchical, if more tightly-knit and

40. Claude Dulong, *Vie Quotidienne à l'Elysée au temps de Charles de Gaulle*, Paris, 1974, p. 92. She remarks that de Gaulle did not wish to have a *chef de cabinet* or a deputy director.
41. Massot, *La Présidence*, p. 169.

more closely linked to the President himself than it had been under de Gaulle.[42] Pompidou also introduced another major element into the structure, by appointing Pierre Juillet to a post outside the hierarchy. Juillet was appointed 'personal adviser to the President of the Republic'. Pompidou's successors have also each included among their staff personal advisers outside the hierarchy.

Giscard kept the same broad organisation of the staff as Pompidou, appointing a deputy Secretary-General and a *chef de cabinet* under the authority of the Secretary-General. Giscard's organisation was, however, even less pyramidal as well as rather smaller than that of his predecessors, for the number of specialist advisers increased and the assistant advisers virtually disappeared. A broad division of labour assigned international affairs to the Secretary-General and all internal concerns to the oversight of the deputy Secretary-General. Each staff member had a clearly defined functional area and equal access to the Secretary-General or his deputy. Giscard moreover abolished the separate status of the Secretariat for African and Madagascan affairs, although Réné Journiac, who had been Jacques Foccart's deputy, continued to work with him as a specialist adviser under the nominal authority of the Secretary-General.

In some respects Mitterrand's organisation of his staff has reverted to de Gaulle's model, in that he has reinstated the post of *directeur de cabinet* and removed the *cabinet* from the Secretariat-General. The *cabinet* includes both a *directeur* and a *chef de cabinet*. Mitterrand retained the notion of appointing personal advisers outside the hierarchy and indeed widened the scope of such appointments. From 1981 until he took up the post of Director of the Bank for European Reconstruction and Development in April 1991, Jacques Attali was 'special adviser to the President', occupying as such, both literally and figuratively, a key position in the operations of the Elysée.

In addition, from 1981, Mitterrand had several 'advisers attached to the President'. It is clear that the nature of the post varies markedly according to its occupant. In the cases, for example, of Juillet under Pompidou or de Grossouvre under Mitterrand, it provided a suitable position for a very close political adviser or a very old friend. For others, the post is related to a specific function and may even be a way of providing a promotion. For yet others such as Edgard Pisani, Director of the Paris Institute for the Arab World, or Elisabeth Guigou when she headed the official body responsible for coordinating France's relations with the European

42. Eric Roussel, *Georges Pompidou*, Paris, 1984, p. 335.

Community, it provides a status within the Elysée for a person who also occupies a prominent function outside it. In addition, since 1982 several staff members have held the title 'adviser to the President.' This has provided a separate structure for specific functions: in African affairs the position was given to Guy Penne from 1982 and subsequently to the President's son Jean-Christophe Mitterrand; and in internal political affairs, including decentralisation and constitutional matters, the position was held by Michel Charasse, who was the director of Mitterrand's electoral campaign in 1988, and who had come to the Elysée after many years as Secretary of the Socialist group in the National Assembly. This title was also held by Gerard Colé, described as the first image-making adviser to be officially installed at the Elysée.[43]

The relatively simple and broadly pyramidal structure of the presidential staff introduced by de Gaulle has become more flexible and more complicated with the proliferation of extra-hierarchical positions. In general, a system which assigns each adviser to a particular sector of activity has persisted because it has proved efficient and limited conflict between staff members.[44] Conflicts have not, however, been entirely eliminated. Examples include the relationship between Jobert, Pompidou's Secretary-General, and Juillet, the special adviser – Juillet retired indignantly to his sheep-rearing activities in central France for months at a time when he felt that his voice was not carrying enough weight – and that between François Polge de Combret and Charles Debbasch, recorded in rancorous detail by Debbasch.[45] Jacques Attali, from his position as special adviser to President Mitterrand, worked with a small group of the staff, who were nominally attached to the *cabinet* in more or less official capacities. As a result, in the early years relationships between the Secretary-General and Attali became very poor.[46] The situation eased when Jean-Louis Bianco, who had known Attali since schooldays and seems to have been able to work more easily with him, became Secretary-General in 1982.

The structure of the Elysée staff has been shaped primarily by the temperament, style and needs of the different incumbents of the Elysée. That it has in essence varied very little since de Gaulle set it up suggests that his original structure was rather well-shaped to suit the primary purpose of the staff, which is to give immediate,

43. Christine Fauvet-Mycia, *Les Eminences Grises*, Paris, 1988, p. 46.
44. Charles Debbasch *et al.*, *La Ve République*, 2nd edn, Paris, 1985, p. 290.
45. Charles Debbasch, *L'Elysée Dévoilé*, Paris, 1982, pp. 165-9.
46. F.O. Giesbert, *Le President*, Paris, 1990, p. 139. See also Pierre Favier and Michel Martin-Roland, *La Décennie Mitterrand; Tome 1, Les Ruptures*, Paris, 1990, p. 433.

practical help and support to the President himself. Similar nuances in style but continuities in purpose have affected the working methods of the presidential staff, to which we now turn.

Behaviour and Working Methods

De Gaulle saw his staff as an administrative, technical and advisory body. Their role was to see that his duties and his household were properly organised, to provide him with the detailed information that he might need, to forward his ideas within the government, and, in sectors in which he was specifically interested, to provide advice and suggestions for action. He was not an easy man with whom to hold a discussion. He discouraged general conversation, but would at times talk over particular issues with members of his staff.[47]

The working methods established by de Gaulle proved well adapted to his concept of the role of the presidency and the President's staff. He insisted that the Elysée should be a calm place where attention could be given to long-term problems. He was himself meticulously punctual and extremely regular in his working habits and expected similar precision in his staff. He hated the telephone,[48] preferring to communicate in writing. His staff prepared notes, which would be passed upwards to him via the head of the section, and then returned, sometimes with directions for further action, sometimes with comments, and sometimes simply with acknowledgement, either from de Gaulle himself or from his *aides-de-camp*. He had no general meetings of his staff, although they all assembled once annually, for the formal exchange of greetings at the New Year. He preserved his distance from most of his staff but the four senior staff members – the Secretary-General, the head of the *cabinet*, the head of the military staff and Jacques Foccart – saw him regularly, usually each evening.

Georges Pompidou's style, developed partly during his years at Matignon, which is by its nature a more frenetic office, more concerned with day-to-day crises, was rather more collegial. While Prime Minister, he had been in the habit of holding an unhurried meeting with his staff every morning, to review the day's news

47. Pierre Lelong in *L'Entourage*, pp. 122–3, and Bernard Tricot, oral communication, Maison Française, Oxford, June 1991.
48. In his memoirs he wrote disparagingly of a meeting he had with the then Prime Minister, Léon Blum, in 1936: 'During our conversation the telephone rang ten times, distracting the attention of Léon Blum with petty parliamentary or administrative matters.' Charles de Gaulle, *Mémoires de Guerre – L'Appel*, Paris, 1954, p. 20.

and give his instructions.[49] As President, he held a general meeting and discussion on Monday afternoons, though most communication with his staff took place on paper. Cohen categorises the staff into three groups. First there were those who saw the President every day or whenever they wished: the Secretary-General and his deputy, the *chef de cabinet* and Pierre Juillet. Then there were who saw him two or three times a week: Jacques Foccart, the chief of the military staff, the press officer and possibly Marie-France Garaud. And then came those who met him only occasionally.[50]

Under Giscard a rather wider range of staff members had ready access to the President, for in addition to the heads of the Secretariat-General and the *cabinet* and their deputies, the 'advisers to the President' also had easy access to him, and the presidential spokesman saw him on most days.[51] Nevertheless, for most of his staff the main means of communication continued to be written notes, since Giscard 'avoid[ed] full meetings of the secretariat except for a short briefing session each Monday morning'.[52] Giscard's staff perceived themselves as being fairly isolated in their work. Although many of the staff had been friends since working for Giscard as Finance Minister and on his campaign team, they all had huge sectors of responsibility and a great deal of work, so, unless there was a particular reason to work closely with a colleague, they functioned on their own and not as a team.[53]

Mitterrand, like his predecessors, also prefers to work with his staff largely through the circulation of written notes. While the Secretary-General and, for as long as he was at the Elysée, Jacques Attali would normally see him every day, as, in his early years as President, did his old friend François de Grossouvre, other advisers see him by request, although they have learnt to use this privilege sparingly. He detests meetings and, in common with de Gaulle, dislikes the telephone. He prefers short notes, and all are passed forward to him via the Secretary-General, who may add his own comments. Unlike his predecessors, Mitterrand does not expect his staff to confine themselves to their particular areas of expertise. Possibly as a consequence, meetings between groups of members of

49. Jobert, *Mémoires*, p. 35.
50. See Cohen in de Baecque and Quermonne, p. 107.
51. *Ibid.*, p. 109.
52. Howard Machin, 'The President's Men; Advisers and Assistants' in Vincent Wright (ed.), *Change and Continuity in France*, London, 1984, p. 87. Schifres and Sarazin (p. 121) contrast Mitterrand with Giscard, alleging that staff meetings were frequent under Giscard and abandoned under Mitterrand.
53. Interview with former member of President Giscard's staff, Paris, Sept. 1991. See also Debbasch, *L'Elysée*, pp. 28–35.

the staff seem to have increased.[54] Attali, especially in the early days of the presidency, headed an informal team of staff members.[55] Mitterrand will receive notes from any of his staff on matters of which they think he should be aware. On complex and controversial subjects he is likely to ask for notes from a range of different people, many of which are returned within twenty-four hours.[56] The comments may be laconic, and this has led to misunderstanding. One of his staff, Gerard Rénon, received back a note on the proposed agreement with the Soviet Union for the Siberian gas pipeline with the instruction to consult the Minister for Foreign Affairs, Claude Cheysson. Rénon assumed that this meant that whatever advice Cheysson gave should be followed. That advice was favourable, and on Rénon's clearance the contract went ahead, Mitterrand himself learning of the agreement from the radio news. Rénon left the Elysée some months later, but the incident did not seem to have damaged his career.[57]

The continuities in the working methods of the Elysée staff, under four different Presidents, each of whom replaced the staff of his predecessor almost completely, are striking. The preference of each President for paperwork, the relative absence of collegiality among the staff, the channelling of work through a small number of senior staff – these characteristics seem common to each presidency, even if there are shifts and nuances in the flexibility and structures involved.

The Functions of the Presidential Staff

The internal working methods of the presidential staff reflect their relationship with the President. Perhaps even more important are the relationships of the staff with the outside world. First, in their role as the channel through which a great deal of information passes to the President an important part of the staff's function is to keep themselves fully informed of developments that may affect presidential policies. 'In addition to the careful reading of huge quantities of documents, they see a very large number of people.'[58] They fulfil this function in a number of ways.

First, they maintain contacts with the members of the Prime

54. I am grateful to Samy Cohen for this point.
55. Samy Cohen, oral communication, Maison Française, Oxford, June 1991. See also Fauvet-Mycia, *les Eminences.*
56. See Schifres and Sarazin, *l'Elysée de Mitterrand*, pp. 121-4, and Favier and Martin-Roland, *La Décennie*, p. 508.
57. Favier and Martin-Roland, *La Decennie*, p. 510.
58. Schifres and Sarazin, *L'Elysée*, p. 162.

Minister's personal staff, with the administrative staff of the ministries concerned in their functional areas, with the ministers'
cabinets, and with other people in the field. 'In this sort of job one
has to know how to spin a spider's web whose strands all lead back
to the President.'[59] The ways in which these relationships can be
developed clearly depends upon the position of the President in relation to the Prime Minister and the government, and the pattern was
distinctly different during the period of *cohabitation* from what it
had mostly been during the Fifth Republic.

Secondly, staff members attend official meetings, and especially the interministerial meetings called by the Prime Minister's
staff at Matignon.[60] These meetings are crucial to the coordination
of the work of the government, and a representative from the
Elysée is present whenever major decisions are taken relating to
the government's policy or legislative programme.[61] 'I attended
all the meetings at Matignon concerning the decentralisation programme and the reform of the civil service laws in the early
1980s. One of the Elysée staff was always there.'[62] Again, under
cohabitation the pattern altered and the practice largely disappeared, but was reinstated with the return of a Socialist government
after 1988.

Thirdly, the Secretary-General of the presidency works in close
liaison with the Secretary-General to the government in establishing
the agenda for the weekly meetings of the Council of Ministers, for
the various formal governmental councils (defence, judiciary)
chaired by the President, and for the meetings on specific subjects
of the ministers concerned, also chaired by the President, which are
known as *conseils restreints*. These differ from the interministerial
meetings held at Matignon in that they are likely to be concerned not
with detail but with the main lines of policy, in areas where the President, for whatever long-term or topical reason, has a particular
interest in establishing a firm direction.

A second function of the presidential staff is to provide the

59. Debbasch, *L'Elysée*, p. 3.
60. Jean-Luc Bodiguel estimated that under de Gaulle a member of the staff of
    the Elysée Secretariat-General was present at just under 20 per cent of the
    meetings of ministers called by the Prime Minister's office. Under Pompidou
    this figure nearly doubled, but dropped back again under Giscard, possibly in
    response to a much higher overall number of meetings. J.-L. Bodiguel, 'Conseils
    Restreints, Comités Interministériels et Réunions Interministérielles' in Francis
    de Baecque and Jean-Louis Quermonne (eds), *Administration et Politique sous
    la Cinquième République*, Paris, 1981, p. 146.
61. Interview with a former member of Giscard's staff, Paris, Sept. 1991.
62. Interview with a former member of a minister's *cabinet*, 1981–3, Paris, Sept.
    1991.

briefing and drafts which the President needs for his public utterances – speeches, interviews and press conferences. Insofar as those events are the occasion for the announcement of the presidential stance on certain issues or even of new policies, this function contains within it an element of policy formulation.

A third function of the presidential staff is to review and prepare briefings for the President on all the matters that will come before the Council of Ministers, including appointments to senior positions. In theory this function could be purely technical; in practice the role and influence of the staff members concerned will depend upon the extent to which the issue is one of particular moment and to which the views and advice of the staff members are taken into account. This was a function which continued even under *cohabitation*.

A fourth function is to keep under review the progress of the development from proposals to legislation and the subsequent implementation of policies in which the President is interested. Again, attendance at interministerial meetings is a crucial means by which this function is exercised, though it will also involve direct liaison with the *directeur de cabinet* of the minister concerned. At the initial stage the staff of President and Prime Minister seek to ensure that the problem has been approached in the same way by both. Once the main lines have been agreed, the Elysée staff watch over the detailed drafting to ensure that the final outcome does not diverge from the intitial intention. Under de Gaulle, Pompidou and Mitterrand, the Elysée representative rarely intervened during the meetings; Giscard's staff were less restrained and tended to take a more active part in the discussions. In all cases the main role of the Elysée representative has been to warn the President if anything was going awry.[63]

The Secretary-General of the Elysée plays a key role in all these functions. He is the chief point of contact for the staff of the Prime Minister and of other ministerial private offices, and the channel through which advice and information, warnings and suggestions reach the President. He is responsible for the smooth running of the office and often for the choice of those who will work within it. It is vital for the Secretary-General to find a concept of his role and a way of managing his relationship with the President that will be found comfortable and congenial by both. Some have managed this tricky process better than others. Claude Pierre-Brossolette left

63. Burin des Roziers in *L'Entourage*, p. 225. Interviews with a former member of Giscard's staff and with a former ministerial *cabinet* member, Paris, Sept. 1991.

Giscard's staff because the relationship had not worked, and while
Pierre Bérégovoy's appointment to a ministerial post in 1982 was
certainly due partly to the President's need for a minister whom he
trusted in a key position, it also reduced conflict among the staff.
The Secretary-General has never been the President's sole adviser,
and seldom his most important confidant, yet in terms of the functioning of the governmental machine in France his role is central.

Influence and Power of the Elysée Staff

Given the wide-ranging role of the President, his staff has frequently
been the subject of speculation and comment. For those inclined to
the notion that history is made and that events are manipulated
by conspiracies behind closed doors the President's closest collaborators seem promising candidates for the role of the 'really' powerful
in France, especially since, at least up till recent years, they were
expected to observe a high degree of discretion. De Gaulle, for
example, required total discretion, and would become irritated if
any of them were mentioned in the press.[64] But questions about
just how powerful the Elysée staff are do not only arise from journalistic exaggeration. The nature of the American presidency and
the very specific role of the White House staff inevitably lead to
comparisons, and at times the allegations have come from those
who are in a position to know. Most striking was the case of Jacques
Chaban-Delmas. His conflict with Pierre Juillet, and his conviction
that it was manipulation by Juillet and Elysée staff that led to his
removal from the office of Prime Minister, were rancorously
described in his book *L'Ardeur*. Cohen refutes the notion that
Juillet was particularly powerful, arguing that he was far from being
able to make everything go his way; for example, he was unable to
prevent his rival Jobert from taking on the Ministry of Foreign
Affairs, or to promote his protégé Chirac as fast as he would have
liked. Equally, President Giscard's limitation of the size of his staff
at the outset of his presidency resulted from his determination that
his ministers should not suffer the difficult relationships with the
Elysée that he had experienced as a minister.

The Elysée staff does not constitute an alternative government or
a super-executive. Nevertheless, it can be highly influential and even
powerful. First, information is itself power. In selecting, filtering
and commenting on it the staff member can undoubtedly influence
the way in which it is perceived. 'The staff member has the power
to point the head of state in a particular direction by causing him

64. Geoffroy de Courcel in *L'Entourage*, p. 105.

to see one person rather than another, by passing on one piece of information and not emphasising another news item.'[65]

Secondly, presentation also conveys power. All the Presidents have insisted on adding their personal stamp to the speeches they make, even if they do not themselves write most of the text, as de Gaulle did. Mitterrand notoriously tends to leave the final version to the very last minute. Nevertheless, in undertaking the preparatory work, staff members may be able to influence the way in which policy is conceived and presented.

Thirdly, the function of overseeing execution is also powerful. If, under most of the four incumbents, the President's representative has only rarely been authorised to speak in the name of his master (a view confirmed by the comment that under Mitterrand the rule is 'and above all avoid "the Elysée thinks that"'),[66] the attitude of the staff member can influence, encourage or inhibit.[67]

Fourthly, in certain circumstances the staff can and do intervene directly. One such circumstance may occur when the participants in a policy decision actively seek such intervention. An example occurred in the early years of the Mitterrand presidency, when the Elysée was directly involved in the negotiation which led to an agreement between two major nationalised companies, Thomson and CGE, which resulted in the CGE subsidiary Alcatel taking over Thomson's telecommunications business in return for CGE's consumer electronics, components and military equipment interests. The chairmen of the two companies both took the view that, having been appointed by the President, they were answerable to him. They ensured at an early stage, through Alain Boublil, the industrial policy adviser at the Elysée, that they had presidential support, which allowed the two chairmen to 'outflank the opposition'.[68] This active role on the part of a staff member angered the Minister of Industry, Chevènement, who complained that Boublil wanted to be the 'chairman of the chairmen' of the nationalised industries and was prepared to say 'the President thinks that . . .'[69]

From his experience on the staff, Debbasch estimated that under Giscard 20 per cent of the measures adopted at the Council of

65. Debbasch, *L'Elysée*, p. 46.
66. Fauvet-Mycia, *Les Eminences*, p. 152.
67. 'It is an integral part of the French politico-administrative system that an interest taken by a member of the President's staff in a particular question spurs on the government body concerned to resolve the matter rapidly.' Debbasch *et al.*, *La Ve République*, p. 290.
68. Alan Cawson *et al.*, *Hostile Brothers: Competition and Closure in the European Electronics Industry*, Oxford, 1990, p. 133.
69. Favier and Martin-Roland, *La Décennie*, p. 454. For Boublil's description of his role, see his *Le Soulèvement du Sérail*, Paris, 1990, especially chapter 2.

Ministers were prepared in the Elysée and some 10 to 15 per cent of senior appointments were determined there.[70] The scope for such active interventionism on the part of the presidential staff is also greatly affected by the extent to which the area concerned is recognised as one that is largely open for direct presidential action (see particularly chapter 6, below). France's policy towards francophone Africa has since 1958 been very largely determined from within the Elysée. Jacques Foccart acted in effect not only as an adviser but also as a minister.[71] All major decisions relating to aid, technical assistance, the appointment of personnel and other matters were made by him, and he could give instructions directly to the French embassies in the African states. He oversaw the direct personal relations of the President with the heads of the African states, receiving them at the Elysée and ensuring that they had privileged access to the President. Foccart's personal position diminished under Pompidou and did not survive the election of Giscard, although its legacy has been the continued close involvement of the President and the appropriate members of his staff in France's relations with Africa, so much so that Mitterrand's initial Minister for Overseas Co-operation resigned with the complaint that the policy decisions in his particular area were being made at the Elysée.

The extent to which in certain circumstances the combination of the President's personal interest and initiative and the resources available to his staff can be deployed both effectively and unaccountably are potentially nefarious in their consequences. During Mitterrand's presidency, a number of scandals came very close to the Elysée. They include the planting of evidence on Irish terrorism suspects, the sinking of the Greenpeace vessel *Rainbow Warrior* in Auckland harbour, New Zealand, and financial scandals surrounding insider trading and take-over bids, as well as problems relating to the financing of the presidential election campaign. Such scandals can be explained, at least in part, by the extraordinary concentration of power within the central executive, including the presidency.[72]

The Constraints on the Power of the Presidential Staff

The power of the presidential staff should not be exaggerated. There are important limitations on it, and it is these which serve to refute

70. Debbasch, 'Les Pouvoirs' in J.-L. Seurin and J.-L. Martres (eds), *La Présidence en France et aux Etats-Unis*, Paris, 1986, pp. 202–3.
71. Cohen, *Les Conseillers*, p. 159.
72. Stephen E. Bornstein, 'The Politics of Scandal' in Peter A. Hall, Jack Hayward and Howard Machin (eds), *Developments in French Politics*, London, 1990, p. 273.

any notion that the staff can constitute a super-government.

First, the staff is small and its workload is enormous, involving extremely long hours, which are not normally compensated for by weekend or holiday breaks. The possibility of acting as a policy-formulating and -implementing executive on anything other than an occasional and spasmodic basis is strictly limited by the need to provide the President with continuous and daily support. None of the four Presidents of the Fifth Republic has wished his staff to form a think-tank or a brains-trust, despite the roles given to certain individuals, most notably Jacques Attali, who for ten years provided Mitterrand with advice, support, stimulation, ideas, encouragement and contacts. The presidential office has consequently never been staffed in a way or at a level that would allow it to usurp the role of the government.

Secondly, the Elysée staff as such has no formal decision-making powers. Even if senior appointments and papers for the Council of Ministers are decided upon by the President and his staff, they will require countersignatures from all the ministers involved.

Thirdly, none of the four Presidents has wished to limit his direct personal links with a wide range of opinion outside his office. The presidential staff have not acted as a barrier around the President. On the contrary, under de Gaulle part of the task of the *cabinet* was explicitly to maintain contacts with a very broad spectrum of interests outside the governmental circles. Other members of the staff saw it as part of their role to listen to what groups who were hostile to de Gaulle were saying and to act, when appropriate, as a channel for these views.[73] Mitterrand, even during the period of *cohabitation*, had regular weekly scheduled meetings with the Prime Minister and the Minister for Foreign Affairs although these were the only two ministers to see the President on a regular scheduled basis during that period.[74] All the Presidents have seen other ministers. President Mitterrand's timetable has included the General Secretary of the Socialist Party in such a weekly meeting. If the President wishes or chooses to work directly with ministers the staff can do little to impede this. Moreover, staff members may not necessarily know about major decisions. When Mitterrand announced the withdrawal of the highly controversial education bill in the summer of 1984 the staff member concerned knew that an initiative was possible (she was asked to remain behind after

---

73. See *L'Entourage*, p. 310–11.
74. Stephanie Mesnier, 'Le Rôle du Quai d'Orsay de mai 1986 à mai 1988', *Revue Administrative*, no. 258 (Nov.–Dec. 1990), p. 491.

working hours) but she did not know what the speech that was being made would contain.[75]

The President's power is exercised through a triangle of relation-ships involving the President, the Prime Minister and the minister or ministers concerned with the subject. This triangle intersects with a complex configuration between supporting staff, involving the Elysée, Matignon, the minister's *cabinet* and the appropriate divisions within the ministry. President, ministers and Elysée staff may well be closely interlinked by political and personal connections. Indeed, as was noted above, ministers have recently been increasingly drawn from among those with Elysée experience.[76] Moreover, the composition of ministerial *cabinets* is an area where Elysée influence can be and often is exercised. The crucial point is that the President's power depends upon his political role and status, which his staff can support but which depends also on many other factors.

The strengths and limitations of the role of the presidential staff were clearly demonstrated during the period of *cohabitation*. It was immediately apparent that the position which the President chose to adopt sharply influenced the possibilities of action. The Prime Minister insisted that direct communication between the ministries and the Elysée should be virtually eliminated, and that matters should be dealt with on a relatively formal basis between Matignon and the presidential staff. The presidential staff accepted the new rules of the game, in keeping with the President's own willingness to do so. Nevertheless in certain areas, particularly foreign affairs, the President was prepared to insist upon his constitutional position and continued to meet the minister weekly.[77] As the months went by, a *modus vivendi* was established between the President's staff and the staff of the Prime Minister, as the President steadily resumed a more confident role in foreign affairs. French policy towards the European Community was an area for a particularly fierce conflict over the control of policy. In these circumstances the Quai d'Orsay was seen as an acceptable and neutral meeting-place where those concerned, including staff members from both Elysée and Matignon, could attempt to arrive at solutions. These were worked out within a European policy group there, and both President and Prime Minister were eventually provided with identical briefings. However, if the President realised this the head of the government was unaware of it.'[78]

75. Schifres and Sarazin, *L'Elysée*, p. 162.
76. I am grateful to Samy Cohen for this point.
77. See Mesnier, 'Le Rôle du Quai d'Orsay'.
78. *Ibid.*, p. 496.

Conclusion

Since the beginning of the Fifth Republic, the President's staff have played a key role in enabling each President to exercise the functions of the presidency as he has conceived them. The staff has always had a solid backbone of administrators, with a profound knowledge of the complex balance of politico-administrative relations within the French system, which both confers a good deal of autonomy upon administrative action and preserves a primacy for political direction. The staff is a part of and (as a result of a web of personal, professional and political connections) deeply enmeshed in the rather small, closely-knit, interlocking Parisian administrative, industrial and political élite that is so marked a feature of the French system, in contrast to the more fragmented élites of Britain and the United States. The function of being the President's eyes and ears, albeit much more rarely his mouthpiece, and of providing him with the tools and means that he requires in order to act as he wishes is a highly intensive one and has resulted in considerable continuities in working methods under Presidents of very different characters and styles. These continuities reflect not only the exigencies of a continuing task but also the continuities in the interpretation of the presidential role.

Nevertheless, styles and approaches and even expectations have varied. De Gaulle's staff partly echoed his somewhat distant and austere style. Pompidou brought to the Elysée his Matignon experience and many of his Matignon staff; their style was more political and more active, a feature that could also be found under Giscard, with his prolonged ministerial experience. Under him the echoing of presidential style extended, it was unkindly observed, to physical characteristics – 'journalists noted, and caricatured, a similar and characteristic manner of speaking and writing, of a "sporting" stance and an elegance of dress.'[79] Mitterrand brought with him a team that came not from the ministries but from the Socialist Party organisation. The style of his office seems more 'open' and the multiplication of sources of information and advice more marked. The activities of the staff have been conditioned by the President's withdrawal, especially after the appointment of Fabius as Prime Minister in 1984 and the period of *cohabitation*, from apparent close involvement in the development of government policies.

The staff are influential. They are always there, and are often the people closest to the President. But they are not the only sources of influence, and no President has allowed his staff to act as a barrier

79. Machin, 'The President's Men', p. 88.

between himself and other parts of the executive and indeed between himself and political life in a broader sense. When they do not inform him of controversial matters, such as the decision in January 1992 to allow George Habash, a prominent Palestinian terrorist, to visit Paris for medical treatment, they are dismissed – the fate that befell Georgina Dufoix in this case. Insofar as they are not merely influential but powerful, their power is an exact emanation of the President's own position. The President and his staff are at their strongest within the governmental machine when they are successful in uniting all those concerned, especially the Prime Minister and the ministries, around the President's overall political line, approach and style. It is upon his political position and success that the staff rely to convert potential into actual power.

4

THE PRESIDENT AND THE PRIME MINISTER:
SUBORDINATION, CONFLICT, SYMBIOSIS
OR RECIPROCAL PARASITISM?

Vincent Wright

'Il est dur de vivre les institutions de la cinquième Republique . . . il faudrait un executif à une tête.'
— Lionel Jospin, 16 July 1990

It is not only active politicians of the French Fifth Republic who find it hard to live with the institutions of the Fifth Republic and who would prefer 'an executive with a single head'. Anyone writing about the hybrid executive of the current French regime is driven to the same conclusion as Jospin. There is a celebrated article on the problems of defining the concept of corporatism. Part of the title summed up the exasperation of the author: it was, he alleged, rather like trying to nail a pudding to a door. In attempting to define the nature of the relationships within the French executive a similar sense of exasperation frequently surfaced. And this is true even if those relationships are restricted to those between the President of the Republic and the Prime Minister.[1]

The President–Prime Minister relationship is examined here from

1. On the relationship see F. de Baecque, *Qui gouverne la France?*, Paris, 1976; Raymond Barrillon *et al.*, *Dictionnaire de la Constitution*, Paris, 1986; Alain Claisse, *Le Premier Ministre de la Ve République*, Paris, 1972; Françoise Decaumont, *La Présidence de Georges Pompidou. Essai sur le régime présidentialiste français*, Paris, 1980; Maurice Duverger, *Le bréviaire de la cohabitation*, Paris, 1986; *L'Entourage et de Gaulle*, publication of the Institut Charles de Gaulle, Paris, 1979; *La Présidence de la République de Georges Pompidou. Exercise du pouvoir et pratique des institutions*, Paris, 1983; Jacques Fournier, *Le Travail Gouvernemental*, Paris, 1987; Marceau Long, *Les Services du Premier Ministre*, Aix, 1981; Jean Massot, *La Présidence de la République en France*, 2nd edn, Paris, 1986; Thierry Pfister, *A Matignon, au temps de l'Union de la Gauche*, Paris, 1985; Thierry Pfister, *Dans les coulisses du pouvoir. La comédie de la cohabitation*, Paris, 1986; Roseline Py, *Le Sécretariat Général du Gouvernement*, Paris, 1986; Jean-Louis Quermonne, *Le Gouvernement de la France sous la Cinquième République*, 3rd edn, Paris, 1987; Stéphane Rials, *Le Premier Ministre*, Paris, 1981; Stéphane Rials, *La Présidence de la République*, Paris, 1981; M. Schifres and M. Sarazin, *L'Elysée de Mitterrand: Secrets de la Maison du Prince*, Paris, 1985; and Patrice Verrier, *Les Services de la Présidence de la République*, Paris, 1971.

three angles: the resources available to each; the sectoral division of responsibilities and influence; and the stages of the policy process most susceptible to the intervention of President and Prime Minister. Such an analysis may enable us to understand, by way of an implicit classification, some of the major structural factors in the relationship. However, the central argument of this chapter is that the relationship is inherently blurred, ambiguous and fluid. In practice, it can oscillate between the extremes of clear presidential primacy to no less clear prime ministerial dominance. Generally, however, the relationship has been characterised by a submerged and tense tug-of-war between the two protagonists (and their respective supporters), with each needing yet resenting the other. Political circumstances combine with ideological and policy dissensions, as well as with personal ambitions and calculations, to make a blurred and shifting situation inevitably unstable.

Resources

Discussion of the resources available in the President-Prime Minister relationship must take into account four basic factors. First, each disposes of an array of resources. Secondly, the nature of the relationship hinges on the ability or willingness of each to exploit or mobilise those resources. Thirdly, each resource is inextricably linked to the other. Each may, in certain circumstances, be seen as a resource for the other: the President-Prime Minister relationship is not *necessarily* a zero sum game. Finally, a 'resource' may be more apparent than real, more troublesome than useful.

An analysis of the resources reveals two broad categories. The first category embraces those which are *structural* in nature, although they may be exclusive to one or the other or shared between them in ambiguous or nebulous fashion. The second broad category is *conjunctural*. It comprises resources which may also be exclusive or shared, depending on political or personal circumstance. The ill-defined nature of the relationship, involving overlapping jurisdictions, leads almost inevitably to a certain conflictual fluidity in the relationship. Matters are complicated by seemingly structural powers proving to be transient, victims of circumstance, while apparently conjunctural powers may ossify into structural ones.

We may identify seven major sets of resources available to both the President and the Prime Minister which help to determine the relationship between them:

– constitutional resources;

- political legitimacy;
- personal charisma and ability;
- patronage;
- party influence;
- bureaucratic leverage;
- control over members of the government.

The Constitution of the Fifth Republic is a hybrid, in the sense that it contains both presidential and parliamentary elements. It confers executive power on a President who is independent of parliament, as well as on a government which is responsible to parliament though provided with certain powers to ensure its own efficacy and stability. Within the government, the Prime Minister is given powers greater than those conferred upon his Fourth Republic predecessors. The Constitution is also ambivalent in that on certain critical issues, such as responsibility for defence policies, it shares power between Prime Minister and President – but in an ill-defined fashion. The very ambivalence of the texts prompts divergent interpretations of the Constitution, making it a source of both flexibility (and hence durability) and tension (and hence instability).

Because the constitutional powers of the presidency are analysed in chapter 2 of this book, we concentrate here on those of the Prime Minister. They are not inconsiderable:

- He is in general charge of the work of the government which 'decides and directs the policy of the nation', and which has 'at its disposal the administration and the armed forces'.
- He is responsible for national defence.
- He ensures the implementation of laws.
- Except as provided for under article 13, he exercises rule-making power.
- He appoints to civil and military posts.
- He may delegate certain of his powers to the ministers.
- He deputises for the President of the Republic when necessary, as chairman of the Higher Council and Committee of National Defence.
- In exceptional circumstances, he may deputise for the President as chairman of the Council of Ministers, by virtue of an explicit delegation of authority and with a specific agenda.
- He proposes the names of members of the government to the President who officially appoints them.
- His signature is required for certain presidential acts.
- He has to be consulted by the President in the event of dissolution of parliament or before emergency powers may be decreed.
- He exercises legislative initiative; may request the calling of an

extraordinary session of parliament; may, after deliberation in the
Council of Ministers, pledge the responsibility of the government
before the National Assembly on its programme or, if it be so
decided, on a general declaration of policy; and may, after deliberation in the Council of Ministers, pledge the responsibility of the
government before the National Assembly on the passing of all
or part of a bill or a motion.
– He may propose a constitutional reform but his proposal becomes
operable only if voted by parliament or approved by way of
referendum.

The Constitution therefore maps out for the Prime Minister a key
mediating role and a general policy role, furnishes him with
wide discretionary rule-making powers, ensures considerable access
to key bodies such as parliament, and provides him with the influence that flows from patronage (ministerial, quasi-judicial and
state service). He has, in effect, four distinct sets of powers: of
consultation; of *certification* (he countersigns certain presidential
acts, 'certifies' the legal authenticity of the acts and assumes responsibility for them before parliament); of *request* (he may ask other
bodies to take action); and of *policy orientation*.

Far from reducing the Prime Minister to the role of a rubber-
stamp, the Constitution, even on a minimalist reading, makes the
Prime Minister a key political and policy actor. Of course, the
constitutional definition of resources does not necessarily imply
that those resources are exploited. Either they may not be available
in practice or there may be reluctance on the part of the Prime
Minister to exploit them. These two factors are explored throughout
this chapter. Yet it is worth stressing that in certain political circumstances the Constitution undeniably affords the Prime Minister
clear preponderance in key areas of decision-making. When, for
instance, Jacques Chirac was appointed Prime Minister after
leading his Right-wing coalition to victory in the legislative elections
of 1986, he was in a position to strip the President of all his domestic
policy power. Shortly after his appointment, on 23 April 1986, he
stated on television that he was 'in possession of all the means . . .
with the entire responsibility' for government policies. This was
clearly not true for foreign, European or defence policies, but it
summarised the situation admirably for all others.

The second resource is that of political legitimacy, that nebulous
yet crucial commodity. For most of the Fifth Republic there has
been a *querelle de légitimité*, which in practice has been resolved
in favour of the President. Since the 1962 constitutional revision,
the President has been truly 'the nation's elect', and he rarely fails

to underline the point. The Prime Minister, on the other hand, owes his legitimacy to selection and not to election. He is chosen by the President who also reserves the right (nowhere defined in the Constitution) to dismiss him (see below, p. 115). Yet the situation which normally prevails can become singularly complicated. Hence, during each legislative election there is theological debate on whether or not the victor emerges with a legitimacy which is higher than, or at least equal to, that of the President. Political legitimacy, it is alleged, is rooted in the results of the most recent election.

The third resource available to President and Prime Minister is personal: leadership qualities such as charisma, political skills and technical competence. It is worth emphasising that all the men who have been elected to the presidency of the Fifth Republic have been sufficiently talented to fulfil their ambition of establishing presidential supremacy. General de Gaulle, whose querulous doubts about the French did not extend to himself, enjoyed an authority within the executive which was never disputed by his supporters. His successor, Georges Pompidou, whose worldly scepticism again never extended to his own abilities, exploited superb political managerial skills to build himself an unassailable position of executive power. Giscard d'Estaing may have been sniped at throughout his presidency by Gaullist members of the ruling coalition, but by the end of his seven-year term, presidential authority had been consolidated and even, in some respects, strengthened. Technical expertise, self-assurance, access to talented advisers, the exploitation of a range of constitutional and political instruments were combined to ensure a dominant presidency.

François Mitterrand's virulent denunciations of presidentialism ceased when he became President. Already as First Secretary of the Socialist Party he had displayed his schizophrenic attachment to both republican ideals and monarchical methods. Whatever general opinions are entertained about Mitterrand they generally concur that he is acutely sensitive to his own status, highly protective towards his own power and a supreme tactical politician, capable of turning apparently difficult situations to his own advantage.

While certain Prime Ministers of the Fifth Republic may have been somewhat lacklustre characters (notably Couve de Murville and Messmer), all have been competent, and some considerable personalities – often too considerable for their own political health. Some Prime Ministers, clearly, have also been intent to leave their mark on French politics and policies. None has been a mere cypher, an automatic rubber-stamp for presidential policies.

Patronage provides the fourth resource available to the two heads of the executive. This extends not only to governmental posts, which are negotiated between the Elysée and Matignon (see below), but also to high-ranking posts in the civil service and in the public banking, industrial, insurance and media sectors. Some of these fall exclusively within the presidential sphere while others belong to the Prime Minister. However, for almost all significant posts (and many seemingly insignificant ones) bargaining is once again the order of the day, and it is often tense, which is scarcely surprising since control over clientelistic networks not only mirrors the respective power positions of the President and Prime Minister but is also seen as a means of strengthening them.

Georges Pompidou as Prime Minister and then as President created a very extensive web of grateful clients in the construction of the so-called 'Gaullist State'. Problems between Giscard d'Estaing and his Prime Minister Chirac were undoubtedly aggravated by Giscard's attempts to dislodge from key state positions the Gaullist *'coquins et copains'* (rogues and cronies – an amiable description by one of the President's closest lieutenants), who looked to the Prime Minister for protection. By 1981 most Gaullists had been replaced by friends of the President: the 'Gaullist state' gave way to the 'Giscardian state'. The accession of Mitterrand to the presidency was almost immediately followed by the placement of Socialist sympathisers in many key civil service and public sector posts. The distribution of patronage has been used by Mitterrand to punish, reward and compensate – also as a means of satisfying the various and conflicting factions of the Socialist Party. Yet a Prime Minister is not totally deprived of patronage: Pompidou, Barre, Chaban-Delmas, Chirac, Mauroy and Rocard all assiduously placed their supporters in strategic state posts.

With control over the dominant party or the ruling coalition in the National Assembly we touch upon the fifth major resource available to the President and the Prime Minister. This is arguably the single most important one, since a parliamentary majority is vital for carrying out the government's programmes. In principle, the President leaves party and coalition management to the Prime Minister, since he must not impair his image of being 'above party'. However, each President has kept a close watch on his party support. De Gaulle was always very well informed of Gaullist party activities, not only by his Prime Ministers but also by the other party 'barons', notably Jacques Foccart. Pompidou loftily reiterated his intention (notably on 22 September 1971) of keeping his distance from his parliamentary majority but a political cell at the Elysée, comprising the 'terrible twins' Pierre Juillet and Marie-France Garaud, enabled him to retain close contact with the party which he had dominated during his premiership.

The faithful lieutenants of Giscard held a hegemonic position in the Republican Party which he had founded, although the relationship between him and the Gaullist party leadership was extremely acrimonious. And Mitterrand, despite one or two setbacks (notably his failure to ensure the election of his candidates to certain posts), has always enjoyed a far closer relationship than any of his Prime Ministers with the Socialist Party. In a very real sense he and his party had always enjoyed a complex yet symbiotic relationship. His faction has always been the single most important one in the Socialist Party and his faithful supporters have been rewarded with key positions in the party hierarchy. Occasional party revolts against President Mitterrand (for instance, over the amnesty accorded to rebel generals of the Algerian war) or over new rules on identity controls) provoked the President to rage – and swift retribution.

Only very rarely has the Prime Minister achieved mastery over party and ruling coalition. The position is summarised in the table below.

Prime Minister	Period	Party	Relations with own party	Relations with coalition partners
Debré	1959–62	Gaullist	difficult	tense
Pompidou	1962–8	Gaullist	mastery	good
Couve de Murville	1968–9	Gaullist	distant	distant
Chaban-Delmas	1969–72	Gaullist	uneasy	friendly
Messmer	1972–4	Gaullist	distant	distant
Chirac	1974–6	Gaullist	increasing dominance	conflictual
Barre	1976–81	Giscardian	distant	acrimonious
Mauroy	1981–4	Socialist	friendly but unstable	first good, then difficult
Fabius	1984–6	Socialist	uneasy	uneasy
Chirac	1986–8	Gaullist	mastery	wary
Rocard	1988–91	Socialist	difficult	easy
Cresson	1991–2	Socialist	strained	non-existent

In other words, only Pompidou as Prime Minister can be said to have used party and ruling coalition as props for his own authority. Indeed, his personal dominance may have been a source of presidential jealousy and thus have contributed to his fall from grace. Other Prime Ministers have kept either a prudent or wary distance from nominally friendly parties, entertained difficult and even hostile relations with them, or had to contend with rivals in trying to establish their control.

The sixth executive resource is administrative: namely control over the bureaucracy. This is the weakest element in the President's armoury: he has very little control over the processing and implementing of policy. He may have friends in high state places, and his staff may keep an eye on many of the major policies of the ministries, but his tentacles spread widely rather than deeply. On the other hand, there is a vast central bureaucratic machine which is organised essentially around Matignon: the Prime Minister is placed at the centre of an extensive web of administrative *services*, all designed to facilitate his policy-making role.

They may be grouped under three broad categories. First, there are the *services propres*, directly controlled by the premiership. Of these the most notable is the General Governmental Secretariat, created in 1935, which is responsible for the overall administrative coordination of the government's legislative programme, for preparing the agenda and taking the minutes of the weekly meetings of the Council of Ministers, and for the servicing of the major interdepartmental committees. It also keeps an eye on the implementation (or non-implementation) of legislation. The Secretariat is small (some fifty people), highly expert and politically neutral (though not hostile). The second group of services are the *services communs* or governmental services which serve all or several departments: the General Directorate of the Administration and the Civil Service and the General Secretariat of National Defence provide two notable examples of such bodies. Finally, there are the associated services – a vast array of institutions officially linked to Matignon, ranging from the office of the *médiateur* (or ombudsman) to those involved in women's rights and occupational training.

In his task of organising and coordinating the vast governmental machine, the Prime Minister is aided by a number of junior ministers (normally three or four) and, more particularly, by his private office (*cabinet*). Recruited by himself, and headed by a *directeur de cabinet*, this is the brains-trust, omnipresent representative, trouble-shooter and general counsellor of the Prime Minister: its members are his eyes, ears and voice. Although officially small in size, with thirty or forty members, it often calls on the help of numerous *officieux* – unofficial members of the *cabinet*. Some prime ministerial *cabinets* have been discreet and essentially bureaucratic, others – those of Chaban-Delmas, Chirac and Fabius – highly interventionist, policy-oriented and dynamic. Mauroy's *cabinet* harboured a group of highly competent *Nordistes*, recruited by the Prime Minister from his local power-base in Lille, while that of Chirac was dominated by a group who had worked with him as Mayor of Paris. The members of Rocard's *cabinet*, technocratic friends of the Premier, had a reputation for ruthlessness: it was Mitterrand who was alleged to have declared: 'Those people are without pity. They are barbarians.'[2]

The final executive resource is control over the government, its personnel and its policies. According to the Constitution, the President of the Republic appoints and dismisses members of the government on the proposal of the Prime Minister. In practice, the government's composition is negotiated between the two. Experience has revealed the following attributes of the President:

– He enjoys total freedom over the choice of the Ministers of Foreign Affairs, of European Affairs and of Defence. In the main, Presidents have appointed either politically friendly experts (such as diplomats) or personal friends (such as Roland Dumas and Charles Hernu). Even in 1986, after the Right-wing victory at the polls, it is said that Mitterrand was able to veto the appointments of Jean Lecanuet and François Léotard as, respectively, Ministers of Foreign Affairs and of Defence, and to negotiate with Prime Minister Chirac the appointment of 'technocrats' to these two areas in which he was determined to defend his prerogatives.

– He may place political and personal friends in other ministerial posts (Jack Lang, whose role is discussed in chapter 7) – sometimes in the teeth of prime ministerial opposition. The appointments of Françoise Giroud and of Jean-Jacques Servan-Schreiber in 1974 were both imposed by Giscard upon an unwilling Prime Minister. As has been pointed out in chapter 3, several ministers have been recruited directly from the President's staff at the Elysée (Pierre Bérégovoy being one of the most prominent of such appointments).

– He may protect ministers against the hostility of the Prime Minister: the best example is that of Alice Saunier-Séité, a particularly combative Minister for the Universities, whose clashes with Prime Minister Barre (a university professor) were as angry as they were public.

– He may encourage direct links between individual ministers and the Elysée, thus by-passing prime ministerial control. The direct link between Fabius, the Budget Minister, and Mitterrand was to

2. Franz-Olivier Giesbert, *Le Président*, Paris, 1990, p. 341.

provide the President with knowledge of French economic policy
and leverage over it.

The Prime Minister may appoint politically sympathetic ministers
but he has constantly to contend with some ministers whose loyalties
are focussed on the presidency. Moreover, in composing the government the Prime Minister has also to be sensitive to the requirements of competence, and of party and coalition politics. Often,
it is better to have party barons in the government, where to some
extent their potentially disruptive behaviour can be contained. The
result is that the Prime Minister can rarely count on the unswerving
support of his ministerial colleagues. An apparent resource may
even become a burden. Such was the case with Chirac and the
government from 1974 to 1976, and to a lesser extent with Rocard
and his government between 1988 and 1991.

The Prime Minister's hold over the government is weakened by
three other factors. In the first place, with the exception of the
1986–8 Chirac government, the President controls the agenda
of the government, and not merely the general guidelines. His
programme forms the basis of government action. Giscard sent
directives to the Prime Minister which outlined the objectives to
be attained by the government, while Mitterrand made clear that
the '110 proposals' of his election platform were to become the
government's priorities. The President may even intervene to impose
his wishes without informing the government, or even against the
wishes of the ministers most concerned. Governmental policies
may be announced at a presidential press conference or television
appearance. Examples abound: the Stabilisation Plan of September
1963 was imposed on a reticent Prime Minister and Finance
Minister; and the Savary Bill on church schools and the Fillioud
Bill on advertising on television, both in 1984, were withdrawn
by the President after only cursory consultation with the ministers
concerned.

The second major factor which constrains the Prime Minister
is the non-collegial nature of the government. Presidents and Prime
Ministers constantly complain about the lack of solidarity of the
governmental team, and are always appealing for greater unity of
action. Yet the frequency of the appeals merely bears witness to
the chronic nature of the problem. At bottom, the President has
a profoundly ambivalent view of the government: he wills its unity
of purpose and action, yet considers its members as *individually*
responsible to him. De Gaulle was very specific on this latter point:
it was to him and him alone that ministers owed allegiance.
Presidents, therefore, frequently deny to the Prime Minister the

means of imposing unity. The result is that many French governments resemble a motley collection of rival and rebellious colonels
taken into battle by a divided leadership. The conflicts in the Chirac
government of 1974–6 and the Mauroy government of 1981–4 were
particularly visible. While Chirac publicly and angrily called his
ministers to order, a more philosophical (or resigned) Mauroy
elevated interministerial squabbles into a system of government.[3]

The second major factor which weakens prime ministerial
leverage over his ministerial colleagues is the extreme sectorial-
isation of public policy-making in France. Ministers tend to resent
prime ministerial interference in the work of their own vast,
sprawling and ill-coordinated empires, and try to circumvent the
coordinating efforts of Matignon. The Council of Ministers,
which meets weekly, is a ritualised and largely rubber-stamping
exercise for decisions taken elsewhere. Ministers are expected to
restrict themselves to the affairs of their own department. Lengthy
discussion is not encouraged. De Gaulle was particularly impatient
with the loquacious: a visible and lively waving of his spectacles
was his method of displaying irritation.[4]

Coordination of governmental policies – a crucial stage, since
it defines priorities – is performed not by the Council of Ministers,
nor mainly by the Prime Minister, but by a wide range of interdepartmental councils and committees, at which both Matignon and
the Elysée are represented. An early experiment with Fourth
Republic-style *conseils de cabinet* – meetings of all the ministers,
chaired by the Prime Minister – collapsed when presidential opposition was made clear. They re-emerged sporadically during the
1986–8 Chirac government but were abandoned after the Mitterrand
re-election in May 1988.

In summary, as with the previous resources, the situation is
less than clear. Both the President and the Prime Minister share
the resource in an imprecise and shifting manner: personality,
political circumstances, calculation and role perception intervene
to determine the distribution of each resource and their interaction.

The Sectoral Distribution of Influence

What are the policy-making consequences of this confused distribution of resources? The question may be answered, at least in
part, by looking at the various policy sectors and policy stakes.
With the exception of the 1986–8 Chirac government, characterised

3. *Le Monde*, 20 April 1982.
4. Quoted in Jean Massot, *op.cit.*, p. 176.

by an uneasy truce between President and Prime Minister, the division of labour may broadly be characterised as follows:

– The President defines the broad parameters of public policy and specifies the major priorities of government action.
– The President dominates entirely the sectors of defence, foreign and European policy.
– In macro-economic policy the President seeks to be involved in all major decisions, and there are numerous examples of the President imposing his options in critical circumstances. In financial affairs, he may choose to influence policies through a close personal relationship with the Finance Minister, or to by-pass the Finance Minister by exploiting a close relationship with the Budget Minister (the case of Mitterrand and Fabius).
– The President may specify the policy objectives of any sector of particular personal interest (Paris and the Paris region, as well as cultural policy; see below, chapter 7).
– The President may intervene in *any* policy area in a sporadic and disjointed fashion. Even de Gaulle intervened in the appointment of French bishops, the price of milk and the management of state theatres. Interventions by Mitterrand have included declarations on doubling the number of students at the prestigious *grandes écoles*, on the need to reduce the length of national military service, on the route of the motorway through the forest of Saint-Germain, and on the restoration of the Tuileries Gardens in the heart of Paris.
– The President decides in all political emergencies (the successive devaluations of the French franc, the church schools crisis of 1984 and so forth).

This list may suggest that the Prime Minister has a minimal policy-making role. That, however, is a misleading impression. In the first place, the Prime Minister enjoys a vast rule-making discretion in domestic policy-making. Secondly, the President has neither the time, the energy nor the staff to control the policy agenda completely. Thirdly, the President may have no interest in a particular area and will be content to leave it to his Prime Minister. Fourthly, political calculation may induce the President to withdraw from certain policy areas and leave greater discretion to the Prime Minister and the government. During the Fifth Republic there have been periods of acute *présidentialisme* and heightened *gouvernementalisme*. Prime Ministers Debré, Pompidou, Barre and Fabius were accorded a greater degree of autonomy than other Prime Ministers, and each left his mark on French domestic policy. Even more constrained Prime Ministers, such as Chaban-Delmas and Michel Rocard, were to give a distinct tone to governmental policies.

Finally, a Prime Minister who controls a parliamentary majority can impose his own domestic policy programme on even the most hostile President. Such was the case between 1986 and 1988 during the Chirac premiership.

If we examine the weight of the President and the Prime Minister in terms of the domestic policy process an equally complex picture emerges:

– Policy *initiatives* emanating from pressure groups are filtered mainly by the sectoral ministries and by Matignon.

– Broad policy *agenda-setting* is established by the President.

– Policy *coordination* generally takes place both at the Elysée and Matignon through interdepartmental councils and committees, with the latter playing the more significant role.

– Policy *formalisation* is concentrated in the hands of the services of the Prime Minister.

– Policy *implementation* lies with the field services of the ministries.

– Policy *monitoring* or *evaluation* is dependent largely on the appropriate sponsoring ministry or on Matignon. This stage is critical, because most policy initiatives spring from the evaluation of existing programmes. The services of the Prime Minister therefore play a crucial role in that murky world of incremental adjustments to the *status quo* – unspectacular, often unpublicised, rarely exciting but representative of most policy-making.

– Policy *legitimation* is divided between the President, who plays an important pedagogical role in setting executive policies (the royal tours of the provinces, the press conferences, the ritualised television appearances), and the Prime Minister who is constantly enjoined by the President to play an active part in explaining government policies.

A look across sectors and an analysis of the stages of the policy process both suggest, therefore, an intimate intermeshing of presidential and prime ministerial powers and power. The weight of each may fluctuate, but the two actors remain inseparable.

Patterns of Presidential-Prime Ministerial Relations

Despite its fluid and shifting nature, the experience of the Fifth Republic suggests three broad patterns of presidential-prime ministerial relations: subordination; conflict; partnership.

The *subordination* of the Prime Minister to the President is alleged to be rooted in the mode of accession to office: election and not selection. Secondly, it is argued that there is a hierarchy of their functions, constantly insisted upon by the President and fully accepted by the Prime Minister: to the President 'high politics', to the Prime Minister 'low politics'. The President establishes the broad parameters and the Prime Minister and the government follow (Michel Rocard, 3 January 1990). Or, as Giscard put it, 'the President is responsible for long-term and vital politics . . . the Prime Minister . . . deals with contingent problems'. By a maximalist interpretation of his rights and by a tendentious reading of the rights of others, Presidents have come to use, misuse and abuse the Constitution. For the President there is no twin-headed executive. De Gaulle stated the position quite clearly at his celebrated press conference on 31 January 1964: 'One could not accept that a dyarchy existed at the top. But, in any case, this is not the case. The President is obviously alone in holding and delegating state authority.' Later, he was to write of his appointment of Michel Debré as Prime Minister: 'I chose my Prime Minister in order that he should be second in command.' He was pointedly to remind Pompidou that, as Prime Minister, he was not the 'head of government but the first-ranking minister'.[5] This Gaullist doctrine has provided the constant underpinning of the relationship between the President and the Prime Minister: even Mitterrand – as President – was to invoke it on several occasions and in very explicit terms.

Thirdly, the subordinate character of the premiership appears to be underpinned by the fact that the Constitution clearly grants the President the right to appoint the Prime Minister. Only in March 1986 was his freedom of action limited. Yet, even though Mitterrand had no effective alternative but to appoint Jacques Chirac, he insisted that Chirac was his own choice. Some prime ministerial appointments have been surprising, as though designed to underline the President's total freedom of choice: the appointments of Georges Pompidou in 1962 and of Edith Cresson in 1991 were totally unexpected. The occasional choice of people with no independent political power-base at the time (the notable exceptions being Chaban-Delmas, Chirac and Rocard) tends to emphasise the personal nature of the appointment. The point could even be driven home with a touch of condescension: thus Laurent Fabius was, for Mitterrand, 'the young Prime Minister whom I gave to France'.

The President is not constitutionally entitled to dismiss the Prime Minister. Indeed, in 1958, during the drafting phase of the Constitution, de Gaulle reassured Paul Reynaud, a member of parliament,

5. Etienne Burin des Roziers, 'Les relations du travail avec le Premier Ministre' in *De Gaulle et le Service de l'Etat*, Paris, 1977, pp. 354–5.

that the President did not have the right to replace the Prime Minister (see above, pp. 49–50). Once again, however, there is a gulf between the practice of the Fifth Republic and its constitutional stipulations. At the 31 January 1964 press conference, de Gaulle was explicit: the President had the right to replace the Prime Minister 'either because the task he gave him is achieved . . . or because he no longer approves of him'. The dismissals of Pompidou in 1968,[6] of Chaban-Delmas in 1972 (shortly after he had received a massive vote of confidence in the National Assembly) and of Rocard in 1991 (after the Prime Minister had made clear his desire to continue in office) all confirm the President's assumption of the right of dismissal. Moreover, successive Prime Ministers have always accepted that right: in his letter of 15 May 1991 to the President, announcing his resignation as Prime Minister, Rocard noted 'that you were good enough to inform me of your intention of forming a new government', which was sufficient to trigger the resignation. No Prime Minister would cling to office if the President asked for his resignation. Otherwise, he would be unworthy of office, a *'triste sire'*.[7] Michel Rocard, in February 1990, summed up a position which had been held by almost all his predecessors: 'I am at Matignon only as long as I have the confidence of the President of the Republic.'

A change of Prime Minister is sometimes a clear presidential signal of his *policy* intentions: the dismissal of Debré constituted the end of the *'hypothèque algérienne'* and a move towards increased presidentialism; that of Chaban-Delmas was the *coup de grâce* to the reformist legislation of the early Pompidou presidency; the appointment of Raymond Barre in 1976 was a clear indication of the President's desire to make the fight against inflation his top priority; that of Laurent Fabius coincided with the President's wish fully to pursue a more market-oriented restructuring of French industry and banking; while that of Edith Cresson was triggered by Mitterrand's wish to 'prepare France for 1993', when the economic frontiers of the European Community would disappear.

In other cases, the change of Prime Minister reflects presidential *political* ambitions: Messmer's appointment was designed to reassure conservatives of the ruling coalition; that of Chirac in 1974 was dictated by Giscard's desire to *'giscardiser les Gaullistes'*; Mauroy's elevation to the premiership was partly motivated by his close identification with the Union of the Left strategy, then being

---

6. De Gaulle, *Discours et messages*, Paris, 1970, p. 323.
7. The reply of Chaban-Delmas to Mitterrand, 15 Oct. 1970.

pursued by Mitterrand; Rocard's appointment, on the other hand, translated the requirement of attracting support from the Centre.

For those who argue the subordination case, the history of prime ministerial appointments and dismissals provides some confirmation: the premiership – 'the most precarious lease in Paris' – is seen as a manipulable commodity in the hands of the President, to be used in the light of his current policy preoccupations and political requirements: a safety valve at the disposal of the President.

The conflict school of presidential-prime ministerial relations may also find confirmatory evidence in the history of the regime. It might even be argued that conflict is inherent in the constitutional and political arrangements of the executive. This is because the effective organisation of executive power requires an active, strong and popular President *and* Prime Minister. Indeed, a weak Prime Minister (Messmer) or weakened Prime Minister (Mauroy) or unpopular Prime Minister (Barre) may do great disservice to the President. However, an active, strong and popular Prime Minister automatically becomes the object of presidential suspicion and this is especially true if the Prime Minister has clear presidential ambitions (cf. Pompidou, Chaban-Delmas and Rocard). Pompidou's brilliant premiership ended in an atmosphere of mistrust and recrimination: he was the 'victim of his own strong personality'. The position of the Prime Minister is thus an intrinsically 'uncomfortable' one.[8] The most flagrant illustration of the conflictual nature of the relationship was, of course, the Mitterrand-Chirac period of 1986–8, characterised by the President's refusal, in 1986, to sign the proposed ordinances on privatisation (14 July), the redrawing of constituency boundaries (2 October) and flexibility in working hours and practices (17 October), as well as his public criticisms of government policy on law and order, immigration, New Caledonia and policy towards television. It was not a period of *cohabitation* but of *cohabitension*, of armed coexistence. The backcloth to these differences was, naturally, the impending electoral battle for the presidency.

No less conflictual was the relationship between Giscard and Chirac between 1974 and 1976: it was marked by 'impatience, incomprehension and irritation' and ended in 'tumultuous conflict'.[9] This conflict culminated in the dramatic resignation of the Prime Minister on 25 August 1976: 'I do not have the means which I consider necessary effectively to carry out my functions as Prime

8. François Goguel, *Les institutions politiques françaises*, Paris, 1981, pp. 465–6.
9. Alain Duhamel, *La République giscardienne*, Paris, 1980.

Minister and in these conditions I have decided to put an end to them.'

If we discount the brief period of so-called *cohabitation*, which of course may recur, it is possible to discern several sources of conflict between President and Prime Minister:

– *Over the general thrust of governmental policies*. Perhaps the best example is provided by the profound differences between the liberalising Chaban-Delmas and the profoundly conservative Pompidou: proposed reforms of local government, the media and the financing of the social security system were among many which encountered presidential hostility. A few weeks after Chaban-Delmas outlined his reformist ideas in a parliamentary speech, the President made clear that they would not be placed on the political agenda, 'adding that I was not Prime Minister in order to make the French dream . . . .'[10]

– *Over specific policies*. Debré clearly felt deep unhappiness about his President's policy towards Algeria, Pompidou was highly suspicious of de Gaulle's more radical ideas on *participation*, and Chirac disliked some of Giscard's early 'social democratic' reforms as well as his pro-European leanings. The generally faithful Mauroy clashed with Mitterrand over industrial and economic policy, and even Fabius made public his unhappiness about Mitterrand's invitation to General Jaruzelski, the Polish leader, to visit Paris in December 1984. Michel Rocard made clear his opposition to the attempt by the state to take a stake in a bank which had been privatised by the Chirac government, while Mitterrand voiced his objections to Rocard's plans to change the electoral system for regional elections.

– *Over political strategy*. Pompidou was much more anxious than his Prime Minister Chaban-Delmas to reassure his conservative supporters. Chirac's attempt to anchor the ruling coalition on the Right was out of tune with Giscard's hope of moving it to the Centre-Left. There was a clear tension after 1984 between Mitterrand who, for electoral purposes, wished to move towards the Centre, and Mauroy who remained wedded to a Left-wing strategy. However, Rocard's taste for forging a coalition with the Centrists was to fall out of favour with Mitterrand after 1990.

– *Over their respective areas of competence*. Most Prime Ministers naturally resent the President's constant attempts to by-pass them and his reliance on unofficial advisers. Chaban-Delmas bitterly complained about 'a mysterious critic' at the Elysée who constantly

10. Jacques Chaban-Delmas, *L'Ardeur*, Paris, 1975.

attacked him, being particularly outraged by the open hostility of certain members of the presidential entourage. Mauroy was visibly upset about the activities of the *'visiteurs du soir'*, members of Mitterrand's court who gave advice to the President which was at odds with that proffered by the government.

It would not be difficult to multiply examples of conflict. Cumulatively, they might tend to confirm the thesis of the conflict school. However, the impression would be misleading. There may be inevitable tension and sporadic conflict in the President-Prime Minister relationship, but the situation described earlier in this chapter suggests a calculated and self-interested attempt by both actors to reach a *modus vivendi*. This leads us to the third pattern of relations: partnership.

The partnership model was probably intended by the drafters of the 1958 Constitution. Certainly, constant collaboration is essential for the smooth functioning of the executive. The significance of the Prime Minister's role has been emphasised by successive Presidents. For de Gaulle, the Prime Minister 'takes part in the conception, organises the preparation and directs the implementation' of government policies. Moreover, successive Prime Ministers have managed to leave their stamp on those policies. It was Pierre Mauroy, Prime Minister during Mitterrand's most interventionist phase, who could declare, in 1987, that the then Prime Minister, Jacques Chirac, 'has had no problem in concentrating all the powers at Matignon . . . they were already there.' This is no doubt a trifle exaggerated, but it does point to an essential truth: that Matignon, as well as the Elysée, has resources to exploit.

Our analysis suggests that it is possible to discern elements of subordination, conflict and partnership in the general relationship between President and Prime Minister, with the emphasis fluctuating markedly. What is more interesting is that all three elements may be seen at work at the same time: they are not mutually exclusive. Partnership precludes neither subordination nor conflict (Giscard and Barre, Mitterrand and Fabius), while subordination prevents neither conflict nor partnership (de Gaulle and Debré). Even the essentially conflictual relationship between Mitterrand and Chirac was characterised by subordination (each to the other in different spheres) but also by a wary and calculated partnership.

Any method of determining the distribution of power between the two would highlight collaboration, however tense, and complementarity, however conflictual. Both President and Prime Minister are leaders, bargainers, jugglers and symbols,[11] locked into complex and constant cooperation which has a constitutional base, an institutionalised structure (weekly meetings, interdepartmental councils and committees) and a political logic. Whether the outcome is one of subordination, symbiosis or mutual parasitism hinges on the interplay of political circumstance and personal chemistry.

11. Georges Jones, 'West European Prime Ministers in Perspective', *West European Politics*, 14 (2) (April 1991), pp. 163–78.

5

THE PRESIDENT, THE PARTIES
AND PARLIAMENT

Howard Machin

In 1958 de Gaulle inherited an undisciplined, fragmented, multi-party system, which had developed over ninety years of parliamentary democracy. In the absence of a presidential constitution, de Gaulle set out to usurp the traditional role played by the parties in structuring political competition. Paradoxically, and in spite of de Gaulle's anti-party diatribes, the political primacy of the presidency depended on presidentialised parties and coalitions. Only with a 'presidential' majority in parliament – a strong coalition of parties, led by the President's 'own' party – could the President have a free choice of Prime Minister, and thereby lead the government himself. In 1962, when one group of parties formed a disciplined presidential coalition behind de Gaulle, other parties quickly appreciated the advantage of competing in a rival alliance. Many party leaders realised the important role they could play in the selection of candidates for the presidency, in the conduct of presidential election campaigns, in coalition-building to create 'presidential majorities', in bargaining parliamentary support for the President's policies against concessions and even in constraining his choices of both government personnel and eventual successors.

The 'presidentialisation' of the parties involved three types of change. The first was that of coalition-building. Before 1958 coalitions had been post-election, parliamentary creations, essentially short-lived, fragile and undisciplined; after 1962 they became pre-election, national, long-term and disciplined. The second change concerned party leadership, for since the presidency became the top prize and the fountainhead of patronage, parties sought to choose people 'of presidential stature' – potential presidential candidates with a moderate, competent, catch-all appeal – as their official or unofficial leaders, while those with presidential ambitions sought to build or to take over their own loyal parties. The third change was that of improved party cohesion. Before 1958, only the Communist Party (PCF – *Parti communiste français*) had operated as a united and coherent organisation; all the others suffered divisions which made disciplined parliamentary behaviour impossible and in some cases led to splits and the creation of new parties. In contrast, the first two decades of the Fifth Republic were marked by party mergers and a general tightening of discipline at all levels in most parties.

The 'presidentialisation' of the parties also had its effect on the presidency. Although de Gaulle may have seen himself as the national saviour, the supreme representative of the national interest, over and above mere sectional, selfish parties, his introduction of the presidential election by universal suffrage as the major political competition of French politics inevitably created a *partisan* presidency. In such presidentialised party competition, it soon emerged that all parties are not equal; some, by their extremist identities, have virtually no hope of fielding a candidate with any prospect of success at the second ballot of a presidential election. Such parties, however, have not faced immediate extinction; the proliferation of non-presidentialised elections since 1978 has permitted their survival, and their continued existence has facilitated their bargaining with 'presidential' parties seeking to build electoral and parliamentary coalitions behind their candidates.

This chapter explores the process of adaptations between presidents and parties. The first section analyses de Gaulle's presidentialisation of political competition and the party system in 1958 and 1962, the subsequent formation of a two-bloc coalition system and the decline of that simplified structure since 1978 as the non-presidential parties reasserted their separate identities. The second section considers the parties as electoral actors, cross-pressured between presidentialised parliamentary and presidential elections and non-presidentialised elections and facing changing constraints as electoral rules were modified. The third section examines the presidentialisation of the role played by parties in parliament and in government. In the fourth section the evolving relations between Presidents, parties and the voters are examined and compared.

The Growth and Decline of a 'Presidentialised' Party System

Between 1958 and 1974, when Giscard d'Estaing was elected to the presidency, the multi-party system of the Fourth Republic was gradually presidentialised into a two-bloc system[1]. There was also

---

1. Much of the factual information in this section is taken from the *Le Monde – Dossiers et Documents* publications on elections. Other important sources are: François Borella, *Les partis politiques dans la France d'aujourd'hui*, Paris, 1990; M. Offerlé, *Les Partis politiques*, Paris, 1987; D. L. Seiler, *Partis et familles politiques*, Paris, 1980; and Yves Mény (ed.), *Idéologies, partis politiques, et groupes sociaux*, Paris, 1991.

a clear decline in the diversity of party behaviour at local as compared to national elections. By the late 1970s, the whole party system appeared to have been 'presidentialised' into two clear blocs. Coalition behaviour of parties in local councils and at local elections was increasingly aligned with the national patterns. Referendums were often treated as national confidence tests for the 'presidential' and 'opposition' coalitions. During the 1980s, however, the two-bloc system fragmented as new, 'non-presidential' parties emerged, the Greens and the National Front. At the same time, disputes between the members of the two blocs became so acute that both the Communists and Centrists disengaged from their former allies. By the start of the 1990s, a schizophrenic, 'semi-presidential' party system seemed to have developed. (See appendix to this chapter for tables tracing these trends during the Fifth Republic.)

Before 1958 political competition in France had been characterised by multi-party rivalry with intense ideological conflict, organisational fragmentation and weak, unstable governing coalitions.[2] Parties and political leaders were almost always divided and weak. Strong leadership was virtually impossible in normal circumstances. Excessive governmental instability (with 108 governments during the seventy years of the Third Republic and twenty-five in the twelve of the Fourth Republic) reflected the acute difficulty of building and maintaining coalitions in a fragmented, multi-party system. Not only were there sharp conflicts between the parties, but factionalism and personal rivalries were rife within almost every party. In parliament, party leaders exercised little discipline over their deputies and senators, and in the country national party organs often had little influence over the strategies and tactics of local organisations.

The one notable exception to this norm of fragmented multi-partyism came during national crises, such as the German invasion in 1914 or the Vietcong victory in Indo-china in 1954, when party leaders declared a temporary truce and invited a 'strong man' to take power at the head of a broad 'national' coalition of parties. Normal party infighting was then suspended, and the 'saviour figure' – Clemenceau in 1917 and Mendès-France in 1954 – was given the necessary disciplined parliamentary support to resolve

---

2. The seminal analysis of the rules of the complex game of party politics in the Fourth Republic was made by Philip Williams, *Crisis and Compromise: Politics in the Fourth Republic*, London, 1964. See also Maurice Duverger, *Les Partis Politiques*, Paris, 1951; Jacques Fauvet, *La Quatrième République*, Paris, 1959; and the classic: François Goguel, *La Politique des Partis sous la Troisième République*, 4th edn, Paris, 1958.

the crisis. Although only Prime Minister, he exercised a quasi-presidential authority during the brief period while the crisis lasted. Once the danger passed, the coalition would collapse and the leader would be thanked, discarded, and thereafter treated with considerable distrust by all. Before 1958, de Gaulle had already played the 'saviour figure' – as leader of the Free French from 1940 to 1944 and President of the provisional government after 1944. In 1946, however, he had resigned from office, in conflict with most political parties over the ideal constitutional arrangements for post-war France. However, his attempt to return as the leader of his own new anti-party party, the RPF (*Rassemblement du peuple français*), failed at the 1951 elections, condemning de Gaulle to a prolonged period of memoir-writing, but allowing the other parties to continue for a few more years with normal political practices.

In May 1958 a new crisis arose and de Gaulle was the only available and generally acceptable 'saviour figure'. A new Gaullist party, the UNR (*Union pour la nouvelle République*), was quickly established by his close disciples, but it did not win a majority in the National Assembly, so an alliance with the Christian Democrats (MRP – *Mouvement républicain populaire*) and Independents (CNI – *Centre national des indépendants*) was formed. De Gaulle quickly realised that the Algerian war and the threat of a civil war meant that the deputies were unlikely to revolt to the point where a majority of the Assembly would reject his policies or his chosen ministers. Indeed, the coalition parties often snarled, sometimes barked but never bit. Ultimately they were calmed by their master's voice from the Elysée palace. Algeria and the risk of de Gaulle resigning proved a functional substitute for common goals and a code of coalition discipline.[3]

In 1962, with Algerian independence decided, the old party leaders saw the departure of de Gaulle and a return to normal practices as highly desirable. Battle was joined over de Gaulle's plan to amend the Constitution to provide for election of the President by universal suffrage. De Gaulle's 'presidentialisation' of the subsequent referendum and general election was a success, but it meant that his myth of the presidency 'over and above the parties' was shattered. Instead the partisan presidency, with the double legitimacy of coincident parliamentary and presidential majorities, was revealed as the core of the political system. Effective presidential dominance was made possible by the victory of a disciplined

3. Philip M. Williams and Martin Harrison, *De Gaulle's Republic*, London, 1960, pp. 121–219 and Pierre Viansson-Ponté, *Histoire de la République Gaullienne*, I. *La Fin d'une Epoque*, Paris, 1970.

presidential coalition in the Assembly elections. That victory
involved both the growth of de Gaulle's 'own' party, the UNR,
to a 'dominant' position, with four-fifths of the deputies in his
parliamentary majority, and the adoption of Giscard's Independent Republicans (RI – they split away from the CNI) as disciplined
junior coalition partners.

The success of this new type of presidential coalition inspired the
other parties to adapt, but it took some time for a simple two-bloc
system to emerge.[4] The parties and clubs of the Centre-Left soon
felt the need to establish their own electoral coalition, either with
the Centre parties (as Defferre proposed in 1964) or with the
Communists. Mitterrand's 'Union of the Left' alliance strategy
prevailed, and he stood as the candidate of both the Socialists
(with the Radicals and clubs formally federated as the FGDS –
Fédération de la gauche démocrate et socialiste – between 1965
and 1968) and Communists in the 1965 and 1974 presidential
elections. In 1971 the new Socialist Party (PS) was formed, and in
1972 the Socialists and Communists agreed a Common Programme
for government.

The Centre parties, however, hoped to remain independent, and
resisted invitations and pressures to join the Left or the Gaullists.
In 1965 the MRP[5] created the Democratic Centre (CD – *Centre
démocrate*), incorporating a few friends from the Centre and Right
to support Lecanuet's attempt to win the presidency. The Radicals
initially opted for alliance with the Socialists in the FGDS, but
some were ill at ease in any alliance with the PCF. After the crisis
of May 1968, the FGDS collapsed and the Radical leaders began
to organise an alliance, the Reformist Movement (*Mouvement
Réformateur*), with the Democratic Centre for the 1973 elections.
Finally the Radicals split, the majority remaining in the Reformist
Movement, but a minority, the Left Radicals (MRG – *Mouvement
des radicaux de gauche*), renewing the old alliance with the
Socialists. In 1973, the dreams of Centrist revival evaporated
as leaders realised that if their parties did not opt for one side
or the other their voters would make the choice for them. Finally,
in 1974, the last non-aligned Centrists climbed down from their
increasingly perilous perch to join the majority coalition of

4. Jean Charlot, *Le Phénomène Gaulliste*, Paris, 1970; Howard Machin and
   Vincent Wright, 'The French Left under the Fifth Republic – the search for
   identity in unity', *Comparative Politics*, 10/1 (October 1977), pp. 35–67.
5. The MRP formally ceased operating in 1967: see Philip M. Williams and
   Martin Harrison, *Politics and Society in de Gaulle's Republic*, London, 1971,
   pp. 63–130; also J. R. Frears, *Political Parties and Elections in the French
   Fifth Republic*, London, 1977, pp. 58–85.

Giscard d'Estaing. Subsequently, the Christian Democrat fragments merged as a single party, the CDS (*Centre des démocrates sociaux* – a confusing title, given their views and values), which in 1978 joined with the Radicals and Giscard's Independent Republicans (by now renamed as the Republican Party (PR – *Parti républicain*) to form the federal UDF (*Union pour la démocratie française*). In short, despite the hesitations and transitional confusion, the Centre was being remorselessly split between the Right and the Left.

The presidentialised, two-bloc system appeared to reach its peak of development in the 1978 parliamentary elections, when the government Centre-Right and opposition Left coalitions each subdivided into two similar-sized parties, fought for a majority. The Centre-Right alliance, of Giscard's 'presidential majority', included the *Rassemblement pour la République* (RPR) and the UDF; the 'opposition' was the Socialist Party and the Communists. All four parties had won just over 20 per cent of the votes, and the margin between the two coalitions was small. Nonetheless, this appearance of symmetry was misleading: Bartolini[6] showed that differences between the RPR and UDF were about tactics and personalities, while those between the PS and PCF reflected a deep ideological gulf. The two-bloc system concealed three distinct ideological positions on a Left-Right axis: Communist, Socialist and Centre-Right. Nor was the system stable; indeed what appeared to be the end-product of a long process of evolution was in fact just a temporary phase.

Since 1978, the number of parties and relative party strengths have changed dramatically. The next stage of the continuing evolution, in 1981, involved both the electoral defeat of the Right and a shift in the party balance within the Left. Mitterrand defeated Giscard to win the presidency, and in the subsequent parliamentary elections the Left gained over 50 per cent of the votes for the first time since 1956. With 37.5 per cent of the first ballot votes, the PS emerged as the new 'dominant' presidential party, with a single party majority in the Assembly, a feat achieved only once before, by the UDR (*Union des Démocrates pour la République*) in 1968. Nonetheless, the new governing coalition included the often difficult alliance partner of the Socialists, the now-declining PCF.

Further changes took place in the 1980s. The Centre-Right parties in opposition faced a new challenge on the Right from Le Pen's National Front (FN – *Front national*), since in the European elections of June 1984 the FN broke their monopoly on representing the

6. Stefano Bartolini, 'Institutional Constraints and Party Competition in the French Party System', *West European Politics*, 7/4 (Oct. 1984), pp. 103–27.

Right. On the Left, the alliance of the PS and PCF disintegrated when the PCF left the governing coalition after Mauroy's government resigned in July. In 1986 *cohabitation* brought a new stage of party development, with the non-coincidence of the presidential and parliamentary majorities, for the first time in the Fifth Republic. Before the election the President had promised to stay in office unless the new majority violated his constitutional powers, but the RPR-UDF alliance won a bare three-seat majority. Chirac, the RPR leader, was appointed Prime Minister with a Centre-Right government. Opposition now came not only from three parliamentary groups (the PS, still the largest single party; the PCF and the thirty-five FN deputies) but also, intermittently, from the President himself.

The re-election of Mitterrand in 1988 ended *cohabitation* and yet another phase began with the presidency and dominant group in parliament again in the hands of the same party.[7] The new Prime Minister, Rocard, began discussions to form an alliance between the PS and the CDS or other elements of the UDF. Only a handful of UDF leaders and a few 'new men' from outside the parties joined the government, so the President dissolved the Assembly. In the June elections, however, the alliance of Socialists and friends which had optimistically dubbed itself a new 'presidential majority' failed to live up to its name, winning only 277 of the 577 seats. With no clear majority in the National Assembly, the PS promptly made a pact with the PCF (to allow the Communists to form a parliamentary group) and a number of policy deals with the CDS (notably over New Caledonia and the budget).

The results of the 1989 municipal elections, however, showed that neither of the 'non-presidential' parties, the Greens and the FN, had lost its electoral appeal. In the European elections, the Greens won seats for the first time, the CDS was the main loser but the PS also lost ground. Divisions in the Centre-Right between potential presidential candidates had clearly not diminished. Furthermore, there was little comfort for the Communists, whose electoral weakness was confirmed, and disappointment for the Socialists whose share of the votes fell, in part a result of the gains of the Greens, who won seats both on many local councils and in the European Parliament in Strasbourg. In 1990 the RPR and UDF formed yet another federal organisation, the *Union pour la France* (UPF) in an attempt to create an institutional mechanism for resolving their divisions. One goal of the UPF was to organise 'internal primary elections' for the choice of a

---

7. Jean-Luc Parodi, 'Le nouvel espace politique français', in Mény (ed.), *Idéologies, op. cit.*, pp. 49–59.

common candidate for the forthcoming presidential elections. In 1991, with the President and his government slumping in the opinion polls, Mitterrand replaced his worryingly popular Prime Minister (Rocard) by the more outspoken Edith Cresson, but no change in the coalition structure ensued from the shock appointment of France's first woman Prime Minister.

In short, political competition was increasingly dominated by the presidency during the 1960s and 1970s. This was reflected in the evolution from a fragmented and undisciplined multi-party system with no stable coalitions towards a two-bloc four-party structure with lasting coalitions. But just as that simplified, presidentialised system had emerged, it began to fragment, leaving for the 1990s a partisan presidency and a two-level party system, with a presidentialised upper tier (PS, CDS, UDF, RPR) and a multi-party lower level of parties not really expecting to share power in a national government coalition, let alone win the presidency (Greens, PCF, FN).

The Changing Rules of Semi-Presidentialised Party Competition

Since 1962, the presidential structuring of political competition has reflected both the coalition pressures inherent in the rules of presidential elections and the parliamentary responsibility of governments. The President is elected by universal suffrage every seven years, through a two-ballot system whereby if no candidate wins an overall majority at the first ballot, only the two candidates who lead at the first ballot can stand at the second. Once elected, the President can only direct the work of the government if his party or coalition has a majority in the Assembly.

Semi-presidential government thus depends on the organising and mobilising abilities of political parties allied in effective coalitions. For, although it is very easy to stand for the presidency, any candidate with serious hopes to win must have the support of at least one major political party at the first ballot, as that party's support and mobilising capacities will help to ensure that the candidate is one of the two front-runners and thus qualifies for the second round. Equally, any party which hopes to play a dominant role in governing France must be able to select a serious presidential candidate from its own ranks. A coalition of several parties is needed to guarantee victory at the second ballot, and this implies that a tactical alliance with some other party or parties should be made before the first ballot. Nonetheless, the paradoxical consequence of the electoral rules is that a candidate competes fiercely against the candidates of his party's *allies* at the first ballot to win the chance to confront the candidate of their common *enemy* at the second.

A presidential election is about personalities and issues as well as party loyalties, and in some ways the campaigns appear to weaken party loyalties. As there can only be two candidates in the second round, the one who pleases the more and displeases the less will be successful. Hence, claims by the candidate of being 'over and above' mere parties is a useful distancing device, if only to ease the anxieties of those transferring at the second round from first-ballot voting for a candidate outside that coalition. A presidential election victory is thus built on both a party (not necessarily the biggest, as Giscard demonstrated in 1974) at the core of a coalition of parties and a candidate who can appeal to some of those who do not normally support any of his coalition partners.

Once victory is achieved, the new President needs a majority in the Assembly if he is to be free to choose his own Prime Minister and direct the work of the government from the presidency. One may already exist, as was the case for Pompidou in 1969, since the Centre-Right coalition had won a large majority in the Assembly in the elections of June 1968. However, if the President faces a hostile incumbent majority in the Assembly, as Mitterrand did in 1981, he can use his power of dissolution and ask the electorate to give him a 'presidential majority' in parliament. Furthermore, the presidential mandate lasts seven years while that of the Assembly is only five years, so most Presidents can expect to face two parliamentary elections and two possibilities of losing their control of the government.

Although de Gaulle had acceded to the presidency by a non-partisan path in 1959, he had realised the need for a strong party base, both in parliament so that he could run the government, and in the country to help win re-election in 1965. Given his distaste for party activity and the Prime Minister's ability at discreet management, the task of party-building fell to Pompidou. Between 1962 and the party conference at Lille in 1967, the Prime Minister transformed the UNR (later known as the UNR-UDT after its merger with the small Left Gaullist *Union démocratique du travail*) from a loose association of enthusiastic disciples of the General into a structured and soundly financed party in its own right. Pompidou's detailed personal involvement in party management was not only effective in establishing the Gaullist party as an organisation which could continue to operate in political life after de Gaulle; he also made himself the unchallengeable heir-apparent to the presidency. When elected to the Elysée in 1969, Pompidou made considerable efforts to retain close contacts with, and the effective leadership of, the presidential party he had done so much to create.

Other politicians with presidential ambitions also saw the need for their own parties as essential vehicles to win election to the presidency and subsequently to wield its powers. Of these Mitterrand was the most successful. As First Secretary of the PS from its founding meeting at Epinay in 1971 until his election to the presidency in 1981, he was the central figure in that party. Despite the apparently democratic party structures, Mitterrand dominated the selection of its top officials, the choice of its tactics and strategy and the preparation of its programmes and platforms. Like Pompidou, Mitterrand sought to continue to manage his party from the presidency, to provide constant parliamentary and public opinion support and later to campaign for his re-election. In contrast, Giscard's attempts to build a presidential party vehicle were less successful. Although he led the Independent Republicans from the time of their split from the CNI in 1962, his party's junior-partner status in de Gaulle's coalition left it little room for growth, especially given Pompidou's efforts to build up the UNR-UDT. The failure of the neo-Gaullists to produce an electable candidate when Pompidou died gave Giscard the opportunity to win the presidency, but it was not till 1978 that he could persuade the Radicals and CDS to federate with his Republican Party (the renamed Independent Republicans). Even then, the impetus to coexist in the UDF was as much that of surviving first-ballot competition from Chirac's RPR as to provide loyal support for Giscard. After 1981, the CDS shifted its presidential hopes to Barre.

The third case of attempted detailed management to establish a presidential party base was that of Chirac in the RPR after 1974. Chirac soon realised that Pompidou's example of successfully running the party from the Prime Minister's office was difficult when the President was doing all in his power to weaken the Gaullists. In 1976 he resigned and became Party Secretary. The next year he won election as Mayor of Paris, which gave him great prestige and considerable resources, besides establishing his ability to defeat a candidate directly supported by Giscard. Like both Mitterrand and Giscard, however, Chirac was to find that his party's loyalty was not absolute; it depended on his ability to win elections. As Mitterrand found in 1978 (like Giscard in 1981 and Chirac in 1988) electoral failure weakens the authority of the presidential party leader and may lead some in the party to contemplate his replacement.

Since there have been only two instances since 1958 (in 1968 and

1981) of a single party winning an overall parliamentary majority, some kind of presidential coalition is essential. Furthermore, in parliamentary elections the candidate who gets the most votes at the second ballot wins the seat, irrespective of his or her share of the poll. The result is that when one group of parties forms an alliance to field a single candidate per constituency at the second ballot, as the UNR and RI did in 1962, the survival instincts of the other parties will push them to form similar second-ballot pacts. This lesson was learned the hard way by the Communist Party, which in 1958, with no electoral alliance, won only ten seats, despite getting 19 per cent of the votes at the first-ballot. In the March 1973 parliamentary elections the Communists had a national pact with the Socialists, so while their share of the first-ballot votes was only 2 per cent higher than in 1958 they won sixty-three more seats.

Logically the parties which form the second-ballot coalition for the presidential election expect to contest the Assembly elections as allies and to serve as the parliamentary majority coalition of the new President. The coincidence of electoral majorities is most simply achieved by the alignment of these core coalitions at the presidential and parliamentary levels. Under de Gaulle it was re-inforced by extending the same coalition arrangements down into local government elections. Before 1979, there had been a high degree of consistency between the presidential, parliamentary and municipal electoral systems. All involved second ballots with restricted access, which encouraged the parties to form alliances at least for the second rounds. The rules of presidential elections, which allowed only the two front-runners at the first ballot to contest the second, pushed the parties to line up into two blocs. Similarly, in parliamentary elections the raising of the threshold of first-ballot votes needed to qualify as a candidate at the second ballot (from 5 per cent in 1958 to 10 per cent in 1967 and to 12.5 per cent in 1976) increased the pressure on the parties to form into broad coalitions. For local elections, the 1964 law provided a 'winner-takes-all' system for the second ballot in larger towns, thus encouraging local coalition-building in parallel to that taking place at the national level. In short, all these electoral rules penalised isolated and small parties (especially if evenly spread geograph-ically) and stimulated coalition-formation and presidentialised 'centripetal' competition between big coalitions.

Then, from the early 1970s, a whole series of institutional changes was undertaken which started to reduce the relative weight of the presidency in the political system, to enhance the prestige and influence of other institutions, and thus to provide opportunities for non-presidential parties to survive or even to prosper. The first small step was an increase in the influence of the Constitutional Council. Until 1971, the Council had never used its power to strike down a law voted by parliament as unconstitutional, but in that year it demonstrated that it could use that power, and it effectively killed off a bill which had the explicit support of the President (Pompidou), his government and a large majority in the Assembly. Then, in 1974, Giscard introduced a constitutional change of considerable impact; the right of referring a bill to the Constitutional Council, which had hitherto been exclusively reserved for the Presidents of the Republic, the Senate and the National Assembly, was given to any group of sixty deputies or senators. Henceforth parties in opposition, which were unable to defeat a bill proposed by a President's government during its parliamentary passage because of the strength of his parliamentary coalition, had a further possibility to block it by appeal to the Constitutional Council. (The Council's decision could only be overridden by an amendment to the Constitution.) This provision was generously used in the 1980s.

A second type of 'depresidentialising' institutional tampering, also decided by Giscard, was the introduction in 1977 of a new type of non-responsible national election – to the European Parliament. The results of these elections had no effect on the composition of the European Commission or the Council of Ministers of the EC. There were very few issues on which Europe-wide coalitions could form, and therefore election campaigns, in France as elsewhere, were fought as national contests. But their 'inconsequential' nature made these elections the ideal channel for the new parties to enter politics. Simply by getting a large share of the votes and a number of seats in Strasbourg, the FN and Greens alike were able to establish a kind of national legitimacy. Party competition in these 'irresponsible' European elections was thus disconnected from that in presidential and parliamentary elections where the results determine who governs and responsible voting is at a premium.

This reform was also significant in that it marked the re-entry of the first element of proportional respresentation into French electoral competition, itself a 'depresidentialising' influence on the parties. Despite the hostility of his RPR allies, Giscard chose to adopt proportional representation within a single national constituency of eighty-one seats for the 1979 European elections. Geographical spread of party support was not penalised in any way. In the 1984 European elections the National Front, by clearing the 5 per cent hurdle, became the main beneficiary of this proportional system. The Greens followed in 1989.[8]

In 1982, the Socialists and Communists took a further step when they decided to modify the municipal electoral rules by the introduction of an element of proportionality. Henceforth, small parties which refused to join coalitions were no longer doomed to total exclusion from council membership. In 1985 the Socialists further complicated electoral structures by a triple innovation. A single-ballot proportional representation system was introduced for the 1986 parliamentary elections, the same system was adopted for the first elections of regional councils and the two elections were scheduled for the same day. The ninety-six *départements* were taken as the multi-member constituencies for both elections, a 5 per cent threshold for representation was fixed, the 'highest average principle' was chosen for the distribution of seats, and the membership of the National Assembly was increased to 577. The result was not proportional but a curious mixture, since many rural *départements* with small populations were given only two or three seats.[9]

When the RPR-UDF leaders condemned the reform as an attempt to reduce their chances of winning an overall majority by allowing the FN to win seats, the election system itself became a campaign issue. The RPR and UDF promised to restore the old system if they won a majority, which they did, although the new rules did allow the FN into the Assembly and the Communists to survive. An early act of the Chirac government was to restore the single-member constituency, second-ballot system, with a 12.5 per cent threshold, as before 1986. The number of seats was kept at 577, and thus many of the constituencies could not be given the same boundaries as in 1981. Some imaginative architecture went into the construction of the new constituencies. However, there were no changes of rules for regional elections, which continue to be contested under proportional representation.

In the 1980s two further 'depresidentialising' innovations were made. The first was the Defferre package of decentralisation reforms, which both enhanced the power and prestige of local elected offices and placed a statutory limitation on the accumulation of elected offices, thereby encouraging the enlargement,

8. 'Résultats des Elections européennes', *Le Monde – Dossiers et Documents*, 1989; *1989 Elections Handbook*, Strasbourg, 1989.
9. Andrew Knapp, 'Proportional but bipolar: France's electoral system in 1986', *West European Politics*, 10/1 (1987), pp. 89–114; 'Les Elections Législatives du 16 mars 1986', *Le Monde – Dossiers et Documents*, 1986; 'How Fabius Lost: The French Elections, 1986', *Government and Opposition*, 21/3 (1986), pp. 269–85.

fragmentation and 'denationalisation' of political élites.[10] The second and most significant institutional innovation took place when Mitterrand and Chirac chose to cooperate in *cohabitation* between 1986 and 1988. The relatively smooth operation of that system of non-presidential government and the satisfaction of the public, as shown by opinion polls, meant that non-coincident majorities became a real alternative to the presidentialised party system of the 1960s and 1970s. In 1988 Mitterrand expressed his preference for a sympathetic and supportive majority, but he could not plausibly argue that a 'presidential majority' was vitally necessity to avoid chaos. The RPR and UDF even proposed a new bout of *cohabitation*. Subsequently, however, the Rocard government showed that stable and effective government may also be provided by a parliament with no clear majority.[11]

As a consequence of all these changes, an inconsistent institutional and electoral environment for party competition had been created by the late 1980s. The strongly 'presidentialised' presidential and parliamentary elections of 1988 were followed by municipal elections in 1989 which were contested under the semi-proportional rules, European Parliament elections later in 1989 under full proportional representation, and the 1992 regional elections under 'semi-proportional' representation (but with very different rules from those for the European elections). The various electoral systems encourage a variety of sometimes non-presidential competitive strategies, and the second ballot of presidential elections no longer imposes a single dominant political cleavage on the party system. Small and extremist parties, the victims of the coalition-building pressures of the two-ballot, single-member (or list), winner-takes-all rules of the pre-1979 period, can now not only survive but also win seats in proportional elections. They could also hope to draw concessions from big parties by fighting first ballots of presidential and parliamentary elections with no hope of winning but simply to demonstrate their hold on some of the voters and influence second-ballot outcomes. The party system thus entered the 1990s in a 'semi-presidentialised' condition, with the core parties – the PS, CDS, UDF and RPR – still primarily focussed on presidential and governing coalition strategies at the

10. 'La Cinquième République', *Pouvoirs*, 49 (1989); Viviane Schmidt, *Decentralising France*, Cambridge, 1991; 'La Décentralisation', *Pouvoirs*, 60 (1992), especially pp. 5–24, 67–78; Andrew Knapp, 'The *cumul des mandats*, local power and political parties in France', *West European Politics*, 14/1 (1991), pp. 18–40.
11. Jean Gicquel, 'La Cohabitation', *Pouvoirs*, 49 (1989), pp. 69–79.

national level, while the fringe of 'non-presidential' parties – the Greens, FN and PCF – pursued other tactics in other arenas.

Parties, Parliament and Presidentialised Government

In the Fifth Republic the initiative for forming governments has been taken by the President, but the parties in parliament can dispose of governments. To rule France the government is required to obtain parliamentary approval for many of its policy decisions. Explicit approval is necessary for new laws and for the annual budget. Ministers are also subject to parliamentary scrutiny of their acts, and must answer the questions posed by individual deputies and senators, or committees. The 1958 Constitution was innovative in France by limiting the domain of parliamentary law-making. Article 34 provides a list of subjects on which parliament can legislate, and on all other matters the government acts by decree. This is typical of the constitutional provisions concerning parliament, which seem designed to limit its powers.

Parliament consists of two houses, which however do not have equal powers. In most circumstances and if the government agrees, the Assembly can outvote the upper house. The Senate cannot censure a government, but equally it cannot be dissolved. It is thus inferior in both power and prestige to the Assembly. The 319 senators are elected indirectly by an electoral college for nine-year terms, with one-third of the seats elected every three years. Since 1986, the 577 deputies in the Assembly are directly elected by universal suffrage every five years. The electoral system for the deputies was not fixed by the Constitution but by law, and in 1958 the single-member, two-ballot system was chosen. The Assembly alone can censure the government, but it can be dissolved by presidential decree.

The institutional practice of government from 1958 to 1986 was that the President chose a Prime Minister who naturally benefited from the support of the President's parliamentary majority. In theory the Prime Minister had a free choice of ministers, but in practice some were imposed by the President. The period of *cohabitation* did not see a shift of influence over the choice of ministers back from the executive to parliament and the parties; the choice of ministers and the allocation of responsibilities were very clearly decisions of the Prime Minister: the key posts went to his closest friends and allies in the RPR – Balladur at Finance, Pasqua at Interior – while the most important ministry given to a UDF leader was only that of Culture and Communications (Léotard). The re-election of Mitterrand and the election of a presidential 'dominant minority' in the Assembly in 1988 was matched by a resurgence of Mitterrand's influence over the choices of ministers. Indeed, the Cresson government of May 1991 was dominated by the 'President's men': Dumas (Foreign Affairs), Joxe (Defence), Bérégovoy (Finance), Nallet (Justice), Bianco (Social Affairs), Guigou (European Affairs) and Charasse (Budget) – who remained a presidential adviser while a minister. In short, neither parties nor parliament played the key role in choosing ministers during the Fifth Republic.

Nor have the parties in parliament played much of a role in initiating legislation. The vast majority of new laws have been introduced as government bills rather than deputies' own bills. The major contributions of the parliamentary party groups have been those of improving government bills and supervising governmental activity. The work of amending laws is shared between the parliamentary committees and the readings before the full house. Since 1958 there have been only six permanent committees, and therefore all have a large membership. After the initial presentation of the bill by the minister responsible, all the members have the opportunity to suggest their amendments. If a majority agrees an amendment (which is relatively easier in a committee with no television cameras present, which removes the embarrassment from cross-party deals) it is included in the text which the committee reports to the reading before the full house. Even if the committee rejects a proposed amendment, the deputy can re-submit it during the session of the full house. The minister may propose an alternative amendment, admitting a compromise with that of the deputy. Although the government has the power to demand a final vote on its text or indeed to by-pass the debate altogether by adopting the 'question of confidence' procedure (under article 49.3 of the Constitution), it rarely uses these weapons, since they are rather too final in their effect as deterrents. Indeed,[12] the government is often rather accommodating towards amendments: in 1989, of 5,181 amendments tabled, 2,285 were adopted and of these 65 per cent were those adopted by the committee and only 18 per cent were government amendments.

It might be argued that the growing influence of amendments, especially during the presidencies of Giscard and Mitterrand, reflects a much more conciliatory attitude of the President and government towards their own supporters. Since 1988, there has also been more consideration of amendments from opposition parties. Nonetheless, the decline of coalition and party discipline

12. Olivier Duhamel, *Le Pouvoir Politique en France*, vol. 1, Paris, 1991, pp. 253–4;

since the departure of de Gaulle is also apparent in this context. While more amendments have been accepted, there has been an increasingly frequent use of the 'question of confidence' procedure. Debré used it only three times in four years, whereas Rocard employed it twenty-five times in three years.

The supervisory role of parliament has also been increasing in recent years. The most vigorous form of supervision – that of dismissal – has only once been used fully and successfully, in 1962. The tabling of a motion of censure is also a means for the opposition parties to impose a media debate criticising the policies of the government. In general this procedure has not been used much, perhaps because it ends in a vote which demonstrates the minority status of the opposition. For in a motion-of-censure vote, an absolute majority of the full membership of the house (577 in 1992) is required for the motion to be carried. Parliamentary questions, however, allow the party groups some opportunity to scrutinise government activities and focus on the Prime Minister and ministers rather than the President. The oral 'questions to the government' (each Wednesday afternoon) and 'questions to the minister' (each Thursday) have proved popular with the deputies, perhaps because they have been broadcast on television.

Since 1958, the parliamentary party organisations have had to learn to live with the presidential leadership of governments and their own involvement in coalitions. The Gaullist-Giscardian alliance of the 1960s had not too many difficulties in this respect; by joining these parties, most deputies had made a clear commit-ment to following presidential leadership. There were some tense moments, and not all were resolved by imposing presidential wishes. But there was a special personal loyalty which many felt for de Gaulle which was not transferred to his successors.

Pompidou at first managed not only to hold his party together and under control but even to enlarge his coalition by drawing in a group of Centrists led by Jacques Duhamel. Difficulties soon set in, especially as Right-wing deputies became hostile to the liberal-isation of television introduced by the Prime Minister, Chaban-Delmas, and as Left-wing Gaullists began to see Pompidou's economic and foreign policies as a betrayal of the goals set by de Gaulle. The Centrists found coalition discipline rather alien to their cultural traditions. Indeed, the basic characteristics of the 'old' parties made their deputies uncomfortable in their subordinate roles as members of presidential majorities. Furthermore, after 1976, when the RPR no longer held the presidency or the post of Prime Minister, they too found that junior-partner status in the presidential coalition – whatever their numerical strength – did not give them as much influence over policy choices as they would have liked. Tension reached a peak in late 1979, when RPR hostility to parts of the 1980 budget forced the Prime Minister, Barre, to use article 49, clause 3, of the Constitution no fewer than six times to secure its passage.[13]

In 1981 wielding power and dominating the Assembly was no easy task for Socialist deputies. They had a radical programme, a difficult ally, and only ten years of existence as a united force; a large number had no previous parliamentary experience and there were few leaders with ministerial experience. One source of tensions was the dominance of the presidency within the political system, for some Socialist deputies had believed that their party, not the President, should guide the government. The choice of ministers clearly showed that the President had not left Mauroy with a free hand. Mitterrand showed more sensitivity to feelings in his party than any of his predecessors, but not enough to quieten all his critics. Some PS deputies saw the regular breakfasts of the Party Secretary and Assembly group leader with the President and Prime Minister not as a useful informal consultative device but rather as a means to allow Mitterrand to keep his grip on the party apparatus.

Relations between PS deputies and their President's governments were never entirely free of tension. While the President hoped to demonstrate that the PS was a moderate and competent 'party of government', some PS deputies saw ideological politics as their *raison d'être*. They hoped not only to continue the tradition of abstract ideological debate while in government, but also to convert their ideological dreams into policy realities. Many were teachers, and the main goal of the pro-Socialist, anti-clerical teachers' unions for over a century had been to abolish the private (mainly church) schools. Hence, it was not surprising that the PS encouraged the government and Education Minister Savary to press on with plans to merge private schools into the state system. Opinion polls indicated that this idea was very unpopular, and there were several huge hostile demonstrations in early 1984. Nonetheless, when Savary made concessions to the private schools lobby in the hope of demobilising their campaign, if not winning their acquiescence, Socialist deputies pushed the Prime Minister, Mauroy, to disown those concessions. The PS vote in the June 1984 European elections dropped to only 20.8 per cent, and the private schools lobby and opposition parties threatened massive public demonstrations against the 'Savary bill'. This crisis was not resolved by the party but by Mitterrand, who scrapped the schools bill, accepted the

13. For details see *ibid.*, p. 254.

resignation of the Mauroy government and appointed a new government led by his talented young acolyte Fabius. This government
included the leaders of every faction within the PS but no Communists. The deputies sadly admitted the folly of their ways, and the
entire party closed ranks behind the President's new government.

In 1986, the narrowness of the Chirac government's majority,
the short period of office before the presidential election and the
willingness of both the parliamentary Socialist group and the
President to exploit any internal differences between the RPR and
UDF, encouraged the deputies of those parties to show a considerable discretion in criticising their leaders. On some occasions, the
government made many concessions but on some key issues it
employed the 'question of confidence' procedure (eight times in all).
The Rocard government, in a minority in the Assembly, made
even more concessions than its predecessor but also used article 49,
clause 3, twice as often. The pattern which thus emerges is that
Presidents and their governments have been growing more willing
to accept criticisms and modifications from parliament in general
and the deputies of their own parties in particular. At the same
time, those deputies have been increasingly willing to use the means
at their disposal to influence governments.

Presidents, Parties and Voters

Many studies have emphasised the 'linkage' function of political
parties.[14] While parties are themselves voluntary associations, with
members, structures, rites and activities like others, they are also
key intermediary and networking organisations. They both reflect
and help to form ever-changing public opinion. They link new social
groups into the political system and place new issues on the political
agenda. During the Fifth Republic, however, parties have been
pushed to adapt to new communication techniques, to deal with
such issues as unemployment, immigration, the environment and
women's rights, but also to resolve their own internal problems,
including the selection of suitable candidates for presidential
elections. Their limited ability to satisfy the electors on all these
accounts, coupled with their growing reputation for corruption,
kindled by the attempts of some individual parties to discredit

---

14. Kay Lawson (ed.), *Political Parties and Linkage: A Comparative Perspective*,
    New Haven, 1980, pp. 2–24; see also Jean Charlot, 'Political parties: Towards
    a new theoretical synthesis', and Jacques Lagroye, 'Change and permanence
    in political parties', both in *Political Studies*, XXXVII/3 (1989), pp. 352–61,
    362–75.

others, has led to a marked decline in public respect for and trust in parties and political élites in general.

Many writers have noted that the semi-presidentialisation of the Fifth Republic was facilitated by its historical coincidence with the growth of mass television in France and the personalisation of politics encouraged by that medium. De Gaulle was the first politician to exploit television widely for political communication, but every subsequent President and presidential candidate has taken professional public relations advice on television appearances. Newspaper journalists have moved into television by taking part in current affairs discussions which have focussed on individual leaders rather than parties or coalitions. Opinion polling has also developed massively since the early 1960s. In short, links between leaders and voters have evolved with the spread of new techniques and technology. The role of the parties – rather than individuals – in election campaigns, public-opinion formation and communication between masses and élites has been modified and generally reduced. Irrespective of television, however, the opinions and values of the electors have also been evolving.

Since the 1960s, there have been a number of changes in the ideological climate and social conditions of the voters to which Presidents and parties have reacted in the hope of increasing their support and influence. But political élites are not merely passive; indeed, changing discourse and actions on the part of those in or near power contribute to the shaping of the ideological framework. Marxism on the Left and Gaullist nationalism on the Right have both declined markedly. A 'New Right' international market liberalism and an authoritarian, racist nationalism have both grown. Post-materialist ideas, especially feminism and environmentalism, have also prospered.[15]

Opinion polls indicated that, after 1979, there was a general fall in public confidence in political parties and a similar decline in identification with individual parties (from 29 per cent in 1978 to 17 per cent in 1984 according to *Eurobarometer* polls). The 1981 elections showed that the RPR, UDF and PCF alike had suffered massive losses of support. Party membership stagnated or declined in almost all parties except the National Front (FN). Party membership figures are notoriously unreliable, since most parties prefer not to publish records, while some have no definition of what

15. Jack Hayward, 'Ideological change: The exhaustion of the revolutionary impetus', in P. A. Hall, J. Hayward and H. Machin (eds), *Developments in French Politics*, London, 1990, pp. 15–32; Sudhir Hazareesingh, *Intellectuals and the French Communist Party*, Oxford, 1991.

constitutes membership. PCF leaders admit that membership has dropped from 650,000 in 1979 to 608,000 in 1989, but outsiders estimate that the real figures are 450,000 (1979) and 230,000 (1989). The PS claimed 195,000 members in 1981, the same number in 1986 and an optimistic but implausible 200,000 in 1989, a success only of survival for the dominant party of the decade. In the UDF, PR members totalled 190,000 in 1986, but only 130,000 three years later, with over one-third of this membership renewed each year. The RPR claimed 850,000 members in 1986 but later admitted that it had no precise definition of membership. In contrast, the FN claimed a big growth in members (up to 100,000 in 1990) and activists, but admitted that often members do not stay for long.

However, this decline in party identification and membership has not been accompanied by declining public interest in politics. An increase in voter volatility has been one consequence. Some voters turned to abstention. After the presidential elections of 1981 there was a big increase in abstentionism; in the 1981 Assembly elections 29 per cent abstained, in 1986 21.5 per cent and in 1988 34.3 per cent. Even in the 1981 and 1988 presidential elections turn-out was lower than in the previous two decades. At the European elections of 1984 and in the 1988 referendum voting figures reached record lows (63 per cent in the November 1988 referendum). Abstention was not, however, the only alternative. Another alternative was voting for a party hostile to the traditional parties; hence, the FN made great gains on the Right. While Right-wing extremism has been found throughout Western Europe,[16] as a consequence of unemployment and xenophobia against immigrants at the end of a long prosperous period, the electoral success of the FN after 1983 was quite exceptional.

The record of failure of the Centre-Right parties to stop the rise of the FN compares unfavourably with the initial success of the PS in dealing with a new ideological challenge to its position from the Greens. With only a loose national organisation, the Greens could barely be said to constitute a party but there was no shortage of local Green candidates at elections. The plan to build a nuclear power station on a seashore site at Plogoff, in Brittany, was one test case by which the PS proved its 'greenness': it supported the weekly demonstrations held at the site, and Mitterrand promised that when elected he would scrap Plogoff and review the whole nuclear programme. In the 1981 elections, many first-ballot Lalonde (Green) voters switched to Mitterrand

16. Klaus von Beyme (ed.), 'Right-wing Extremism in Western Europe', *West European Politics*, 11/2 (1988), pp. 1–18, 47–64.

at the second ballot and again voted PS in the subsequent parliamentary elections. Mitterrand kept his promise to cancel Plogoff, but the report of the nuclear review, which recommended continuing a reduced building programme, disappointed many. Nonetheless, the PS was the least 'environment-destructive' and most friendly of the big parties, and some Greens could still make pacts with the PS.

However, the Greens were not the only new socio-political movement with which Mitterrand and the PS managed to create ties. One other of importance was the feminists. This linking with feminists was neither inevitable nor entirely successful. The feminist movement, a loose network of organisations and individuals striving to enhance women's rights and political consciousness, first had hopes of sweeping reforms when Giscard appointed a 'special delegate' and later a junior minister 'for the feminine condition' and Simone Veil as Health Minister with responsibility for the legalisation of abortion. Mitterrand attempted to outbid his predecessor by promising, and creating, a Ministry for Women's Rights. This title and the choice of a dynamic minister, Yvette Roudy, suggested a more radical approach. Furthermore, the dynamic and hard-hitting Edith Cresson was appointed to a traditional male preserve, the Agriculture Ministry. Within a year of taking office, the Socialist government proposed changing the municipal electoral law to ensure that women candidates occupied one-third of the places on all party lists. It was prevented from implementing this measure only by a ruling from the all-male Constitutional Council. The new ministry gradually built up contacts with the feminist movement, the PS and Mitterrand gathering the electoral fruits. The President seemed to turn again to feminism as a source for new friends and allies in 1991 when he appointed Cresson as the first woman Prime Minister in French history and made a series of appointments of women to senior posts in his staff at the Elysée.

Yet another group which Mitterrand and his party targeted for networking was *SOS-racisme*, one of the organisations founded to oppose the FN and campaign for equal rights for immigrants after 1984. Its symbol – an open hand – and its slogan, 'Don't touch my mate', were soon widely known. It won massive support from young people of all ethnic origins but especially from the *beurs* (North African immigrants' children with French citizenship). Many immigrants and *beurs* had already been pro-Socialist before 1981, in part because both the RPR-UDF coalition and the PC had gained reputations of hostility to immigrants. From 1983 to 1988, Mitterrand's support for immigrant rights often seemed aimed to divide the parties of the Right as much as to aid the immigrants. Mitterrand often discussed (but did little towards actually enacting) voting rights for immigrants in local elections. In 1988 Harlem Désir, the charismatic leader of *SOS-racisme*, openly supported Mitterrand, and on the night of his re-election the celebrations were often led by *beur* activists. The Rocard government soon modified the immigration law and circulars of its predecessor. However, the rising unemployment figures and spreading riots in immigrant urban areas during late 1990 and early 1991 showed that PS governments have certainly not solved all problems faced by *beurs* in education, housing and employment. Mitterrand's response of appointing first an 'interministerial delegate' then a Minister for Towns and concentrating funding on potential trouble-spots (more than 300!) illustrated his awareness of the social and political danger.

Mitterrand and his party also made great efforts to establish close links with the principal student organisation, which led the 1986 strikes, sit-ins and demonstrations which persuaded the Chirac government to scrap its university reform plans. Indeed, the minister responsible for the project resigned after a student was killed by a policeman's baton. The student leaders were openly pro-Socialist and the PS attacked the government project and handling of the demonstrations. Student demonstrators hailed the President as their hero. Mitterrand coopted Isabelle Thomas, an articulate, photogenic student leader, to his 1988 campaign team, and later to his staff in the Elysée. Hence, while in 1986 the RPR-UDF had overtaken the PS in winning the support of younger voters, by 1988 the situation had been reversed.

In 1988, the Socialist net was cast very wide. The President's proposal for a new wealth tax to provide a guaranteed minimum income was designed to appeal to those who supported the winter soup-kitchens created by the comedian Colluche to feed the 'new poor' of the age of industrial restructuring. Rocard stressed that his proposed 'broadening' of the governing coalition was not just towards Centrist politicians but also towards any elements of 'civil society' not hostile to the PS. New ministers included Bernard Kouchner (leader of an international humanitarian doctors' move-ment), Roger Fauroux, a successful industrialist, and Pierre Arpaillange, a respected magistrate who in the 1960s had worked with four Centre-Right Ministers of Justice. While this policy was not a complete success, it represented an effort towards widening support for the PS and the President.

In short, it was in part the ability of the Socialists, through social and political 'networking', to adopt new social movements which allowed them, in the 1980s, to retain their dominance within the party system. The failures of the RPR, UDF and PC in this respect facilitated the electoral success of both the PS and the FN. Nonetheless, in other respects the PS had major problems. In 1981 it was still highly factionalised. Increasingly the factions became clans around prominent leaders struggling to assume the role of heir-apparent. This leadership contest had dominated the 1979 party conference at Metz, when it seemed that Mitterrand might not run in 1981. At the 1981 party conference at Valence, only months after the election, there were calls for much more radical policies and changes of administrative personnel. In 1984, when Mitterrand seemed too unpopular to be re-electable, a new race for recognition as the PS presidential candidate began, largely conducted by factions organised as informal political 'clubs', including Rocard's *Convergences*, Fabius' *Démocratie 2000*, and Chevènement's *République Moderne*. All claimed to be merely think-tanks for new policy ideas, but no one was fooled into thinking that the real competition was about policies. As Mitterrand's popularity increased again after 1985, this clan warfare diminished, a clear sign that the contest for the presidential candidature had been called off. Once Mitterrand had been re-elected in 1988, however, the 'war of succession' began again and the inter-clan rivalry soon emerged into full public view, notably at the party Congress in Rennes, when the President attempted but failed to impose his 'favourite son', Fabius, as Party Secretary and heir-apparent.

Faced by a series of scandals, particularly implicating Socialists, Mitterrand tried to save the situation by suggesting an all-party agreement on public funding for political parties and the publication of party accounts. After 1988, new scandals appeared and even the Justice Minister (Nallet) was attacked for misuse of funds as treasurer of Mitterrand's presidential election campaign in 1988. An inquiry was held and yet another party finance act was voted, but the Socialists could not shake off the public image of corruption.

In 1981 the PCF joined the Socialists in government, having decided that this was the best way to stabilise their waning influence. As the Mauroy government lost popularity, the PCF appeared to act increasingly incoherently with its governmental and opposition personalities barely in coexistence. By 1984, when unemployment and governmental unpopularity were both growing at alarming rates, Communist leaders decided that remaining in office could only cost votes. They left the ruling coalition and attempted to take over the leadership of the discontented. This decision was no more fruitful for their revival plans than their previous choice: in

1986 they lost almost one-third of the voters who had supported them in 1981.

The continued decline of the PCF was again clear in 1988, with the poor performance of the lacklustre official PCF candidate Lajoinie in the presidential contest. Even many who had voted Communist in 1986 opted for Mitterrand at the first ballot, showing loyalty to the notion of unity of the Left and awareness of the futility of voting PCF in a presidential election. The party could no more direct its voters than control its members. After the elections, with only twenty-seven seats, the PCF had not even enough to form an independent group in the Assembly. To avoid total marginalisation in debates, it made a truce with the Socialists who did not have a majority in the Assembly: the PCF voted with the PS to elect Fabius as Speaker of the Assembly, and the PS responded by changing Assembly rules to allow a group to be formed with only twenty-five deputies. The 1989 municipal and European elections brought no solace: the PCF was surviving but not reviving, yet their support would still be necessary for a future presidential victory of the Left.

In opposition, the situation for the Centre-Right parties was very different, although relations between the RPR and UDF were no more cordial than those between the PS and PCF. The parties of the new opposition sought to reconstruct themselves for an eventual electoral revenge by simultaneously competing against each other and together against the Socialists. Both aspired to presidential and dominant party status, although the UDF had additional problems of holding together its constituent parties. A return to the 'golden age' of de Gaulle and Pompidou was the dream of the RPR after 1981: to recapture both the leadership of the Centre-Right alliance and the presidency and to dominate both government and parliament. The initial frustrations of facing opposition were great after twenty-three years in office, especially as almost half its deputies had lost their seats. Nevertheless the situation was not hopeless. The RPR had at least a clear leader, Chirac, with open presidential ambitions. With Giscard then disgraced, there appeared to be no real leadership challenge from the UDF. Furthermore, the economic crisis was unsolved, so a medium-term increase in both unemployment and voter discontent was probable. The RPR thus strove to lead the parliamentary opposition, to ensure that Chirac remained the sole presidential candidate of the Centre-Right, and to win the support of all those dissatisfied with the PS by offering attractive alternatives.

The RPR's failure to regain alliance domination also reflected the unexpected resilience of the UDF. After the defeat of 1981, many PR, CDS and Radical leaders had agreed that, whatever their differences, continued coexistence within the UDF federal structure was essential to avoid becoming mere acolytes of the RPR. Some, ambitious or far-sighted, saw that the UDF could provide a base for a presidential candidate in 1988. The resuscitation of the presidential hopes of the UDF, however, was mainly the work of old rather than new leaders. In 1983, as the PS government set new records of unpopularity, its immediate predecessors, Giscard and Barre, staged their own political comeback, after months avoiding publicity and rebuilding networks of allies. However, the two returned to public life as rivals. Each saw himself as a future President and strove to win the support of the entire UDF to that end. While the policy differences between them were small, their intense personal rivalry became a divisive factor within the UDF. Barre was backed by the CDS, while Giscard, despite the reluctance of Léotard (who himself had presidential dreams), regained the support of his old party, the PR. This leadership rivalry thus reinforced the interparty competition within the UDF, but as both men hoped eventually to harness the electoral support of the whole federation, neither sought to dismember it. In the 1986 election campaign, Barre differed from both Chirac and Giscard with his demand to force the resignation of the incumbent President in the event of a RPR-UDF victory. Rivalry continued during *cohabitation*, although only Chirac and Barre were serious candidates for the presidency. The result was that Chirac, as Prime Minister, campaigned on his record in power, while Barre ran against him on a platform explicitly critical of that record.

However, the campaigns of both 1986 and 1988 were singularly complicated by the competition from the National Front after its electoral breakthrough in 1984. The failure of the RPR and UDF to regain support when the popularity of Mitterrand and the PS plummeted after 1982 partly explains the take-off of the FN, as its leader Le Pen showed remarkable skill in exploiting the weakness of the old parties and the worries of the electorate. Having inherited a fortune and taken professional advice on his image, Le Pen led the great FN electoral upsurge. After 1984 the Front found that holding itself together and growing were real challenges. At the élite level, several deputies who had defected to the FN from the RPR or UDF were ill at ease with Le Pen's anti-semitic utterances and authoritarian leadership, and his closest lieutenants had different strategies for expansion. The 1986 vote was high, but over one-third of the 1984 FN voters had moved to other parties. The 1988 presidential first ballot also brought more new voters, but the parliamentary elections again showed that voter loyalty

was weak. The rise of the FN thus destroyed the RPR-UDF monopoly of representation of the Right and Centre and reduced their
chances of returning to power.

In the 1988 presidential elections, the FN divided the two presidential candidates of the Centre-Right. Barre opposed any concession to the FN on the grounds that it would push moderate and
liberal voters to back Mitterrand, while Chirac seemed more
worried about the abstention of FN voters. The RPR and UDF
had failed either to destroy or to coopt the rival on the Right,
and their own supporters had been divided and weakened. In
1988 some were scared back to Mitterrand. In the months following
the 1988 elections, different RPR and UDF leaders drew very
different conclusions about the causes and consequences of the
defeat. Several suggested that to avoid such destructive public
rows the RPR and UDF should merge as a single party, the UPF.
In contrast, CDS leaders, encouraged by Barre, rejected this idea
and called into question the need to keep the UDF united. The
CDS deputies formed their own group in the Assembly and
expressed willingness to support any policy of the Rocard government with which they agreed. In 1989 the parties of the Centre-Right
seemed further away than ever from the 'unity behind a single
leader' which so many saw as essential for the reconquest of the
presidency and a majority in the Assembly. The RPR and UDF
leaders might declare that the UPF was an ever-closer union but
not all their followers agreed.

The repeated inability to find agreed new presidential candidates
and the growing scandals of corruption and internal rigging of
decision-making condemn the main parties to lose public confidence
and respect. They facilitate the task of new parties, like the Greens
and National Front, of breaking into the traditional system. Nonetheless, their difficulties do reflect a very real problem of adapta-
tion to new institutional rules in a changed economic and social
environment.

Conclusions: a Partisan President and a
Semi-Presidentialised Party System?

At all elections, political competition is about ideas, policies,
personalities, social alliances, votes and posts, but the relative
weights of these factors vary considerably according to the type
of election in question. Political parties and coalitions structure and
simplify the choices available to citizens, especially in European,
local and regional elections. However, presidential elections are primarily structured by presidential candidates, as were parliamentary

elections until the success of *cohabitation* in 1986. But presidential candidates are also members and leaders of political parties. The decades of the Fifth Republic have witnessed major changes in the parties and party system. Relations between parties and the presidency have been profoundly modified, and alternation in power now poses few problems.

The President of the Republic has emerged as the supreme partisan, although he continues to be challenged by rival contenders for this role. His partisanship is not only crucial to his election; it is also an indispensable element of his exercise of power as President. Detailed personal involvement in party (and coalition) management has been a permanent presidential preoccupation since Pompidou. On the Right, the role of parties in the proposed selection of the would-be single presidential candidate by primary elections is an augury of the continuing need to counterbalance the President's state functions with party support and partisan choices. So, whoever becomes Mitterrand's successor, party will continue to play a pivotal role in the way by which candidates accede to the presidency and the way in which presidential power is exercised.

APPENDIX

Table 5.1. THE PRESIDENTIAL AND EUROPEAN PARTY SYSTEMS

PRESIDENTIAL VOTES AT FIRST BALLOT (%)

	PCF	PS+ MRG	Other Left	Green	Centre (MRP/CD)	UDF	RPR	Other Right	FN
1965	⟨32.2⟩				15.8		43.7	2.9	5.3
1969	21.5	5.1	4.8		23.4		44.0	1.3	
1974	⟨43.2⟩		3.7	1.3		32.6	15.1	3.8	0.9
1981	15.3	28	5.6	3.9		28.3	17.9	3.0	
1988	6.7	34.1	4.4	3.8		16.5	19.9		14.4

EUROPEAN VOTES (%)

	PCF	PS+ MRG	Other Left	Green	Centre (MRP/CD)	UDF	RPR	Other Right	FN
1979	20.5	23.5		4.4		27.6	16.3		1.3
1984	11.2	20.8		3.4		⟨43.0⟩			10.9
1989	7.7	23.6		10.6	8.4*	⟨28.9⟩			11.7

* CDS list.

Howard Machin

Table 5.2.   THE PARLIAMENTARY PARTIES

FIRST BALLOT VOTES (%)

	PCF	PS	Other Left	Green	Centre	UDF (RI)	RPR	Other Right	FN
1958	19.2	15.7	8.3		11.1		19.5	22.9	
1962	21.7	12.6	10.2		9.1	⟨ 37.8 ⟩		8.6	
1967	22.5	19.0	2.1		13.4	⟨ 37.7 ⟩		4.9	
1968	20.0	16.5	4.7		10.3	⟨ 44.7 ⟩		3.5	
1973	21.4	20.8	3.6		13.1	⟨ 36.0 ⟩		5.1	
1978	20.6	24.7	4.4	2.1		21.5	22.6	3.0	0.9
1981	16.1	37.5	2.0	1.1		19.2	20.8	2.8	0.4
1986	9.8	31.6	2.6	1.2		⟨ 42.1 ⟩		2.7	9.8
1988	11.3	35.9	2.0	0.4		18.5	19.2	2.9	9.7

SEATS IN THE NATIONAL ASSEMBLY (%)

	PCF	PS	Other Left	Green	Centre	UDF (RI)	RPR	Other Right	FN
1958	10	44	32		57		199	133	
1962	41	66	39		55	35	233	13	
1967	73	116	4		41	44	201	8	
1968	34	57			33	64	296	3	
1973	73	101	1		34	55	183	12	
1978	86	114	1			134	159	2	
1981	44	283	6			62	84	11	
1986	35	214	1			129	146	14	35
1988	27	278			41	90	130	13	1*

* Expelled from the FN after the elections for indiscipline.

Table 5.3.   PARTIES, COALITIONS AND
GOVERNMENTS SINCE 1959

	President & PM	Governing parties	Oppositions
1959	De Gaulle Debré/UNR	UNR +MRP + CNI SFIO* (crisis coalition)	PCF
1962 April	De Gaulle Pompidou/UNR	UNR + CNI + MRP (semi-presidential coalition)	SFIO PCF
1962 Nov.	De Gaulle Pompidou/UNR	UNR + RI (presidential coalition)	CNI MRP SFIO PCF
1966	De Gaulle 2 Pompidou/UNR	UNR + RI (presidential coalition)	CNI MRP SFIO PCF
1967	De Gaulle 2 Pompidou/UNR	UNR + RI (presidential coalition)	CD FGDS + PCF
1968	De Gaulle 2 Pompidou/UNR	UDR + RI (dominant-party system)	CD FGDS + PCF
1969	Pompidou Chaban-Delmas/UDR	UDR + RI + CDP† (dominant-party system)	CD PS + PCF
1972	Pompidou Messmer/UDR	UDR + RI + CDP (dominant-party system)	CD PS + PCF
1974	Giscard d'Estaing Chirac/UDR	UDR + RI + CDP + CD (two-bloc system)	PS (& MRG) + PCF
1976	Giscard d'Estaing Barre/UDF	RPR + UDF (PR + CDS) (two-bloc system)	PS (&MRG) + PCF
1981	Mitterrand Mauroy/PS	PS (& LMRG) + PCF (dominant-party system)	RPR + UDF
1984	Mitterrand Fabius/PS	PS (& LMRG) (one-party majority)	PCF RPR + UDF (FN)
1986	Mitterrand Chirac/RPR	RPR + UDF (*cohabitation*)	PCF PS (&MRG) FN
1988	Mitterrand 2 Rocard/PS	PS (& LMRG) (minority)	PCF CDS RPR + UDF (PR-Rads)
1991	Mitterrand Cresson/PS	PS (& LMRG) (minority)	PCF CDS UPF (RPR + UDF)
1992	Mitterrand Bérégovoy/PS	PS (& LMRG) (minority)	PCF CDS UPF (RPR + UDF)

* Section Française de l'Internationale Ouvrière
† Centre pour la Démocratie et le Progrés

6

THE PRESIDENT'S SPECIAL ROLE
IN FOREIGN AND DEFENCE POLICY

Jolyon Howorth

'My name is Ozymandias, king of kings:
Look on my works, ye mighty, and despair!'
—P.B. Shelley

Of all the leaders of the Western world, the French President undoubtedly enjoys the most extensive range of real powers. In chapter 4, Vincent Wright outlines the various resources available to the executive. Of these, by far the most significant derive from the Constitution, from the legitimacy conferred by universal suffrage, and from presidential charisma and patronage. These resources, enhanced by a seven-year mandate, are particularly rich in a country with a strong statist tradition like France, which, unlike the other great presidential regime, the United States, also lacks the countervailing influence of institutions designed to keep a check on central authority. Under the Fifth Republic, executive powers are greatest in the realm of foreign and defence policy where, convention has it, the President benefits from a *domaine réservé*, a concept we shall use throughout this chapter as a shorthand for the problematic referred to in the title. Given the resources available and given that Presidents of the Fifth Republic are inevitably quite exceptional individuals, their 'special role' in foreign and defence policy is widely perceived as amounting to virtual *carte blanche* where diplomacy and security policy are concerned.

And yet no single individual in a democracy could reasonably aspire to personal control over so vast an area of public policy. The free will of the President's decision-making powers is in fact constrained in a variety of important ways. A President does not come into the Elysée out of a vacuum. His (or her) world-view/ temperament/method of working will already have been massively shaped by long experience. Moreover, at the moment when a given individual inherits the presidential mantle, France's world interests are not in a state of limbo, but deeply structured as a result of centuries of effort. So too are its armed forces, its weapons systems, and its military capabilities. The external world in which it exists constitutes a major constraint. The margin of manoeuvre for genuinely original or creative diplomacy is very limited. Only an exceptional man can take the world by the scruff of the neck and shake it.

In addition to the structural constraints imposed by the situation a new President inherits, a whole set of other-institutional-constraints also comes into play. These involve not only the forces – diplomatic, political, military – which will push and pull him in different ways, but also the mechanisms – informational, bureaucratic, managerial – allowing him to make decisions and to implement them. Thousands of men and women in various positions of influence will, according to their identity and their disposition, help him or hinder him. Ideally, therefore, in order to assess the truth of the *domaine réservé*, one would have to analyse every single presidential decision in the light of these various factors. How much genuine margin of manoeuvre did the President have? Whom did he consult about his options? Whom did he not consult? What were the sources of the information on which he identified those options? How accurate was that information? How strong were the pressures exerted upon him to take a particular decision? How much information of a contrary nature was available? How strong were the countervailing pressures? How strong was his own commitment to the particular course of action chosen? The questions are endless.

Such an exercise, apart from being impossibly tedious, if not impossible, would not necessarily tell us much more than we can find out by simpler methods. Of course bureaucrats are going to behave in a certain way; naturally the President is dependent on information supplied by others; and inevitably some people will seek to put spokes in his wheels while others loyally promote his cause. Life is never simple. But these factors exist in any decision-making situation.[1]

In order to understand the workings of the *domaine réservé*, we therefore address four specific issues:

– *Constitutional factors*: What can the President, as well as the other actors involved, do and what can they not do and how does it work out in practice?
– *Personality factors*: What sort of man is the President, what are

1. In *La Puissance et les Rêves*, Paris, 1984, Régis Debray argues that in the jungle of international affairs, a French President has little more direct control over events than the pilot of a Boeing 747 programmed to fly a pre-ordained route. See, in particular, chapter III. Samy Cohen offers a vigorous refutation of Debray's thesis in *La Monarchie nucléaire*, Paris, 1986, chapter X.

his passions, how secretive is he, how narrow-minded, how vain, how authoritarian?
– *Court politics*: With what sort of people does the President surround himself? How representative, how competent, how young/old, how many?
– *Corporate constraints on presidential power:* which lobbies have access to him? Which services effectively escape his control? How strong is political opposition? How much attention does he pay to public opinion and polls?

Constitutional Factors

The Constitution of 4 October 1958 contains a degree of genuine ambiguity over the specific powers and responsibilities of President and Prime Minister in matters connected with defence. Articles 5 and 15 confer enormous power on the former while articles 20 and 21 confer equivalent power on the latter. Under the premiership of Michel Debré, at a time when the presidential nature of the Fifth Republic was still a subject for discussion, the ordinance of 7 January 1959 attempted to tip the balance of power in favour of the Prime Minister who thereby exercised 'general and military control over defence' (article 9).

However, Debré's 'challenge' was both unique and short-lived. Three factors in particular have, over the years, combined to consecrate presidential supremacy over defence. The first is *constitutional amendment and refinement*. Here, the most important element was the 6 November 1962 amendment on election of the President by universal suffrage, which confers legitimacy and *de facto* power of unrivalled quality on the incumbent. Shortly after the departure of Debré, the decree of 18 July 1962 had already made it clear that the President, by chairing the Defence Council, controlled 'the overall framework of national defence and, in the event of war, the conduct of operations' (article 1), while the Prime Minister merely oversaw 'the implementation of these decisions', even seeing some of his former responsibilities siphoned off to the Defence Minister (article 3). Although the General Secretariat of National Defence (SGDN), which was set up by this same 1962 decree, is formally attached to the Prime Minister's office, the fact that its main function is to service meetings of the Defence Council ensures that it has traditionally been an irreplaceable resource for the Elysée. This situation was clarified by a new decree on 25 January 1978 (several weeks before elections which might have brought in the first instance of *cohabitation*), stating that the SGDN may receive orders from the President. As for the Defence Minister, his function, as defined by article 16 of the January 1959 ordinance, and by article 3 of the decree of July 1962, is clearly that of a specialist, concerned with organising, administering and managing the tentacular structures of the civilian and military wings of the armed forces. Finally, the decree of 14 January 1964, conferring on the President sole responsibility for firing a nuclear weapon, and that of 10 December 1971 placing the Joint Chief of Staff under the authority of the President, eliminated any residual uncertainty as to who was in charge.[2] Each constitutional amendment since 1962 has therefore enhanced presidential power over national defence.

The specific arena of foreign policy (as distinct from defence policy) calls for rather less constitutional exegesis, in that there is no explicit reference to diplomacy as being within the terms of reference of anybody other than the President. Nor has there been the type of subsequent clarification through ordinances and decrees which one finds with defence policy *per se*. To separate these two areas is to some extent an artificial exercise since defence policy and foreign policy cannot be divorced from each other. This is all the more true when the French President is not only elected for seven years by universal suffrage, but also carries with him, wherever he goes, the code for firing the nuclear weapon: 'It is because he benefits from the undisputed confidence of the electorate that the head of state can govern, that is to say, can assume responsibility for his actions, foremost among which is the responsibility for deciding on the use of nuclear weapons. That is what governing means. [. . .] If that responsibility is diluted, the President doesn't govern, he manages. *The nuclear deterrent cannot be in the hands of managers* [emphasis in the original].'[3]

There remained, however, one supreme test of this constitutional evolution. *Cohabitation* has proved to be the second factor tending to confirm presidential supremacy.

2. In addition to the text of the Constitution itself, see, on these constitutional niceties, *Organisation générale de la défense*, Paris, 1989; Bernard Chantebout, *La Défense nationale*, Paris, 1972; Hubert Haenel, *La Défense nationale*, Paris, 1982; Alain Lebougre, 'Les responsabilités politiques de défense sous la Cinquième République' in Jacques Robert (ed.), *L'Esprit de défense*, Paris, 1987; Philippe Ardant, 'L'article 5 et la fonction présidentielle' in *Pouvoirs*, no. 41 (1987), special issue on *'Le Président'*.
3. Alain Lebougre, p. 47.

Trial by 'Cohabitation'

The impact of *cohabitation* on the *domaine réservé* has become
a subject of some controversy and it is instructive to look at the
situation in detail. Some observers have argued that the clash
between Mitterrand as President and Chirac as Prime Minister
was resolved to the clear benefit of the former. However, France's
foremost specialist on these matters, Samy Cohen, considers that
the conflict between Elysée and Matignon resulted in a significant
loss of presidential control.[4] Once it became clear that *cohabitation*
was going to happen, commentators were agreed that the *domaine
réservé* would constitute the great test case.[5] In what could only
be called a pre-emptive strike, which immediately made it clear
that he had no intention of abdicating, Mitterrand set down, in
July 1985, certain conditions for *cohabitation*, foremost among
which was that he would retain tight control over foreign and
defence policy. His statement that anything else would amount to
a *coup d'état* gave rise to angry protests from the opposition.[6]
Only a week later, Roland Dumas tested the water in less polemical
fashion by pleading for 'the logic of consensus'. On most major
foreign and defence issues, he suggested (not entirely disingenu-
ously) that a consensus had evolved which allowed France to speak
to the rest of the world with one voice.[7] The opposition was not
slow to pick up the challenge. A former Foreign Minister, Jean
François-Poncet, in a mordantly ironical reply, rehearsed a long
list of problems on which he took issue with Socialist foreign

4. Jean Gicquel, 'De la cohabitation', *Pouvoirs*, no. 49 (1989), asserts: 'External
coexistence led unquestionably to an increase in the stature of the President';
Franz-Olivier Giesbert, *Le Président*, Paris, 1990, p. 299, notes: 'Apart from
defence and foreign policy, Mitterrand had little control over anything.' For
the most subtle and nuanced account, see Samy Cohen, 'La Politique étrangère
entre l'Elysée et Matignon', *Politique Etrangère*, no. 3/89 (Autumn 1989),
pp. 487–503. The most detailed account is to be found in Pierre Favier and
Michel Martin-Roland, *La Décennie Mitterrand*, II: *'Les Réconciliations'*,
Paris, 1991.
5. *Le Monde* special section entitled 'A qui la politique étrangère?', 23–24 March
1985; Jacques Amalric, 'Diplomatie. Un domaine réservé à partager', *Le Monde*,
26–27 Jan. 1986. In a final chapter to his book *La Monarchie nucléaire*, Samy
Cohen adopted a rather pessimistic stance, predicting that ambition would
get the better of reason – even *raison d'état* – and that it was not unthinkable
that 'the Prime Minister would end up taking over the powers of the President',
op. cit. p. 251.
6. Alain Rollat, 'M. Mitterrand fixe les limites de la cohabitation avec la droite',
Le Monde, 12 July 1985. Note that in preparation for the 1986 elections,
Mitterrand chose to write just one book: *Réflexions sur la politique étrangère
de la France*, Paris, 1986.
7. Roland Dumas, 'La logique du consensus', *Le Monde*, 25 July 1985.

policy.[8] It is true that much of his criticism was petty and superficial rather than substantial, but the combative mood revealed
by such an urbane man as François-Poncet did not augur well for
cohabitation.

The electoral platform agreed upon by the united Right in
January 1986, while remaining sufficiently vague on foreign/
defence issues to allow for flexibility in implementation, nevertheless pointed to several areas of potential conflict between the
outgoing and incoming administrations. There were calls for a
major increase in defence expenditure (to rise as soon as possible
to 4 per cent of GNP), for participation in the Strategic Defence
Initiative (SDI), otherwise known as 'Star Wars', for the production
of the neutron bomb, for a shift in the strategic doctrine underpinning what had recently been renamed pre-strategic nuclear
weapons (and which the Right-wing document pointedly re-
christened 'tactical'), for radical reorganisation of the recently
created FAR (*Force d'Action Rapide* – Rapid Action Force), for
a massive injection of resources into conventional weapons, and
for a tougher line on the Soviet Union. There were calls for a major
acceleration of European integration, for the strengthening of
bilateral relations with certain African states, for a new peace
initiative in the Middle East and for firmer defence of France's
interests in the Pacific.[9] It can be said at once that virtually none
of this happened. But that was no foregone conclusion. In his
presidential campaign *Lettre à tous les Français* in 1988, Mitterrand
noted that, in March 1986, 'I had reason to fear, as a result of
the political platform on which the right-wing parties had been
elected, and because of campaign speeches by their leaders, a major
battle over the broad lines of foreign and defence policy.'[10]

Much has been written since the late 1970s about the so-called
'consensus' in France on foreign and defence policy. Space does
not allow us to embark upon that particular issue, but it is clear
that broad agreement has existed on the major outlines of France's
approach to the rest of the world. Yet, as the above paragraphs
may suggest, considerable differences of opinion and policy have
surrounded the details, and it was on these that Chirac engaged
in a vigorous challenge to the President. The contest was intense

8. Jean François-Poncet, 'Sur l'air du consensus', *ibid.*, 2 Aug. 1985.
9. RPR/UDF, *Plateforme pour gouverner ensemble*, 16 Jan. 1986, pp. 15–17. It
   is noticeable that one major item did not appear in that platform: the call for
   a new mobile missile (SX) to replace the ageing missiles on the Plateau d'Albion.
   However, this was highlighted in Chirac's major defence proposals, 'Construction de l'Europe et défense commune', *Le Monde*, 28 Feb. 1986.
10. *Lettre à tous les Français*, p. 8.

and there is no doubt whatever that the presidential monopoly came under severe attack. On some issues, such as the Middle East, where the route to diplomatic success was still shrouded in obscurity, or African policy, where the old Gaullist networks directed by the legendary Jacques Foccart had never been disbanded, the President elected to let the Prime Minister walk the tightrope. On virtually every other issue, however, the President resisted – and beat off – Chirac's challenge. The challenge itself came from many different directions.

First, there was the matter of official appointments. After the narrow victory of the Right, it was widely reported that Mitterrand had vetoed Chirac's original choices for Foreign Minister (Giscard, Lecanuet) and Defence Minister (Léotard). Eventually, mutually acceptable 'technicians', Jean-Bernard Raimond and André Giraud, were agreed by Mitterrand.[11] More significantly, however, Chirac broke new constitutional ground by establishing a full-scale 'diplomatic cell' at Matignon, headed by François Bujon de l'Estang, a structure which complemented his 'personal' control of various foreign-policy dossiers such as cooperation, overseas trade and African and Pacific affairs, through the appointment of close RPR associates: Michel Aurillac, Michel Noir, Jacques Foccart and Gaston Flosse.[12] The Prime Minister also sought to maximise his own control over ambassadorial and other top-level diplomatic appointments.

Secondly, there was the matter of information. Throughout the period of *cohabitation*, the normal flow of diplomatic and defence-related dossiers and documents between the Elysée, Matignon, the Quai d'Orsay and rue Saint-Dominique* was considerably reduced. It is, however, difficult to assess the real impact of this. It would seem that nothing of any real significance was withheld from the

* The last two named are the locations of, and hence shorthand for, the Foreign Ministry and the Defence Ministry respectively.
11. Thierry Pfister, *Dans les Coulisses du Pouvoir. La comédie de la cohabitation*, Paris, 1986, pp. 44–7, insists that both Giscard and Lecanuet were proposed for the Quai d'Orsay. Franz-Olivier Giesbert, *Le Président*, pp. 279–80, gives Chirac's version, which denies that any of these names was proposed. Although Mitterrand's story has varied from that of Chirac, the latter does recognise that Mitterrand told him that had he suggested Lecanuet and Léotard, the President would have vetoed them.
12. Jacques Amalric, 'M. Chirac s'est doté d'un instrument efficace', *Le Monde*, 26 April 1986, p. 3.; Jill Lovecy, '*Cohabitation* and the "presidentialisation" of Matignon', *Modern and Contemporary France*, no. 27 (Sept. 1986), pp. 12–17. See also on the beginnings of the diplomatic tug-of-war, Pfister, *op. cit.*, chapter 6: 'Diplomatiquement vôtre'. It should be noted that, in making Michel Aurillac (at cooperation) a full minister, Chirac was breaking new ground.

President, who benefited in any case from an extensive network of parallel sources of information, as well as from the confidence if not the actual connivence of many heads of state/government and most of the foreign ambassadors in Paris. There is no doubt that the workload and autonomy of the President's diplomatic advisers at the Elysée were considerably reduced, although relations between the President and his Foreign Minister remained close and mostly harmonious.[13]

The third and in some ways most visible area of challenge was stylistic. The new Prime Minister began at once to behave like a President, albeit one housed at Matignon. He insisted on receiving all visiting foreign dignitaries, embarked immediately on a round of European and African visits and, most significant of all, announced unilaterally his intention of attending summit meetings. This decision proved counterproductive. At summits there is always, by definition, one leader and a number of 'retainers'. Not only did the protocol of meetings such as the G7 or the European Council consecrate presidential supremacy, but Mitterrand's newly-appointed image-maker, Jean-Louis Chambon, skilfully arranged post-summit press conferences in such a way as to accentuate Chirac's inferiority. Few in France were impressed by Chirac's rather too blatant early attempts to claim precedence (such as his insistence that he, rather than Mitterrand, had taken the decision to refuse permission for US bombers to overfly French territory on their way to Libya on the night of 14–15 April 1986, or his claim during his first television appearance on 23 April that he alone had the 'totality of responsibility for all aspects of government').[14] Thus, in

13. Interview with Mitterrand's current *conseiller diplomatique*, Pierre Morel, Paris, 19 July 1991. Jean-Bernard Raimond, *Le Quai d'Orsay à l'épreuve de la cohabitation*, Paris, 1989, attempts to minimise the degree of conflict between himself and Mitterrand to such an extent that the book actually tells us nothing about the struggle for control.

14. At the 1986 G7 meeting, television coverage was eloquent: 'Every TV set throughout the land brought home the reality of presidential pre-eminence in diplomatic affairs. As for the Prime Minister, he appeared to be merely passing through' (Giesbert, *op.cit.*, p. 282). At the press conference after the European Council meeting at The Hague in June 1986, Jean-Louis Chambon arranged to have Mitterrand flanked by the Prime Minister and the Foreign Minister, thus establishing a visual equivalence between these two (largely silent) 'retainers'. Chambon considers that Chirac's biggest mistake in this regard was to insist on accompanying Mitterrand for the traditional wreath-laying ceremony at the Arc de Triomphe on 8 May 1988, as the presidential election campaign was reaching a crescendo. The television cameras made it quite clear that one man was the President and the other an intruder (interview with Jean-Louis Chambon, Paris, 19 July 1991). On the Libyan bombings, see Jacques Amalric, 'La petite histoire d'une double épreuve', *Le Monde*, 29 April 1986, and Raimond, *op.cit.*, pp. 72–6. On Chirac's press conference, see *Le Monde*, 25 April 1986.

a variety of ways, Jacques Chirac sought to make maximum use of
the powers conferred upon him by articles 20 and 21 of the Constitution. To what extent did he affect the substance of policy?

On defence and security issues, Chirac made an early bid for
supremacy. During a visit to the army camp at Suippes (Marne) on
10 July 1986, he declared: 'National defence is the responsibility of
the Prime Minister. As such, it is my intention, in this area as in
others, to exercise to the full my constitutional role.'[15] In a speech
to the National Defence Institute on 12 September 1986, he spelled
out yet again the notion he had highlighted in his pre-electoral
foreign policy interview in *Le Monde*: that of redesignating France's
'pre-strategic' short-range nuclear weapons as 'tactical', battlefield
weapons for military use on the central front.[16] Such an approach
to nuclear weapons was anathema to Mitterrand. At the same time,
Chirac's Defence Minister, André Giraud, was becoming outspoken
in his support for two programmes with which Mitterrand had
little sympathy: the mobile SX missile (the so-called 'second component' scheduled to replace the ageing missiles on the Plateau
d'Albion) and a joint Franco-American variant of the F-18 fighter.
The President, true to his style, bided his time, and it was not till
13 October 1986 that he chose to blow the whistle. On a visit to
a parachute regiment training camp at Caylus (Tarn-et-Garonne),
shortly before a crucial Defence Council meeting at which the main
lines of the Chirac five-year military programme law were to be
decided, he reminded his audience that in matters of military
doctrine and procurement 'authority rests with the President of
the Republic.' He also refuted both Chirac's approach to short-
range nuclear weapons ('These weapons are [. . .] not just a pro-
longation of a classical or conventional battle, but an integral part
of the strategic "whole"') and Giraud's predilection for the hugely
expensive SX ('There will be no second nuclear component [i.e.
nuclear submarines] at the expense of the first'), adding by way of
conclusion: 'I hope I have made myself fully understood. This is a
point on which I stand by the authority vested in me by my
office.'[17]

In his *Lettre à tous les Français*, Mitterrand commented
laconically on this Caylus speech: 'It had taken six months to bring
the whims of the new majority back into line. The discussion was

15. Jacques Isnard, 'M. Chirac veut exercer pleinement son rôle de premier ministre
    en matière de défense', *Le Monde*, 12 July 1986, p. 8.
16. J. Chirac, 'La politique de défense de la France', *Défense Nationale*, Nov. 1986,
    p. 12. Compare these statements with those in the *Le Monde* article cited in
    note 9.
17. Jacques Isnard, 'M. Mitterrand prend ses distances envers la politique de défense
    préconisée par MM Chirac et Giraud', *Le Monde*, 15 Oct. 1986, p. 8.

over. And that was that' (p. 10). In reality, matters were by no means so simple. It is true that, from about the late autumn of 1986, Chirac appeared to abandon his more overt attempts to challenge the President's supremacy in defence policy. On SDI, for instance, the new Prime Minister had, before his election, noisily denounced the President's refusal to join the Pentagon research bandwagon; by April 1986, he already appeared to have changed his mind.[18] But his Defence Minister, André Giraud, kept up the struggle, in particular by keeping alive the SX missile (which, in defiance of presidential orders, he covertly funded out of other budgets). Mitterrand and Giraud were also at loggerheads over the construction of the new aircraft-carrier (Giraud being opposed, Mitterrand in favour). Giraud lost that round, as he did with his attempts to keep alive the F-18 option which Mitterrand ruled out at the Paris air show in June 1987.[19] On the other hand, it was the Defence Minister who vetoed Mitterrand's attempt to prolong General Saulnier's tenure as Joint Chief of Staff until the end of his presidential term. The Giraud defiance is in some ways more interesting than the half-hearted Chirac challenges in that Giraud had less to lose and knew more lucidly than Chirac what he wanted. Giraud's being politically close to Raymond Barre did not help his case with Chirac. Indeed, on many defence issues, there was what amounted to an objective alliance between Chirac and Mitterrand against Giraud.[20]

In any case, Mitterrand could play Giraud at his own game, allowing the grossly programme-inflated 1987-91 military programme law to pass unchallenged since he knew full well that the real choices would have to be made later and that this would give him important powers of arbitration when he felt the time was ripe. On the INF treaty, Mitterrand made the running from the start with a subtle and sophisticated response. André Giraud led the opposition to INF with mutterings about 'Munich'. Chirac, who by March 1987 had begun – either through genuine alignment or political caution – to side with the President on most defence issues, made a totally unconvincing attempt both to coordinate the chaotic responses of the 'majority' and to elicit the support of Margaret Thatcher and Helmut Kohl for a cause (rejection of the

---

18. Jacques Isnard, 'Défense. Cohabitation stratégique', *Le Monde*, 11 April 1986.
19. Jean Guisnel, *Les Généraux*, Paris, 1990, pp. 220-2.
20. On Saulnier, see Jean Guisnel, *op. cit.*, p. 125. I am grateful to François Heisbourg for insights into some of these other clashes (interview in London, 10 June 1991).

'zero option') in which neither he nor they believed.[21] By the end
of 1987, Mitterrand felt so confident of his control of defence
policy that, when questioned by Jean Daniel on Chirac's alleged
predilection for flexible response, he was able to state categorically:
'There is no question of flexible response for France. That is also
the view of the Prime Minister.'[22]

   In foreign affairs, it is clear that François Mitterrand allowed
Chirac to try his hand in a number of areas where the President
himself had no firmly established strategy (particularly the mine-
field of terrorism and relations with Iran). Samy Cohen lists several
issues on which Chirac had to make do with 'minor modifications'
(relations with Turkey, South Africa and Iran) but accepts that
there was no clear difference of approach between the Chirac and
the Fabius governments in any of these cases. Indeed, the former
Prime Minister Pierre Messmer, who was chairman of the parliamentary Foreign Affairs Committee throughout the period of
cohabitation, claims that, on every occasion when Mitterrand and
Chirac actually clashed, it was the Prime Minister who drew
back.[23] In his major foreign policy interview in *Le Monde* on 8
July 1987, Chirac seems to have abandoned any public attempt to
differentiate his foreign or defence policy from that of Mitterrand:
'Since we are fortunate enough in France to have general agreement
on these matters, there have been no difficulties between the President and the government. [. . .] It is always possible to stress such
and such a nuance, but these have been of no importance whatsoever.' Although he occasionally demonstrated irritation at the fact
that Mitterrand, in protocol terms, was invariably regarded as the
senior interlocutor by foreign statesmen, particularly in Franco-
German relations, Chirac made little effective use of his extensive
'diplomatic cell' and deferred increasingly to the President. Further

21. Jolyon Howorth, 'France and Gorbachev: Old problems, new questions and
    the quest for correct answers' in J. Howorth and G. Ross (eds), *Contemporary
    France*, vol. 2, London, 1988.
22. *Nouvel Observateur*, 18 Dec. 1987, p. 42.
23. Interview with the author, Paris, 19 July 1991: 'From what I saw, it is difficult
    to say that Chirac had much influence over foreign affairs. [. . .] Whenever there
    were differences over detail, it was Chirac who gave way.' Messmer cites the
    case of South Africa where, according to him, Mitterrand wished to give
    maximum political support to the ANC, while Chirac went along with Pretoria's
    preference for dealings with men like Chief Buthelezi. When Mitterrand learned
    that Chirac had invited Buthelezi and Angola's Jonas Savimbi to talks in Paris,
    the President demanded that the Prime Minister refrain from seeing them.
    Chirac acceded to this presidential veto and asked Messmer to take the two
    visitors out to dinner! They returned to Africa furious with both Mitterrand
    and Chirac.

research is necessary in order to establish whether there were really any major differences of opinion – leading to actual clashes – on Middle Eastern and African issues. It is fairly clear that, when the Right was in opposition before 1986, it had made as much political capital as possible out of Mitterrand's difficulties in Chad and Lebanon, and had been highly critical of his pro-Iraq stance in the Iran-Iraq war. However, between 1986 and 1988 the course of events in Chad as well as the heightening of tension between Paris and Tehran ruled out any prospect of a radical shift in policy. In a recent book highly critical of Mitterrand's entire record on foreign affairs, Louis Wiznitzer replicates (without acknowledgement) Cohen's claim that during *cohabitation* 'Mitterrand kept control of defence, disarmament and German affairs, had to hand over to Chirac cooperation, Africa and the Middle East, and shared responsibility for the Arab-Israeli conflict and France's overseas territories.'[24] But neither author substantiates this claim with precise examples of policy clashes resulting in 'victory' for the Prime Minister. The present state of our knowledge therefore leads to the conclusion that, while the challenge from Chirac was vigorous and multi-faceted, and while Mitterrand's task in these areas became much more complicated, presidential pre-eminence remained almost total in the realm of defence and was substantially unaffected in the most important areas of diplomacy.

In his *Lettre à tous les Français*, Mitterrand took a malign pleasure in portraying Chirac's 'abnegation' as opportunistic rather than principled. Assuming that this portrayal is correct, there are a number of reasons for it. First, as Mitterrand had made clear before March 1986, he was utterly determined to fight off any challenge to presidential authority in these key areas of the *domaine réservé*. Secondly, he knew that he possessed considerably greater mastery of the foreign/defence dossiers than did Chirac. Had there been a real contest, it would not have been one on equal terms. Chirac's priorities were in any case elsewhere: in economic and industrial policy. Thirdly – and crucially – Mitterrand knew that there were major divergences *within* the Right (over resources, between the Defence and Finance Ministries, over policy and strategy, between Chirac and Giscard, and indeed within the RPR

24. Louis Wiznitzer, *Le Grand Gachis, ou la faillite d'une politique étrangère*, Paris, 1991, pp. 218–19. Wiznitzer's book is a violent anti-Mitterrand diatribe with no footnotes or other form of reference, and must be taken with a very large pinch of salt, but up till the time of writing it is the only book purporting to deal with the whole of Mitterrand's foreign policy, including the period of *cohabitation* and on to the Gulf war. His claim on the sharing out of responsibility is taken from Cohen's article in *Politique Etrangère*, *loc. cit.*, p. 494.

itself). It would have been relatively simple for the President to play on those divisions in order to spike Chirac's guns. Fourthly, Chirac wanted passionately to be President. The last thing he intended was to provoke a constitutional crisis which might undermine his own legitimacy if he ever got to the Elysée. Fifthly, the period of *cohabitation* was in reality very short, and everyone was preoccupied with the forthcoming presidential election. Indeed the extent to which the horizon of 1988 dominated the politics of *cohabitation* from late 1986 onwards is itself an interesting reflection on the real locus of power in the French Constitution.[25]

The experience of *cohabitation* between March 1986 and April 1988 did nothing to diminish the French President's claim to a monopoly of foreign and defence policy. Most of the efforts deployed by the Chirac government to transfer power in these areas from the Elysée to Matignon went on behind closed doors and were invisible to the general public. There is no doubt, and here Samy Cohen is surely correct, that their efforts led to some confusion in the chancelleries, to much duplication and waste of effort in the corridors of power, and to potential risks for the overall coherence of France's external policy. What certainly ended with *cohabitation* was the cooperative and constructive working relationship which had previously existed between the different centres with responsibility for defence (ministry, SGDN, Elysée and General Staff). Some argue that that relationship has never been re-established, favouring an increased concentration of power in the Elysée.[26] There is evidence also that the reappointment as Foreign Minister of Roland Dumas ensured the 'revenge' of the Elysée over the Quai d'Orsay.[27] As we see below, the Gulf war provided a providential opportunity for Mitterrand to reassert total supremacy over a major issue of diplomacy and defence. And yet to the extent to which the President did 'hang on' to his prerogatives in these areas, he did so not because of the Constitution (except to the extent to which Chirac, as a presidential aspirant, did not wish

25. See, on this point, Peter Morris, 'Review of the Year 1987' in J. Howorth and G. Ross, *op. cit.*, p. 7: 'The first lesson of 1987 was that the presidency remains the key political prize within the French political system and that the post-1986 loss of some of its policy-making powers has in no way diminished its attractiveness.'
26. Author's interview with François Heisbourg, London, 10 June 1991.
27. Samy Cohen, in *Politique Etrangère, loc. cit.*, pp. 497ff., speaks of 'the revenge of the Elysée' and rightly contrasts the post-1988 reality with the much more emollient, power-sharing attitude expressed by Mitterrand in his 1988 interview with Olivier Duhamel of *Pouvoirs* (in which he suggested that henceforth the President would lay down the broad lines of foreign and defence policy and the Prime Minister implement them).

to challenge the canon) but for conjunctural, almost fortuitous reasons. Although the experience will have made it very difficult for any future Prime Minister under conditions of *cohabitation* to mount an effective challenge to a President determined to resist, the fact remains that the ambiguities in the Constitution remain as striking as ever and another experience of *cohabitation* with different actors under different circumstances could well produce a very different result.

Personality Factors

The second factor which has consecrated presidential supremacy has been the *personality and practice* of the various incumbents. This introduces our second main set of considerations. The four Presidents of the Fifth Republic have all possessed exceptionally powerful personalities, albeit remarkably different ones.

It is impossible in a few words to characterise a man as exceptional as Charles de Gaulle. Jean Lacouture sees him as extraordinary in six ways: in physique, as a soldier, as a politician, as an intellectual, as a human being and as an artist.[28] Unlike any of his successors, he came to the presidency from the very heights of historical achievement, having already changed the course of French foreign and defence policy. As a soldier – and an extraordinary one at that – command was his profession. As a soldier, too, he had confidence in his subordinates and assumed that they could be trusted to run their departments. As early as 1922, at the *Ecole de Guerre*, he had adopted as his motto *De minimis non curat praetor* (the leader is not concerned with details).[29] His closest collaborators insist that the notion of *domaine réservé* as it is normally understood (restricted to foreign and defence policy) did not exist under de Gaulle: whatever was the urgent matter of the moment rapidly became part of the *domaine réservé*.[30] However, it cannot be doubted that, of all the issues to which de Gaulle turned his attention, foreign and defence issues were closest to his heart. At the same time, it is probably true that, for the reasons

28. Jean Lacouture, *De Gaulle, I. Le Rebelle, 1890–1944*, Paris, 1984, pp. 815–18.
29. *Ibid.*, p. 120. Lacouture recounts how de Gaulle responded when his professor of tactics, Colonel Moyrand, tried to catch him out on the details of a manoeuvre: 'Colonel, you entrusted me with the responsibility of commanding an army corps. If, in addition, I had to take on the tasks of my subordinates, I would not have the necessary peace of mind to carry out my mission correctly: *de minimis non curat praetor*.'
30. See *L'Entourage et de Gaulle*, Paris, 1979, pp. 118–19, 124.

outlined above, his direct and detailed control over policy was less absolute than that of any of his successors.

Georges Pompidou was in many ways the opposite of de Gaulle. A private and unflamboyant man, conservative and predictable, he was nevertheless a *bon viveur* and a devotee of modern art. Foreign policy in general (with the exception of European policy) and defence policy in particular held few attractions for him. Although he is said to have basically disagreed with most of de Gaulle's foreign and defence policy, he made no attempt as Prime Minister to influence that policy and (with the exception of Europe) did little to change it when he became President.[31] Because he was a banker through and through, the two great policy areas in which he was passionately involved – economic/industrial policy and European integration – induced him to exercise a *domaine réservé* in some ways more watertight than that of the General, whose trust in his subordinates Pompidou did not have the confidence to share.[32] Of the four Presidents, Pompidou was probably the one whose personality and interests were least suited to the demands and responsibilities of the office, particularly where overall foreign and defence policy was concerned.

Valéry Giscard d'Estaing presented another major contrast with his predecessor. Haughty and patrician, supremely confident of his own intellectual and personal skills, youthful and energetic, interested in everything and determined to make his mark wherever he went, Giscard came to the Elysée as a technocrat, confident that a small group of carefully selected experts, working as a team, could find the correct solution to any problem. Typical of the man was his comment to the élite of France's defence establishment, the National Defence Institute, on first addressing them in June 1976. His ignorance of defence issues was well known, but so eager was he to impose himself in this area that he began his speech by saying: 'Naturally, I have taken the trouble to acquire a basic

31. Author's interview with Maurice Couve de Murville, Paris, 30 May 1991. On the other hand, Pompidou's Prime Minister, Pierre Messmer, while recognising Couve's views about Pompidou, refutes them. He accepts that, while Prime Minister under de Gaulle, Pompidou had no influence whatever over foreign and defence policy, and asserts that de Gaulle did not even discuss these matters with him. On the other hand, Messmer insists that when Pompidou became President he asserted tight control over foreign and defence policy. He explains the lack of distinction between the policy orientations of de Gaulle and those of Pompidou by arguing that in fact Pompidou agreed wholeheartedly with de Gaulle's approach. Interview with author, Paris, 19 July 1991.
32. See, on Pompidou, François Decaumont, *La Présidence de Georges Pompidou. Essai sur le régime présidentialiste français*, Paris, 1979, pp. 151-5 ('Les "domaines d'élection" de Georges Pompidou').

knowledge of the nature of the concrete decisions a President of the Republic must take; *with perfect organisation, such knowledge can in fact be acquired in just a few hours* [emphasis added]'. Fifteen years later, he was able to confess that mastery of the defence dossier had been a long and difficult learning process,[33] one which he was never able fully to control because of political factors to which we shall return. In foreign policy, Giscard was tempted to feel that his own personal charm could overcome many obstacles. On the positive side were his relationships with Helmut Schmidt of West Germany and, possibly, also with James Callaghan of Great Britain. On the negative side was his misjudgement of African leaders in general and of Jean-Bedel Bokassa in particular, his inability to fathom the character of Jimmy Carter and his unwarranted confidence in his ability to influence Brezhnev. His supreme blunder was precisely in the field of foreign and defence policy: his ill-fated trip to Warsaw to meet Leonid Brezhnev in May 1980.[34] As one of his own advisers put it, it was not that he was incapable of learning – on the contrary – or that he did not wish to listen, but simply that 'the President did not surround himself with enough people of independent judgement, capable of giving him, no matter what the circumstances, a detached and independent view, even if they knew that he did not agree with it.'[35]

This was not to be Mitterrand's Achilles heel. Unlike his three predecessors, Mitterrand arrived at the Elysée 'from the bottom up' as the epitome of the consummate politician, the arch-survivor. In addition, his lawyer's training produced in him a fine sense of the importance of detail. Often referred to as the 'Florentine', he borrows from Machiavelli an acute sense of political strategy, a finely tuned consciousness of balances of power (both national and international), a trust in almost nobody, an uncanny capacity to keep his cards close to his chest (or even out of sight), an obsession with detail, an ability to bide his time and strike at precisely the right moment, and a ruthlessness in the strike itself. At the

33. Giscard's speech reproduced in *Défense Nationale*, July 1976. By contrast, see his own extraordinary account of his ignorance in these matters in vol. 2 of his *Le Pouvoir et la Vie. L'Affrontement*, Paris, 1991, pp. 176–212.
34. See, on this, Samy Cohen, *La Monarchie Nucléaire, op. cit.*, pp. 126–35. Giscard himself claims, contrary to Cohen, that he personally remained agnostic until after wide consultations, in particular with Raymond Barre and Helmut Schmidt, both of whom urged him to go to Warsaw, and that, far from being a fiasco, his trip was successful in that his firmness of tone ensured that there was no Soviet invasion of Poland the following year – see *Le Pouvoir et la Vie. l'Affrontement, op. cit.*, pp. 386–440.
35. Charles Debbasch, *L'Elysée devoilé*, Paris, 1982, p. 64.

same time he has demostrated an absence of rigidity and a degree
of flexibility which have served him well during a period of extreme
international turbulence. A 'President in waiting' for almost twenty
years, he had, far more than either Pompidou or Giscard, refined
his own mastery of the defence and foreign policy dossiers long
before entering the Elysée. During the 'Mitterrand decade', he has
gradually monopolised the *domaine réservé* to an extent greater
even than de Gaulle. Above all, Mitterrand makes it extremely difficult for even those close to him to read his innermost thoughts.
'François Mitterrand is determined to remain his own master. He
refuses to be a slave to anything, either to a piece of advice or to an
agenda. He will not allow anything to be imposed upon him. He
protects himself from lobbies and never reveals all his cards to a
single individual. And he always ensures that he has several possible
courses of action.'[36] The down-side of this, especially on the
foreign and defence front, is that he has become such a master of
reacting to events that it is unclear whether he has any proactive
policy of his own, any 'grand design'.

In sum, it could be argued that, with the possible exception of
Georges Pompidou, each successive President has deployed his
personality to adapt the powers of the Elyseé to his own ends,
thereby constantly increasing them. The personality factor in the
functioning of the *domaine réservé*[37] cannot be totally divorced
from what I have called 'court politics'.

Court Politics

In the discharge of his duties, the President has constant interaction with a number of key individuals, among whom are, first and
foremost, the Prime Minister, the Foreign Minister, the Defence
Minister, the Secretary-General of the presidency and his personal
Chief of Staff. What role do they play in foreign and defence
matters?

The Prime Minister. From Georges Pompidou to Pierre Bérégovoy,
the Prime Minister's function has essentially been one of faith-
fully coordinating the overall policy of the government, as determined by the President. Although, as we have seen, the Constitution
nominally affords the Prime Minister important powers over
foreign and particularly defence policy, and although the Prime

36. Pierre Favier and Michel Martin-Roland, *La Décennie Mitterrand*, I. *Les
    Ruptures*, Paris, 1990, p. 529.
37. On the 'personality' factor in French presidential politics, see Vincent Wright,
    The Government and Politics of France, London, 1979, chapter 2: 'The Exten-
    sion of the Presidential Sector: the personal factor'.

Minister's office benefits from the services of the General Secretariat of National Defence, almost all Prime Ministers have voluntarily taken a back seat on this issue. The exceptions were Michel Debré, who considered himself as Prime Minister to be, in effect, also a *de facto* Defence Minister,[38] and Jacques Chirac, who attempted to challenge both Giscard and Mitterrand in this area. The failures of both men to impose themselves on the President in the *domaine réservé* have contributed to the weakening of Matignon's position. Of course, all Presidents will normally (but not invariably) consult the Prime Minister on important issues of foreign and defence policy, and there are many occasions – budgetary arbitration in particular, but also overseas visits, and general statements of policy either in interviews or in set-piece speeches, such as in the National Assembly, or at the National Defence Institute – when the Prime Minister appears to take a lead in foreign and defence policy. Yet it is almost unheard-of for Matignon to distance itself from the Elysée in these matters.[39] Naturally, as potential presidential candidates, Prime Ministers need to acquire national visibility in the areas of diplomacy and defence. However, while they remain at Matignon, this is normally done with the utmost discretion. Perhaps the most interesting case in this regard – and potentially the most significant in terms of continued consolidation of the presidential *domaine réservé* – is that of Michel Rocard. Of all the Prime Ministers of the Fifth Republic, he was by far the most credible *presidential* candidate. As such he might have been expected to adopt, from Matignon, a high-profile stance in foreign and defence policy, but he seemed rather to be going almost to extreme lengths in order not to tread on Mitterrand's toes. During the Gulf war, the Prime Minister hardly seemed to exist. It is arguable that the self-effacement of a potential presidential candidate like Rocard (whether voluntary or compulsory) has further contributed to the shoring-up of the *domaine réservé*.

38. The author was assured by Pierre Messmer, in an interview on 30 May 1991, that Michel Debré considered himself to be *Ministre de la Défense Nationale* (under article 21 of the Constitution) – just as de Gaulle, the last Prime Minister of the Fourth Republic, had been. As for Messmer, he was 'merely' *Ministre des Armées*.
39. The exception which proved the rule about Prime Ministerial deferrence was Fabius's criticism of Mitterrand for meeting General Jaruzelski in 1985. See, on this, Samy Cohen, *La Monarchie Nucléaire, op. cit.*, pp. 24–6. On the role of the Prime Minister in general, see Robert Elgie and Howard Machin, 'France: The Limits to Prime-ministerial Government in a Semi-presidential System', *West European Politics*, vol. 14, no. 2 (April 1991), pp. 62–78.

The Foreign Minister, of course, exists at the very heart of the *domaine réservé*. Yet, as François Mitterrand asserted in 1983 shortly after parting company with his outspoken Minister for Overseas Development, Jean-Pierre Cot, 'It is I who determine France's foreign policy, not my ministers'[40] – words which epitomise the basic attitude of all Presidents of the Fifth Republic. Yet there are important differences between the degree of influence exercised by each of the ten Foreign Ministers of the Fifth Republic.[41] Much the most influential was Maurice Couve de Murville, who presided over the Quai d'Orsay for ten tumultuous and diplomatically seminal years (1958–68). His influence derived not only from the working style of the General (who allowed his ministers far greater personal latitude, kept them far better informed, engaged in far less personal telephone contact with other heads of state, and used far fewer personal emissaries than his successors), but from the fact that there existed between the two men 'a kind of spontaneous and instinctive agreement'.[42] Couve de Murville claimed that there was only one issue on which he and the General fell out: that of the modalities for pulling out of NATO.[43] This degree of complicity between the President and the minister, coinciding as it did with a veritable revolution in French diplomatic relations, nevertheless had its negative side: it gradually inculcated in the staff – and indeed introduced into the culture – of the Quai a conformism, a lack of creative imagination and responsibility which all subsequent Presidents, but particularly Giscard and Mitterrand, were to regard, probably with excessive suspicion, as being inherently hostile. At the outset of each new seven-year term, this suspicion actually fuelled presidential determination to exercise an even tighter grip over foreign policy.[44]

Maurice Schumann, who acted as Pompidou's Foreign Minister for almost four years, was a perfect choice. As a 'pedigree' Gaullist, Schumann was able to reassure the many conservatives, particularly in the National Assembly where his parliamentary skills were legendary, that the one foreign policy issue which dominated the period – British entry into the EC, on which he and the President were at one – was a legitimate policy objective. Even so,

40. Jean-Claude Pomonti, 'M. Mitterrand entend dédramatiser les relations franco-africaines', *Le Monde*, 20 Jan. 1983, p. 3.
41. The following discussion owes much to Samy Cohen, *La Monarchie nucléaire*, *op. cit.*, pp. 83–163.
42. M. Couve de Murville, *Une Politique étrangère, 1958–1969*, Paris, 1971, p. 9.
43. Author's interview with Couve de Murville, Paris, 31 May 1991. See, on this quarrel, *L'Entourage et de Gaulle, op. cit.*, p. 237.
44. See, on this, Samy Cohen, *op. cit.*, pp. 11, 92.

Pompidou's suspicions of the Quai were such that, in spite of having a Foreign Minister committed to European integration, he short-circuited official diplomatic channels, including Schumann himself, and used the Secretary-General of the Elyseé, Michel Jobert, as a personal negotiator, thereby inaugurating the tradition of 'parallel diplomacy' which each successive President has built on and expanded. When Schumann resigned after his defeat in the parliamentary elections of 1973, Pompidou appointed his own *alter ego*, Michel Jobert, thereby inaugurating another significant move which would have been unthinkable under de Gaulle: the ministerialisation of the 'entourage'.[45]

Giscard d'Estaing made three attempts to recreate the symbiotic relationship between de Gaulle and Couve. In Jean Sauvagnargues he chose a weak and ineffectual career diplomat who simply evaporated before Giscard's determination (based in equal parts on insecurity and over-confidence) to prove that he was in charge. In Louis de Guiringuaud, he swung to the opposite extreme, appointing a man who singularly failed to appreciate who was in charge. And in Jean François-Poncet, formerly (like Jobert) the Secretary-General of the presidency, he found a man who was so forcefully his master's voice that 'unconsciously, he wound up betraying the Gaullist model he sought to emulate'.[46] The François-Poncet appointment was a further step towards explicit recognition of the growing importance in this area of presidential advisers. Both Pompidou and Giscard, who began their presidential terms with relatively little direct experience of foreign affairs, were so mistrustful of the Quai that they gradually concentrated even greater power in the Elysée.[47]

Strangely François Mitterrand, who is often charged with having engineered a greater concentration of presidential power than any of his predecessors, may well be judged by history as having been the one President who was most influenced – at least on detailed aspects of foreign policy – by one of his ministers. With Claude Cheysson (1981–4) he seemed consciously to seek out his own opposite. Cheysson's impact was undoubtedly greatest (particularly

45. After Pompidou's death, Jobert described his relationship with the President thus: 'For eleven years, I worked with the same man, gave him eleven years of myself, with no regrets, acted effortlesly as his shadow, and constantly aspired to serve him . . .' *Mémoires d'Avenir*, Paris, 1974, p. 9. On Jobert, see Cohen, *op. cit.*, pp. 104–11.
46. Cohen, *op. cit.*, p. 124.
47. For Giscard's policy-making, see Samy Cohen, 'La politique extérieure de la France de 1974 à 1981. Un seul homme? Un homme seul?', in S. Cohen and M.-C. Smouts (eds), *La Politique extérieure de VGE*, Paris, 1985.

on Middle East policy) in the early years when Mitterand was still finding his way and when domestic issues dominated his agenda. It is probably the case that Cheysson's own 'extremism' (pro-Arab, pro-Third World, anti-American, 'pacifist') helped to nudge Mitterrand dialectically towards his own complex form of pro-Atlantic and pro-European Gaullism. In exchanging Cheysson for Roland Dumas in 1984 (Dumas repossessed the post in 1988 after the hiatus of *cohabitation*) Mitterrand probably came as close as any President to appointing his mirror image.[48]

At the same time, the enormous increase in summitry over the last ten years (G7, CSCE, European Councils, bilateral meetings etc.) and the collapse of the world order created by the Cold War since 1989 have resulted in a quantum leap in presidential travel. There can be no doubt that the state of the world itself has conferred on the French President an ever-increasing personal role in international diplomacy. One clear consequence of this has been the concomitant whittling away of the importance of the Quai d'Orsay, which probably reached its nadir under *cohabitation*, when the Elysée and Matignon were vying with each other to win control of every aspect of foreign policy. According to at least one seasoned observer, the nature of international relations has recently changed to such an extent that all foreign ministries (not only the French) have degenerated into 'technical' ministries geared to producing little more than an endless succession of briefing papers.[49]

The Defence Minister plays a very different role from the Foreign Minister. Under the Third Republic, the post changed hands no fewer than seventy-five times, involving fifty-three different individuals, of whom thirty-three were generals and twenty civilians. The generals tended to predominate in the earlier years of the Republic and the civilians later. This rhythm was actually stepped up under the Fourth Republic, no fewer than nineteen different individuals presiding over the increasingly unmanageable affairs of the rue St.-Dominique (compared with effectively only two Foreign Ministers – Bidault and Schuman – from 1944 to 1954). What is striking about the Third and Fourth Republics is that

48. Gabriel Robin, in *La Diplomatie Mitterrand, ou le triomphe des apparences*, Paris, 1985, p. 10, writes: 'Roland Dumas is the President's man as a result of long familiarity; the two men are like intellectual blood brothers.'
49. Dominique Moïsi, 'Le Quai d'Orsay et la crise du Golfe', *Pouvoirs*, 58 (1991), pp. 47–52, analyses the growing sense of powerlessness among the diplomatic corps. On the Quai under *cohabitation*, see Thierry de Beaucé, 'Le Quai dépossédé', *Le Monde*, 5 Sept. 1987; Thierry Bréhier, 'Affaires étrangères: la grande misère du Quai d'Orsay', *ibid.*, 7 Nov. 1987.

the minister was either a professional soldier or a career politician, but in the Fifth Republic he has mostly been neither. In 1958 de Gaulle set the tone (as he had done in 1944) by amalgamating the posts of Prime Minister and Defence Minister. Technically, once he became President, his Army Minister assumed the post – but not the title – of Defence Minister, but the job was overtly redefined as essentially technical, the incumbent being, according to the ordinance of 1959, 'responsible . . . for the organisation, the management, the upkeep and the mobilisation of the armed forces'. With the exception of Michel Debré's term at the rue Saint Dominique (see below), there has never been any serious doubt since 1958 that the real Defence Minister in France is the President.

De Gaulle, in appointing first an administrator from the Atomic Energy Commissariat, Pierre Guillaumat (June 1958-February 1960), and then a colonial administrator, Pierre Messmer (February 1960-June 1969), deliberately removed from the minister any responsibility for the formulation of defence policy. Messmer (the longest-serving Defence Minister since Louvois, who held the post from 1677 to 1691) himself considers that his sole function was to provide the administrative and technical back-up to de Gaulle's grand decisions. Yet one major development took place which emanated directly from Messmer's office: the development of the short-range *Pluton* nuclear weapons system, and the doctrine of the 'warning shot' which accompanied it. In that this development, much more than the deployment of the French strategic deterrent itself, served to differentiate France's defence doctrine from that of NATO, here was a major 'breach' of the principles of the *domaine réservé*.[50]

Georges Pompidou, in appointing to the rue Saint Dominique the highly political Michel Debré, had three main aims, all of which dovetailed with each other: first, to keep Debré away from involvement in economic or foreign (i.e. European) policy; secondly, to secure himself the support of the Gaullist 'legitimists'; and thirdly, to ensure that defence, which was probably the President's own weakest area, was properly overseen. Debré's conditions for playing thus into Pompidou's hands were that the ministry be retitled

50. Interview with the author, Paris, 30 May 1991. Pierre Messmer asserted not only that de Gaulle himself had virtually nothing to do with the *Pluton* decision, but that he appeared to regard it – and the doctrine of *coup de semonce* (warning shot) – as of little significance. On the decision concerning *Pluton*, see Institut Charles de Gaulle, *L'Aventure de la Bombe*, Paris, 1985, pp. 103, 157-8, 192-3.

Ministry of National Defence and that he himself be given the
rank of *ministre d'état* (a unique instance under the Fifth Republic).
Once again, if there has been any exception to the rule about
domaine réservé, it came between 1969 and 1974. In the event,
Debré will be remembered chiefly for his reform of military service,
his attempts to cut the number of those exempted, bringing down
upon his head the wrath of an entire generation of school-leavers.
On Debré's replacement by Robert Galley in 1973, both the title
and the rank of the minister reverted to the 'normal' Fifth Republic
specifications. In fact, owing to Pompidou's declining health, it
seems likely that most defence-related decisions were taken between
1973 and 1974 by the Prime Minister Pierre Messmer.

Giscard d'Estaing, determined to break with the all-round defence
logic of late Gaullism, tried hard to be his own Defence Minister,
in spite of being obliged by political reality to appoint a succession
of Gaullists to the rue Saint Dominique. His first 'official' minister,
Jacques Soufflet (May 1974-February 1975), was a company director (albeit with previous experience as an air force officer); his
second, Yvon Bourges (1975–80), like Messmer, was a former
colonial administrator who had held junior office in the Atomic,
Space and Foreign Ministries under de Gaulle; his third, Joel Le
Theule (October-December 1980), a former geography professor,
died in office after only two months; and his fourth, Robert Galley
(December 1980-May 1981), like Guillaumat a CEA administrator,
performed for Giscard the same function as he had for Pompidou
(April 1973-May 1974), namely that of a stop-gap minister pending
forthcoming elections. However, although it is probably true that
Giscard's Defence Ministers had little direct influence over his
decisions, he was in fact very unsure of himself, particularly in
the early years, and held regular consultations on defence issues,
involving a wide range of experts (Raymond Aron, François de
Rose, André Giraud, and Generals Beaufre, Buis, Gallois and
Méry).[51] As we shall see below, Giscard initiated a new method of
attempting to maximise presidential control over defence
policy – through strategic use of his personal Chief of Staff.

Francois Mitterrand, as with foreign affairs, began by making
what was undoubtedly the most high-profile political appointment
of the Fifth Republic. In one way, Charles Hernu's entire career
had been preparation for the Defence Ministry. It had been largely
he, during the 1970s, who had 'converted' the Socialist Party to
a policy of deterrence which dovetailed easily with Gaullism. Moreover, in launching the *Conventions pour l'armée nouvelle* (1974),

51. See Samy Cohen in *La Politique Extérieure de VGE, op. cit.*, p. 28.

he had successfully reconciled the Left and the military. But for the
death of a Portuguese photographer in Auckland harbour, New
Zealand, in July 1985, he might well have been – in his lifetime –
the only Socialist Defence Minister of the Fifth Republic.[52]
As minister, Hernu was in fact relatively influential. Although
Mitterrand was obliged to call him to order over East-West relations, and, in the early years, used his close friend François de
Grossouvre as a permanent watchdog over developments at the
rue Saint Dominique,[53] the most important reform of France's
defence structures since de Gaulle – the Rapid Action Force –
emanated from Hernu's office rather than from the Elysée. Indeed,
Hernu's credibility among the armed forces was greater than that
of the President himself, and there is abundant evidence to suggest
that between 1981 and 1984 defence policy in France was a result
of constant synergy between the ministry, the Elysée and the chiefs
of staff.[54] Hernu then became too self-confident and the rest of
the story is well known.

After being forced (much against his will) to make Hernu the
scapegoat of the *Rainbow Warrior* affair, Mitterrand reverted to
more traditional managers in the case of Paul Quilès (September
1985-March 1986) and André Giraud (March 1986-May 1988). After
the return of the Left to power in 1988, he experimented
with another political appointment in Jean-Pierre Chevènement,
partly as a way of keeping Chevènement happy (he has always
taken a keen interest in defence matters), partly as a way of keeping
him out of harm's way (his earlier ministerial career had been very
controversial), and partly as a means of keeping him under control
(the *cognoscenti* insist that Mitterrand attached only one condition
to the offer of the defence portfolio: that Chevènement do as he

52. There is little doubt that Hernu personally allowed the attack on the Greenpeace
    vessel *Rainbow Warrior* to happen. He was thereby forced to resign in
    September 1985. He died in January 1990.
53. In 1980 Hernu had written a book, *Nous . . . les Grands*, in which he ridiculed
    American suggestions that the Soviets were superior in any single area of
    defence. Once Mitterrand became President, he ordered the book to be removed
    from circulation. On Grossouvre, see Guisnel, *Les Généraux, op. cit.*, p. 147.
54. This, at any rate, is the assertion of Hernu's *conseiller technique* François
    Heisbourg (interview with author, 10 June 1991). The story of the FAR is a
    remarkable tale of political and military intrigue, revealed by Guisnel, *op. cit.*,
    pp. 145-59. Heisbourg disagrees about the centrality of General Fricaud-
    Chagnaud to the story, but in an interview in Paris on 30 May 1991 the General
    informed the present writer that, after Hernu had proposed the FAR to the
    President, Mitterrand immediately summoned Fricaud to the Elysée in order
    to satisfy himself about the details of this reform . . .

was told and refrain from controversy[55]). After Chevènement's dramatic but hardly unexpected resignation at the height of the Gulf war (30 January 1991), Mitterrand renewed the experiment with a 'manager' in Pierre Joxe. In sum, while Mitterrand needed and relied on Hernu in the early years of his presidency, a time when the rue St.-Dominique was highly influential within the *domaine réservé*, the Greenpeace affair and *cohabitation*, coming as they did on top of one another, ensured that the President did not repeat the experiment in collective control over defence policy. Since 1988, the Elysée has been in complete control. As we see below, Mitterrand, like Giscard, also made very special use of his personal Chief of Staff.

The Elysée Staff. The individuals with the greatest scope for influencing the President on matters concerning the *domaine réservé* are arguably the Elysée staff. Foremost among these are the Secretary-General of the presidency and the personal Chief of Staff (CEMP), with a growing army of special advisers playing an increasingly important role. Special mention must also be made of African affairs with the specific role within the Elysée of the diplomatic adviser on African and Madagascan affairs. There is no doubt that the role of the Elysée 'entourage' has shifted dramatically over the years, with ever greater real influence accruing to it, especially in foreign and defence matters. There are several reasons for this, some already alluded to.

The first, and undoubtedly the single most important factor has been the very different role which has fallen to the entourage under the different Presidents. De Gaulle saw his Secretaries-General – Geoffroy de Courcel (1959–62), Etienne Burin des Roziers (1962–7) and Bernard Tricot (1967–9) – as loyal servants of the presidency, performing essentially administrative, service and facilitating tasks, all geared to optimising the correctness of the President's decisions (see also above, chapter 3). He did not see them as in any way performing ministerial functions or substituting for the minister, still less attempting to interfere with or influence the minister's work.[56] Moreover, he insisted that his collaborators maintain the utmost discretion, never being 'visible' to the public – via the media or in any other way – and never speaking on behalf of the President or the government.[57] He believed it necessary to

55. The author was assured of this by a highly-placed source in the Defence Ministry in an interview in Paris in April 1989.
56. On this whole question, see *L'Entourage et de Gaulle, op. cit.*, especially pp. 84–107. Author's interview with Bernard Tricot, Paris, 3 June 1991.
57. See Geoffroy de Courcel's comments on this in *L'Entourage, op. cit.*, p. 105.

change his Secretaries-General from time to time, both to allow them to pursue their own careers and to bring in fresh ideas to the Elysée. Finally, he insisted that the numbers of the Elysée staff be very limited (ten in 1959, fifteen in 1969) and that they function in a formal way with a strict hierarchy, only the four most senior officers having direct access to the President.[58] In short, under de Gaulle the influence of the Elysée staff, insofar as it existed, was personal/incidental rather than structural/institutional.

It was a similar story for the CEMP. De Gaulle saw the function of this senior officer as being strictly one of liaison between the presidency and the other defence institutions (ministry, Secretariat-General of National Defence, Matigon etc.). The post carried with it no automatic guarantee of promotion or special status. It was usually occupied by an officer of middle rank and alternated between the three services. Although the General consulted daily with this officer, the individual himself had virtually no influence whatsoever over defence policy. Indeed, so 'faceless' were de Gaulle's CEMPs that their names rarely appear in the history books and have indeed largely been forgotten by their surviving contemporaries.

Things changed somewhat under Pompidou. The role of the Secretary-General became both more influential and more explicitly linked to foreign affairs. Michel Jobert was already Pompidou's most loyal and longest-standing collaborator; at the Elysée, he was given the task of organising the President's personal control over European policy, before becoming Foreign Minister (two highly significant departures from de Gaulle's practice). Had Schumann not resigned as Foreign Minister, Jobert would probably have been the only Secretary-General of Pompidou's presidency, underscoring the growing power and continuity of the post. Pompidou also innovated in employing a small number of personal emissaries. As for the CEMP, Pompidou appears to have continued with de Gaulle's practice. His two CEMPs, Generals Deguil and Thenoz, made no particular mark on history.

The major change came with Giscard. This was not so much the case with the Secretary-General, two of Giscard's three (Pierre-Brossolette and Wahl) being essentially specialists, reflecting the President's own background (Finance Inspectorate). With the other, Jean François-Poncet, Giscard essentially replicated his predecessor's initiative in bringing foreign policy into the Elysée before taking the Elysée to the Quai d'Orsay. Where Giscard broke new ground was in the appointment of special foreign policy

58. *Ibid.*, p. 87.

emissaries, particularly his close associate Michel Poniatowski, as personal ambassadors for sensitive operations.[59] Moreover, where de Gaulle's staff had involved a maximum of fifteen and Pompidou's had risen to twenty, Giscard appointed as many as twenty-five special advisers and assistant advisers.[60] But his greatest innovation was with his CEMP. Where Pompidou had been content to continue with de Gaulle's last appointment, Giscard immediately brought into the Elysée the man who was already the chief military adviser to the Independent Republican Party, the overtly non-Gaullist General Guy Méry. Within a year, he had appointed Méry to the top post of Army Chief of Staff (CEMA), at once underscoring the significance of the post of CEMP – as a springboard to the most senior position in the armed forces – and of his intention to take close personal command of the armed forces themselves. Between 1974 and 1975, the heads of all three armed forces – previously impeccable Gaullist appointees – as well as the CEMA, were replaced by Giscardian nominees. Giscard used General Méry as the spearhead of his campaign to de-emphasise nuclear deterrence, to redefine French defence doctrine and to upgrade the conventional elements of the army in the context of a realignment with NATO and an attempt to locate a role for the French army in any European war.[61] It is significant that all three of Giscard's CEMPs were *army* generals. When Méry was forced to retire in 1980 at the mandatory age of sixty, Giscard repeated his previous manoeuvre and appointed his current CEMP, Claude Vanbremeersch, to the post of CEMA, even though Vanbremeersch had only a year to serve before retirement.

Unfortunately for Giscard, this was not enough to guarantee him control of defence policy. The Gaullist watchdogs were out in force, men like Pierre Messmer and Michel Debré orchestrating a major campaign against the President when the details of his policy became known in 1976. Although he managed to channel extra resources into the army (a policy which had become inescapable anyway), his decision to cut the sixth nuclear submarine ran up against a Gaullist veto, the President being informed that if it were not immediately reinstated, the RPR would vote against his defence budget and bring him down. Thus the Chief of Naval Staff, Admiral

59. See Cohen, *Monarchie Nucléaire, op. cit.*, p. 39.
60. Charles Debbasch, *L'Elysée dévoilé, op. cit.*, pp. 20–23, for list of collaborators and functions.
61. See Méry controversial speech to the National Defence Institute in May 1976 ('Une armée pour quoi faire et comment?', *Défense Nationale*, June 1976), followed only a few weeks later by Giscard's equally controversial speech to the same body, published in *ibid.*, July 1976.

Lannuzel, who had been a major contributor to the decision not
to build the sixth submarine, learned one day that it was back on
the stocks again when opening his newspaper over breakfast.[62]
Giscard's presidency is a good example of the limitations of the
domaine réservé in a case where a President is attempting to implement policy which is rejected by a sizeable political group on which
he is dependent for survival in parliament. It is, in many ways,
the most significant example of constraints on the *domaine réservé*
in the entire history of the Fifth Republic.

François Mitterrand has broken still further with the original
Gaullist customs where the entourage is concerned. His first choice
as Secretary-General was typical. As one of Mitterrand's closest
advisers and confidants, Pierre Bérégovoy's job was to 'protect'
the President from the hostile state environment into which 10 May
1981 catapulted him. By July 1982, Mitterrand felt secure enough
to put Bérégovoy into the Government and to take on as Secretary-
General the thirty-nine-year-old member of the Council of State,
Jean-Louis Bianco, whom Jacques Attali had brought into the
Elysée in 1981. Bianco was to remain in the job longer than any
of his predecessors, only leaving in May 1991 to take up a ministerial post in Edith Cresson's government. He was then replaced
by his *alter ego* Hubert Védrine, whom Mitterrand had talent-
spotted in 1981 as his diplomatic adviser. The preoccupations of
the presidential Secretariat have increasingly reflected those of the
President himself, foreign and defence issues predominating. Under
Bianco, the post of Secretary-General became, in association with
the special adviser Jacques Attali and the diplomatic counsellor,
backed by an ever-growing profusion of special and assistant
advisers, an extremely important locus of foreign policy coordination. With the recent explosion of summit meetings (all of which
are prepared by the Secretary-General and his staff), there has been
a major crystallisation of the nascent division of diplomatic labour
between the Elysée (policy formulation) and the Quai d'Orsay
(back-up).[63] Nowadays, and this marks a fundamental departure
from Gaullist practice, the Elysée staff have a public image border-
ing on star status, subjected to constant media exposure and

62. Author's interview with Admiral Paul Delahousse, Paris, Dec. 1984.
63. Although there are currently about fifty special advisers at the Elysée, about
half of whom deal in one way or another with foreign or defence policy,
Mitterrand's *conseiller diplomatique* at the time of writing, Pierre Morel, insists
that there is no possibility of 'diplomatic autonomy' in the presidential
entourage. The 'official' diplomatic staff number only four, of whom two deal
permanently with European affairs. Interview, Paris, 19 July 1991.

fequently commenting, with varying degrees of discretion, on all aspects of foreign and defence policy.[64]

However, where Mitterrand differs from all his predecessors is in the range and diversity of his sources of information. His unofficial advisers are probably as numerous as his official ones. Not only does he retain close personal friends from right across the political spectrum (a testimony to the trajectory of his political career), but he also refuses to allow his collaborators to work collectively in the style of his predecessors' *cabinets*.[65] Mitterrand seeks maximum information, often assigning two or even more individuals to a specific problem, sometimes without their knowledge.[66] On an issue as complex and shrouded in secrecy as the *Rainbow Warrior* affair, it is clear that, from the moment the scandal broke, Mitterrand was well informed about every aspect of the secret service operation.[67] What is more, he actively discourages ministers from discussing issues (particularly foreign and defence ones) with each other. The flow of information and comment is from the minister via the Elysée staff to the President and back again. It is nowadays not uncommon for ministers to receive notes and memos offering proposals and even instructions direct from the Elysée staff, a procedure which would have been anathema to de Gaulle. Here again, therefore, the passing years have seen an increasing accretion of powers to the President's Office.

Mitterrand has also made very special use of his personal Chief of Staff. In the air force general, Jean Saulnier, he found a man after his own heart: discreet, independent, influential, cultivated, original and absolutely loyal. Saulnier had been proposed by Mitterrand's brother Jacques, himself an air force general and latterly head of *Aérospatiale*. In addition to initiating the President into the subtler aspects of military theory, Saulnier played a crucial role in persuading the military that Mitterrand was a man with

64. See, for instance, the special issue of *Globe*, May 1991, with extended interviews of both Jacques Attali and Jean-Louis Bianco. Mitterrand loves to surround himself with brilliant and highly visible, increasingly young and increasingly female collaborators who will give him a wide range of extremely well-distilled advice. Many an eyebrow was raised in April 1991 when he replaced Jacques Attali with the vivacious and colourful thirty-one-year-old Anne Lauvergeon. See *Le Monde*, 12 April 1991, pp. 27–9.
65. Christine Fauvet-Mycia, *Les Eminences grises*, Paris, 1988, p. 103.
66. Pierre Favier and Michel Martin-Rolland, *La Décennie Mitterrand, op. cit.*, p. 509. A good example of this was that in January 1991 special envoy Michel Vauzelle, who had been sent to Baghdad to visit Saddam Hussein, did not know that Edgard Pisani had, for months, been opening up separate channels of communication with Saddam.
67. Franz-Olivier Giesbert, *Le Président, op. cit.*, pp. 242, 260–1.

whom they could do business. Although clearly implicated in the
Greenpeace scandal, Saulnier was rewarded for his service to the
President by being made CEMA in 1985, thereby virtually institutionalising the special promotion initiated by Giscard. During the
period of *cohabitation*, Saulnier played a crucial role in stimulating
the defence information flow to and from the Elysée. His replacement as CEMP was army General Gilbert Forray who, as Director
of the Military Academy at Coetquidan, had helped promote the
credibility of Socialist military thinking and, as first commander
of the Rapid Action Force (FAR), been instrumental in helping to
break the resistance of the military establishment to the FAR.
Forray was later to be rewarded for his services by being appointed
CEMA, just as his successor, another air force general, Jean Fleury,
went straight from the Elysée to the post of Chief of Air Staff.
Fleury's successor, and Mitterrand's fourth CEMP, Admiral
Jacques Lanxade, after virtually overseeing from the Elysée the
military details of the Gulf war, was in his turn, in March 1991,
appointed CEMA. In this way, Mitterrand has ensured that his
personal military advisers at the Elysée have gone on to take all
but one (Chief of Naval Staff) of the top military jobs in France.
Such close control over the military, given the harmonious relationship between Hernu and the defence establishment, might seem
unnecessary. But in 1988, forty-five senior officers broke with
the tradition of political silence expected of *'la grande muette'*
and published political support for Jacques Chirac, thus revealing
the extent to which Mitterrand remains an adversary in the eyes
of a generation of military officers trained under de Gaulle.[68]
Mitterrand's response was to increase his own personal control
over defence-planning and doctrine and to encourage Chevènement
to hasten plans to slim down the armed forces.

It would be necessary to conduct a thorough study of the role
of the CEMP in order to establish with precision how its evolution
has contributed to the process of presidential supremacy in the
realm of defence policy. The pool of candidates from which the
post can be filled is far narrower than for the other major presidential posts, and to some extent the degree to which President and
CEMP 'hit it off' depends on the accident of personal chemistry
(Mitterrand found he had far more in common with Saulnier and
Lanxade than with Forray and Fleury). But it cannot be doubted
that the changing importance of the CEMP has been one of the
cardinal features of the story of the *domaine réservé*. All in all,

68. See, on this incident, Guisnel, *op. cit.*, pp. 60–3; Jacques Isnard, 'M. Chevène-
    ment rappelle à l'ordre quarante-cinq généraux', *Le Monde*, 9 July 1988.

180   *Jolyon Howorth*

the use made by the Elysée of presidential advisers of one sort or another has, in different ways, added up to a constant increase in presidential intrusion, influence and real power.

Thus on the general situation regarding the President's ministers and staff, one must conclude that there is a clear distinction to be made between de Gaulle and the others. The latter have all evolved throughout the course of their mandate(s), via a process of experimentation with different individuals, in the direction of greater and greater direct control over foreign and defence policy.[69] Yet there are significant areas of foreign and defence policy which, despite this vast array of powers, remain beyond the President's direct control.

Corporate Constraints on Presidential Power

Perhaps the greatest single lobby a President has to contend with is the *military-industrial complex* (MIC). This is a vast and sensitive subject, too intricate to allow for more than a glimpse in this chapter. Edward Kolodziej has broken important ground concerning the lack of democratic accountability of the MIC; his masterly study of the French experience in making and marketing arms, in addition to offering the clearest guide to the economic and industrial imperatives behind France's armaments export drive, shows how all Presidents of the Fifth Republic have constantly found themselves swept along in directions they had not intended as a result of the inertial thrust of the military-industrial complex.[70] Perhaps the most telling example of this type of pressure is afforded by the Rafale combat aircraft, a highly controversial weapons system with an astronomical price-tag which was successfully imposed not only on a highly reluctant military establishment but even on a sceptical President. The story of how François Mitterrand, who believed passionately in European defence cooperation, and who was desperate to find savings in his defence budget, was bamboozled by a trio of aeronautical friends and family into pulling out of the proposed five-nation European fighter aircraft (EFA) and into channelling 150 billion francs into the already overflowing coffers of Marcel Dassault – and of how he subsequently came to regret

69. The cumulative effect of this can be seen in that, whereas de Gaulle was caricatured as a military dictator and Giscard as an *ancien régime* monarch, Mitterrand's role in the *Bébette* show is that of God.
70. Edward A. Kolodziej, *Making and Marketing Arms: The French experience and its implications for the international system*, Princeton, 1987, pp. 59–60, 193 and *passim*.

his decision – is a sobering insight into this particular lobby.[71] The entire question of the structure of the armaments industry, and of its internationalisation – and consequent loss of national control – is a major factor to be taken into consideration in assessing the reality of presidential power over a key area of defence and foreign policy.[72]

A second area where it has been clear that the President is by no means in control has been that of the *secret services*.[73] In most countries the espionage and counter-espionage networks tend to be laws unto themselves. In France, they beat all records for lack of accountability. Most Presidents of the Republic, and none more than Mitterrand, have regarded them as at best a necessary evil, and at worst a cancer within the state. Officially under the 'control' of the Ministry of Defence, the Counter-Espionage Service (SDECE) gradually evolved, during the 1960s and 1970s, into an autonomous body run by a coterie of high-ranking officers with allegiance to nobody. There is no direct chain of command between the Elysée and the service, no links at all with either Matignon or the Ministry of the Interior. When Mitterrand first came to power in 1981, he was determined to bring the organisation to heel, but his first choice as head of the SDECE, Pierre Marion, proved far from equal to the task, and the battle appears to have been lost. There is considerable evidence to suggest that in the early days of the Mitterrand presidency, at least, the SDECE was manipulating evidence in such a way as to persuade the President to intervene massively in Chad. It appears that the secret services have at least two rival organisations operating in Africa, neither of which is subjected to any effective political control from Paris. It is also abundantly clear that, whatever the original intentions of Mitterrand and Hernu with respect to the *Rainbow Warrior*, the DGSE (as it was by then called) massively overstepped the mark, perhaps partly even *in order* to embarrass the President. Eventually, thoroughly disillusioned with the existing secret services, Mitterrand attempted to put in place a

71. On the Rafale, see Guisnel, *op. cit.*, chapter 10, '150 milliards pour Dassault'; Pierre Marion, *Le Pouvoir sans Visage. Le complexe militaro-industriel*, Paris, 1990, p. 43; Jean-Michel Boucheron, *Rapport fait au nom de la commission de la défense nationale et des forces armées sur le projet de loi de programmation 1990-1993*, Assemblée Nationale, annexe 897, 2 Oct. 1989, pp. 315-324.
72. Jean-Paul Hébert, *Stratégie française et industrie d'armement*, Paris, 1991; Pauline Creasey and Simon May (eds), *The European Armaments Market and Procurement Cooperation*, London, 1988; Andrew Moravcsik, 'The European Armaments Industry at the Crossroads', *Survival*, XXXII/1 (Jan./Feb. 1990).
73. See, on this, Jean Guisnel and Bernard Violet, *Services secrets. Le pouvoir et les services de renseignement sous François Mitterrand*, Paris, 1989; Pierre Marion, *La Mission impossible. A la tête des services secrets*, Paris, 1991.

parallel structure at the Elysée, but the real secret services were too clever for him and led him straight into an embarrassing trap involving the false arrest of suspected IRA terrorists.[74]

The third area of corporate constraint derives from *political pressures* of one sort or another. Although we have examined the extent to which the main ministers with responsibility for defence and foreign affairs may or may not interfere with presidential policy, we have not assessed the influence of other ministers, in particular the Finance Minister. There are certainly documented instances where the technical arguments of the controller of the purse-strings have overruled the will even of a man like de Gaulle.[75] In the annual wrangling with the spending departments, the Finance Ministry enjoys considerable power over budgets, as does the Prime Minister in his subsequent arbitrations. Furthermore, as we have seen in the case of Giscard, a President's hands can be effectively tied in a situation where he does not command an overall majority in parliament. On the other hand, there is virtually no pressure whatever on the President from the political parties (either his own or the others) as such. It is a strange feature of French political life, undoubtedly exacerbated by the existence of the *domaine réservé* itself, that all too few politicians express any interest whatever in foreign or defence policy.[76]

A fourth – and growing – area of pressure derives from *investigative journalism*. The role of dedicated journalistic sleuths was crucial in bringing to light details about Bokassa's diamonds, about Greenpeace, about the Luchaire affair, the Carrefour scandal and many others.[77] Although the predominant culture in a country like France militates against over-intensive media scrutiny of the actions of the state, on occasion international comparisons can bring home to French journalists just how spoon-fed and gullible they can often

---

74. See also Franz-Olivier Giesbert, *Le Président*, *op. cit.*, p. 119, and Favier and Martin-Rolland, *op. cit.*, pp. 513–16.
75. In discussions over the funding of the second military programme-law (1965–70), de Gaulle insisted that there be annual adjustments made in order to compensate for any cost overruns. His Finance Minister, Giscard, deployed a range of technical arguments to defeat this proposal. Interview with Bernard Tricot, Paris, 3 June 1991.
76. Those with genuine specialist knowledge of the subject in any given party can be counted on the fingers of one hand. Even some members of the parliamentary Defence and Foreign Affairs Commissions would be hard put to make a telling speech on the subject. As Jean-Pierre Cot ruefully remarked, a deputy who gets too interested in foreign affairs is heading for electoral defeat.
77. See Stephen E. Bornstein, 'The Politics of Scandal' in P. Hall *et al.*, *Developments in French Politics*, London, 1990, pp. 269–81; Jacques Derogy and Jean-Marie Pontaut, *Enquête sur trois secrets d'état*, Paris, 1986.

be. This was felt with particular acuteness during the Gulf war when French correspondents in the Middle East realised that their Anglo-Saxon colleagues had access to far more detailed and more accurate information about the conduct of the war than was being fed to the French through the official channels of the Army Information and Public Relations Service (SIRPA).[78]

Finally, one must not forget the issue raised at the beginning of this chapter: that of the 'power' which may or may not be exerted – individually or collectively – by the thousands of civil servants, administrators and other officials who are involved, at whatever level, in processing foreign and defence policy. The President receives, as do his ministers, all relevant papers and documents. What the President does not have is the army of functionaries and civil experts available to the Quai d'Orsay and the rue Saint Dominique who actually interpret that information. It is not difficult to imagine a situation similar to that which actually existed during the Gulf war when the President and the Minister of Defence were on a collision course. It is theoretically possible for a Defence or Foreign Minister, if he felt so inclined, to withhold vital information from the President. The fact remains that even the sizeable team available in the Elysée is dependent not so much on raw information from civil servants as on loyalty in supplying its necessary interpretation. After all, the vast majority of the still comparatively limited staff at the Elysée are on 'leave' from other ministries, on which their career ultimately depends. France has nothing equivalent to the American National Security Council, and all Presidents have rejected suggestions that such a structure be introduced at the Elysée. There could come a time when these repeated rejections become a source of regret to a future President.

The French President, therefore, despite the very considerable powers at his disposal, does not and cannot have everything entirely his own way, and yet in specific instances the conduct of France's foreign and defence policy can be and has been run as though it were the personal creation of the man in the Elysée. There can be few better illustrations of this than the 1991 Gulf war.

78. G. Seidel, 'Un premier regard sur les Médias français et le Golfe. La responsabilité des journalistes en temps de crise', *Modern and Contemporary France*, 44 (Jan. 1991). For good insight into the difficulty the government experienced in controlling press coverage of the Gulf war, see Josette Alia and Christine Clerc, *La Guerre de Mitterrand*, Paris, 1991, pp. 300–2.

François Mitterrand, the Gulf Crisis and War

François Mitterrand was at his country residence and most of his ministers were on vacation when the news came in on 2 August 1990 of Saddam Hussein's invasion of Kuwait. From his family retreat in the Landes, the President immediately began to take personal control of the crisis. Almost every day, from August until the end of February, he discussed events on the telephone with world leaders from George Bush and Mikhail Gorbachev through Margaret Thatcher/John Major and Helmut Kohl to Hosni Moubarak and King Fahd, occasionally acting as honest broker between them. Most of them he met personally, often on more than one occasion. Rarely can a President have been involved so incessantly, so directly and so personally in the management of an international crisis. During those seven months, in addition to presiding over almost daily meetings of the diplomatic and military Chiefs of Staff (at which he personally decided on the minutest details of France's involvement), he held seven *conseils restreints*, seven individual press conferences and ten or a dozen joint press conferences with other world leaders, engaged in four major television interviews, addressed parliament on two occasions and the nation on two others, and delivered a crucially important speech at the United Nations.

To understand Mitterrand's intense involvement in the Gulf war, one must understand the sort of man he is. Fundamentally a jurist, he believed intensely that the problem of Kuwait was a test-case in international law on which hinged the entire prospect of creating a new world order. From start to finish, his was a strategic reaction which took account of the short, medium and long terms, which recognised the conflicting claims of First, Second and Third Worlds, and the contradictory and complementary aspects of superpower and European aspirations and capabilities; which appreciated how diaphanous is the veil between diplomacy and war; which understood the complex issues of Muslim pride and Western arrogance; and which sympathised with both Arab and Israeli. Here was an issue, he felt, which spoke to the very heart of France's world influence, in which the chaotic claims of history and geography, of rights and aspirations, of force and persuasion, of pragmatism and ideology were central. Mitterrand seemed convinced that the other major nations involved in the crisis would not, could not, or did not wish to achieve the complex objectives he had set himself. America was too crude, Russia too distracted and enfeebled, the Arab world too divided, Britain too tied to Washington's apron-strings. He was persuaded that France alone could induce Saddam Hussein to come to his senses.

From the outset, Mitterrand's objectives were ambitious: to avoid war, to obtain the restoration of Kuwaiti sovereignty, to free all hostages, to safeguard Arab dignity across the 'Arab nation', to preserve France's special relationship with the Maghreb, to use the crisis to re-launch the stranded Middle East peace process, to defend right, and to lay the foundations stones of a new international order. He therefore engaged in discourse which spoke (either at one and the same time or sequentially) both to Washington and to Baghdad, to Saddam Hussein and the Emir of Kuwait, to the Arab world and to Israel, to North and to South, to France and to Europe; which spoke of preserving peace while preparing for war, of respecting national sovereignty while imposing international law, of using this very crisis to help the transition from forty years of universal tension towards a new era of universal understanding.

To that end, he spared no effort to bring about his objectives. He toured the Middle East personally, visited the United States and many European countries, despatched to the four corners of the globe a dozen personal emissaries from across the French political spectrum,[79] and spoke constantly to everybody. It took him more than six weeks to devise in his own mind the peace formula which was to underpin his crucial speech at the United Nations on 24 September which was to remain on the table, in one form or another, till 15 January 1991. The UN speech, every word of which he drafted himself, is a masterpiece of Mitterrandesque diplomacy, in which there is both a carrot and a stick for almost everybody – especially for Saddam Hussein. Its crucial component was the acceptance of 'linkage' between the Kuwait crisis and the Arab-Israeli conflict.[80] For almost six months Mitterrand performed a personal balancing act between war and peace, between Washington and Moscow, between the United States and Western Europe, between the two sides of the Arab world. In this activity he was subjected to many contradictory and confusing pressures: from his Defence Minister to reverse the war machine and rely solely on diplomacy; from his Foreign Minister (after an initial, failed

---

79. Among these emissaries was the man Mitterrand is reported to have refused as Foreign Minister under Chirac, one of his most bitter political adversaries, Jean Lecanuet. The Plantu cartoon in *Le Monde* showing Lecanuet explaining to some foreign potentate that 'François Mitterrand's policies are absolutely brill – iant!', while thinking to himself 'What on earth am I saying?', says it all.
80. On the French peace plan, see Jolyon Howorth, 'France and the Gulf War: From pre-war crisis to post-war crisis', *Modern and Contemporary France*, no. 46 (July 1991), pp. 3–16.

attempt to create a Franco-Soviet approach) to step in line with James Baker and the State Department; from the Arab world to detach himself from American policy; and from most of Europe to align himself more closely with that policy. Through it all he pursued his own chosen course.

Although the Quai d'Orsay continued throughout the crisis to prepare briefings, particularly concerning the impact of France's position in the Arab world, it is clear that from about mid-August Mitterrand personally defined and expressed that position.[81] By September the Quai, which was in any case deeply divided internally into a pro- and an anti-Arab lobby, felt marginalised and considered that the minister, Roland Dumas, was behaving more as the President's right-hand man than as the leader of the French diplomatic corps. Arab diplomats soon came to realise that their various attempts to exploit sympathetic contacts at the Quai or in the media were to no avail.[82] Mitterrand's diplomacy rested almost entirely on the massive use of personal emissaries, whose missions were usually conducted in the greatest secrecy. Unknown to all but a couple of his closest advisers, various lines of communication were opened up between the Elysée and Baghdad (including via Yasser Arafat in Tunis). The most significant of these was undoubtedly the series of cloak-and-dagger meetings which his special adviser Edgard Pisani, Director of the Paris-based Institut du Monde Arabe, held in various locations in Switzerland with Saddam's brother Barzan Takriti.[83]

The aim of these 'discussions' was to get Saddam to announce unequivocally his intention of withdrawing from Kuwait. As the deadline for war approached, the risks of engaging in such dialogue grew with each day. A succession of world leaders, past (Edward Heath, Willy Brandt) and present (James Baker, Perez de Cuellar), met for discussions with Saddam himself or his Foreign Minister Tariq Aziz. On the central issue of a guarantee to withdraw from Kuwait, all encountered a blank wall. Yet Mitterrand seemed convinced that he could succeed where all others had failed. There is evidence that Saddam was prepared to listen to the French overtures, but demanded a face-saving price: the visit to Baghdad of Foreign Minister Dumas or even the President himself. Before

---

81. See, on this, Dominique Moisi, 'Le Quai d'Orsay et la crise du Golfe', *op. cit.*
82. Josette Alia and Christine Clerc, *La Guerre de Mitterrand*, *op. cit.*, pp. 118–20.
83. It was not until after the Gulf war that the existence of this 'parallel diplomacy' was leaked to the public – see *Le Canard Enchaîné*, 6 March 1991. I am grateful to Edgard Pisani for several personal interviews which have clarified his role in the crisis.

Mitterrand could consider such a perilous course (which no other country even contemplated), he needed a clear signal from the Iraqi leader that movement on the central issue was forthcoming. Until the very last moment, Mitterrand kept all his options alive. As the seconds separating peace from war were ticking away, he summoned Roland Dumas and Edgard Pisani to his office in the small hours of 14 January. He asked each to rehearse the reasons why he thought (Pisani) or did not think (Dumas) that diplomacy should be carried – via Concorde – to the banks of the Tigris. By then Pisani felt that he had cast-iron reassurances from Saddam's own brother that a peace agreement would be signed, whereas Dumas felt that the diplomatic and above all military risks of failure were too great. Mitterrand decided in favour of Pisani: the two men were ordered to leave that morning (14 January) for Baghdad on the ultimate peace mission. But before they could depart, Perez de Cuellar called on Mitterrand and convinced him that the cause was futile. Critically, Mitterrand changed his mind one last time, not at the eleventh but virtually at the twelfth hour. Abandoning a peace he more than anyone had struggled to preserve, he embraced with fortitude a war which he had foreseen earlier than most as being the inexorable logic of Saddam's behaviour.

The war found France ready. For, in parallel with his diplomatic efforts, Mitterrand had carefully prepared his military options. And here the role of his CEMP, Admiral Lanxade, was paramount, being of far greater significance than those of the Defence Minister and the Chief of the General Staff put together. It was Lanxade who, already thinking of the long term, suggested to the President in early August the despatch to the Gulf of an aircraft-carrier, bearing the helicopters which would play such a vital role in the eventual land offensive. It was also Lanxade, in mid-September, who persuaded the President to cross the military Rubicon and commit ground forces to the conflict. This was at a time when Mitterrand was under under intense pressure from his Defence Minister to reverse the military escalation.[84] It was Lanxade, fluent in English, who – at the behest of the President – criss-crossed the Atlantic and burned the telephone wires between Paris and Washington, liaising in the minutest detail with National Security adviser Brent Scowcroft and General Colin Powell. During the course of the war itself, every evening without fail at six o'clock, Mitterrand presided over a war council at the Elysée which brought

---

84. Alia and Clerc, *op. cit.*, pp. 99–102, reveal how this was Mitterrand's most difficult decision of the entire crisis, involving something almost unheard-of for the sanguine President: a sleepless night.

together, in addition to Lanxade, the Prime Minister, the Defence
Minister, the Chief of the General Staff, the heads of the three
armed forces and of the SGDN, and the Secretary-General of the
Elysée. All testify to Mitterrand having personally selected the sites
for French bombing missions, the exact size and composition of
the French forces, the precise timing and location of their activities.
In the most literal sense, François Mitterrand played fully the role
conferred upon him by the Constitution as *'chef des armées'*.[85]

The Constitution, his personality, the practice of his entourage
and the lack of any corporate or political constraints combined to
turn this quite naturally into Mitterrand's crisis and Mitterrand's
war. The Prime Minister's voice was hardly to be heard; the
Foreign Minister's was indistinguishable from his own; the Defence
Minister's, although (but also, in part, became) dissident, was
hardly relevant; the opposition was inaudible or incoherent, or
both; parliament became essentially a formality; and the press, with
only the most marginal exceptions, and the public were massively
on the President's side. It was a classic and perfect case of *domaine
réservé* politics, illustrating both the potential and the illusions
of such personal power. The President does indeed appear to have
the world in the palm of his hand. His scope is vast, his sense of
destiny awesome, his forms of action almost infinite. But ultimately
a situation involving foreign and defence policy actually depends far
more on other people than it does on the man in the Elysée. Judgement and luck are present in equal parts. But no amount of judgement can counteract the effect of just a very small dose of luck.

Conclusion

We have suggested that the French President's special role in foreign
and defence policy is a highly significant feature of French political
culture. Implicit in the Constitution and consecrated by practice,
the *domaine réservé* has assumed different forms and has operated
in differing degrees of intensity and totality from one President
to another. To some extent, this is a function of the personality
of each particular President and of his relationship with those
around him. But increasingly it is also a feature of the evolution
and, above all, the predominant interpretation, of the functions
of the other great offices and institutions of state, as well as of

85. See, on this, Samy Cohen, 'Le Président chef des armées', *Pouvoirs*, 58 (1991),
    33–40. I am grateful to a variety of leading actors in the Elysée and in the
    Defence Ministry for interviews which have allowed me to reconstruct these
    events.

the practice of international relations with its increasing emphasis on summitry. Since the resignation of de Gaulle and certainly since the death of Pompidou, the picture is one of almost constant increase in executive control. This may well not be the intention of the Presidents involved (essentially Giscard and Mitterrand). It is certainly not an automatic consequence of the text of the Constitution. As *cohabitation* showed, nothing guarantees that this situation will continue indefinitely. Indeed, the experience of those tense years 1986–8 suggests that at the heart of the Constitution there lies a glaring and potentially dangerous contradiction, which could one day land France in trouble. Meanwhile, the accumulated tradition of the *domaine réservé* continues to confer on the tenant of the Elysée powers in the field of foreign and particularly defence policy which go far beyond those enjoyed by any other world leader.

7

THE PRESIDENT, CULTURAL PROJECTS AND BROADCASTING POLICY

Martin Harrison

Of the many indicators of political power few are more persuasive than the capacity to set a political agenda and then implement it. While Presidents of the Fifth Republic have displayed this capacity in considerable measure in a number of fields, earlier chapters also underline the constraints imposed by institutional resistances, informal pressures and France's second-rank international status. In contrast, the constraints on presidential action over broadcasting and cultural affairs have been fewer and weaker – the 1986-8 *cohabitation* excepted. Unimpeded (so far) by external alliances or significant encroachment by Brussels, Presidents have been almost untroubled by ministers with substantial personal or institutional strength, constitutional or bureaucratic impediments, pressure groups or public opinion. Indeed, the ambitious presidential construction projects of recent years have enjoyed wide acceptance because they stand in a tradition reaching back to the *Ancien Régime*. François Mitterrand has readily acknowledged his approach as being monarchical. Presidential intervention in broadcasting, without enjoying such supportive public attitudes, could at least claim continuity with the 'republican' tradition of subordination to the interests of the government of the day and the absence of any vigorous counter-tradition of fairness and public service.

So, for such mainly extra-constitutional reasons, broadcasting and cultural affairs have been marked by the consistent, overt and arbitrary deployment of presidential prerogative power. This is not to suggest that Presidents have decided everything – far from it – but they have enjoyed almost total freedom to decide whatever they chose to decide. Most notably, de Gaulle's successors have chosen to mark out a *domaine réservé* of major cultural projects where their writ has run supreme; other aspects of cultural policy have remained largely under orthodox ministerial control. Lines of responsibility have remained reasonably clear and patterns of decision-making relatively settled. By contrast, there has been a pattern of occasional imperious presidential interventions in major broadcasting decisions, as unheralded as they have been arbitrary.

This erratic pattern has made decision-making processes precarious and unpredictable, undermining the authority of ministers and nominally independent regulators.

With such relatively unconstrained presidential prerogative power, court politics has inevitably flourished. In broadcasting this was most overtly marked in the layers of ministers and officials, more royalist than the King, vying to stifle material that might incur presidential displeasure, reducing the system to craven conformism. Those days have passed but the courtly manoeuvring continues in more oblique forms. In cultural affairs, each new project has attracted its micro-politics among those seeking the ear of the sovereign. That ear remains crucial even on matters where he does not directly involve himself. There are many reasons for the relative failure of André Malraux as minister and the relative success of Jack Lang, but not the least of these was Malraux's unwillingness to play the courtly game and Lang's uninhibited engagement in it.

In many respects, then, Presidents have been able to assert their unfettered will in the areas under discussion here. Yet, as de Gaulle once put it with his characteristic scepticism, if politics is first of all 'a matter of will', then it is a matter of 'realities'. Presidential absolutism is a style of rule rather than a guarantee of success. Although the presidential will has usually prevailed, the gap between aspirations and outcomes has often been cruelly wide, indicative of the limitations of presidentialism as practised in the Fifth Republic.

Cultural Projects

In more than a decade at the Elysée de Gaulle made just three major decisions on cultural matters – but they were of great importance: to create a full-scale Ministry of Cultural Affairs, to appoint André Malraux head of it with the rank of *ministre d'état*, and to maintain him at this post throughout his presidency. The creation of the ministry brought to being an idea that had been canvassed for decades, one of many apparently lost causes of the Popular Front. Yet, ironically, it was apparently an afterthought, hastily devised by Georges Pompidou to find a place for Malraux after de Gaulle decided to replace him at the Ministry of Information by Jacques Soustelle.[1] Nevertheless it was an inspired improvisation. A writer with an international reputation, *amateur* of Asian art and involved

1. A. Peyrefitte's testimony in *Georges Pompidou, Hier et Aujourd'hui*, Neuilly-sur-Seine, 1990, pp. 202–3. Criticisms and suggestions from Roland Cayrol, Jean-Luc Parodi and Jack Hayward are gratefully acknowledged.

in the cinema, Malraux was the most selflessly loyal of all de Gaulle's ministers. Yet he also brought an aura of revolution and a whiff of notoriety from his escapades in Indo-China in the 1920s, his involvement in the Popular Front and his commitment to the anti-Fascist cause in Spain. The background that invested him with an odour of sulphur among the orthodox Right created a capital of sympathy beyond the customary bounds of Gaullism. He was not a man to confine cultural life in a straitjacket of 'official' art. 'The State', he said, 'does not exist to direct art but to serve it.'[2] Considering how governments of the time were so unsentimentally domesticating broadcasting, fears on such grounds – inherent in the very notion of a Ministry of Culture – were by no means baseless. In that respect at least Malraux was the man for the job. De Gaulle's readiness to retain him despite all his deficiencies as a minister was no less important, giving the ministry time to establish itself in the face of resentments by the departments from which it was carved that might otherwise have swept it away.

Malraux voiced the eminently Gaullist ambition of ensuring that France was 'once more the leading cultural country in the world' and of making her into a 'cultural third force' between the United States and the Soviet Union – 'between a culture which knew what it wanted and one that did not' – allying the notions of 'rank' and French exceptionalism. His emphasis on preserving the artistic 'heritage' was no less congenial to de Gaulle. Yet, although de Gaulle was politely respectful of the arts, he had little interest in them and hardly ever intervened in matters within Malraux's province. Nevertheless, from time to time he lent his prestige to Malraux's endeavours by opening an exhibition or a new *maison de la culture*, and called on his unrivalled talent for elevated if at times impenetrable oratory on occasions like the transfer of Jean Moulin's ashes to the Panthéon. A note to the Prime Minister in 1963 seeking funds 'to restore the Opéra and the Opéra-Comique to their rightful rank' is notable precisely for its rarity.[3]

The one area where de Gaulle staked a personal role was urban planning. When Paul Delouvrier expressed anxiety about opposition by vested interests to his development plan for the Paris region, the President reassured him with a characteristic sweep of the arm that 'in relation to the Paris region . . . nothing is to be decided, still less undertaken, without my explicit approval.'[4] His

2. Cited by B. Anthonioz in Institut Charles de Gaulle, *De Gaulle et Malraux*, Paris, 1987, p. 206.
3. C. de Gaulle, *Lettres, notes et carnets, 1961–3*, Paris, 1986, p. 331.
4. *Ibid.*, p. 313.

subsequent role was more modest, but at times decisive. Thus he intervened in the controversy over the Montparnasse Tower. Malraux told hostile officials on his behalf, 'Gentlemen, if people in the thirteenth century had thought like you, we would have had no cathedrals.' De Gaulle also contemplated a 'grand design' for Les Halles after the transfer of the central markets to the suburbs, including 'lyrical, rounded skyscrapers' to house the Ministry of Finance, which would have had to move out of the Louvre. Opposed by the City Council for its high density, the idea was abandoned shortly before de Gaulle's resignation.[5] He also involved himself in the controversy over the future of the disused Gare d'Orsay, where French Railways wanted to build an international hotel. Le Corbusier proposed a 105-metre tower. De Gaulle admired Le Corbusier but considered his scheme inappropriate for a site 'so steeped in history'.[6] Claudius-Petit, the minister directly concerned, could not change his mind. This was well before the era of *les grands projets présidentiels*. De Gaulle's concern for his place in history was not one that sought expression in steel and concrete. The nearest he came was, typically, promoting the construction of a number of patriotic memorials and instructing his Prime Minister to establish a body that would be responsible for erecting and maintaining national monuments to the armed forces and the Resistance.[7]

De Gaulle let his ministers get on with their jobs outside areas marked out for his personal attention. However, this did not mean he was unimportant in other matters. That Malraux survived is only explicable on the basis of his close relationship with the President: a man of sudden inspirations rather than long campaigns, he was impatient with parliament, at odds with much of his staff, rapidly wearied by detail, and in later years diminished by ill-health and family tragedy. With no personal following, viewed with suspicion by many in the governing majority and without strong presidential backing, Malraux had little prospect of meeting his ambitious brief: 'to make the greatest works of the human race – and first and foremost those of France – accessible to the largest possible number of people in France, to ensure the widest possible audience for our cultural heritage, and to encourage the creation of works of art

5. F. Chaslin, *Les Paris de François Mitterrand: Histoire des grands projets architecturaux*, Paris, 1985, pp. 113–14.
6. E. Claudius-Petit in Institut Charles de Gaulle, *De Gaulle et Malraux*, pp. 249–50.
7. S. Barcellini in *ibid.*, p. 251.

and of the mind to enrich that heritage'.[8] Such democratisation
of cultural enrichment called for vastly increased funding, but
although initially his share of the national budget rose from 0.33 to
0.43 per cent, eleven years later it was exactly the same proportion
(albeit of a larger total). Almost all his programmes, even his cher-
ished *maisons de la culture* which are remembered as his greatest
achievement, suffered chronic financial anaemia. This was in no
small part because, although Malraux enjoyed exceptional access to
de Gaulle and was one of the very few who spoke with him as an
equal, he apparently never pressed him for more money. Indeed
they scarcely ever discussed matters within his ministerial brief. He
occasionally raised matters with members of the Elysée staff, but
because the cultural affairs advisers of the period had little impact
on policy, this availed him little.

So, far from de Gaulle dominating cultural policy, the fact that
for most of the time he was *le grand absent* was fatal to many of
Malraux's ambitions. Malraux's proposal to give the Louvre its
'full cultural dimension' was thwarted, because without firm presidential backing he had no hope of evicting the Finance Ministry
from quarters it had 'temporarily' occupied for decades. Success
had to await a less inhibited minister, Jack Lang, a quarter-century
later. Again, in the court politics of the period, absence of presidential support blighted Malraux's hopes of improving the visual
dimension in education and reforming the regional art schools
and the teaching of the plastic arts, all of which were blocked by
the highly conservative bureaucracies of the Ministry of Education.
So too with the Ministry of Information (controlling the most
potent cultural medium of all, television), and the Foreign Ministry
(responsible for external cultural policy, where again the President's
aid was neither offered nor sought) Malraux declined to disturb
de Gaulle with such secondary matters. In view of Malraux's other
deficiencies as a minister his policy failures cannot be attributed
to a single factor. Nevertheless, with little personal political standing and heading a weak ministry, his delicacy about using the
President as a resource was crucial on a number of occasions.

For better and worse, then, during the first eleven years of
the Fifth Republic the minister rather than the President was the
most important actor in cultural politics. However, in the twelve
years between his departure and the Socialist victory of 1981, the
pattern was more complex. None of the eight holders of the culture

8. Decree 59–889 of 24 July 1959, *Journal Officiel, Lois et Décrets*, 26 July 1959.
   For a swingeing 'high culture' attack on the Malraux-Lang promotion of mass
   culture, see M. Fumaroli, *L'Etat Culturel, Essai sur une religion moderne*,
   Paris, 1991.

portfolio, all chosen or approved by the President, enjoyed a relationship with the President approaching that between de Gaulle and Malraux, and none brought any great political standing to the job. It was demoted first to 'minister', then to junior minister, then combined with environment as a full ministry, and finally bracketed with communication. These vacillations reflected the continuing uncertainty about the status and direction of cultural policy in the wake of the upheavals of 1968, the fading of Malraux's vision of democratisation and the unresolved tensions between the 'modernising' and 'heritage' wings of the arts community.

Georges Pompidou's election marked the emergence of the Elysée as a major actor in cultural policy and the ascendancy of the modernisers. He saw that important issues came to interministerial councils under his chairmanship; previously they had rarely reached so high a level. Publicly and privately he expressed a strong commitment to promoting culture, but not to higher public spending. Indeed, the first budget of his presidency cut expenditure, particularly on the theatre and the *maisons de la culture* which were still in deep disfavour for biting the hand that fed them in 1968. At a stormy reception for members of the world of the arts shortly after he had taken office, Pompidou personally delivered the message that ambitions must be more modest. Yet he was also prepared to listen. On that same occasion he told one of his most outspoken critics to set down his views on paper, and speedy action on a much-delayed reform of the terms of employment in decentralised theatre companies ensued. Such encounters were exceptional. While Pompidou – and his wife – had the widest social circle of any Fifth Republic President, his acquaintance with cultural bodies remained limited and wary, although he was in his way as hostile to 'state culture' as the Left-wing culture lobby. For the most part, he preferred to deal with them through a former member of Malraux's staff, Bernard Anthonioz. His preference for an arm's-length relationship was confirmed by his experience with a major exhibition of contemporary creative work, which was staged in Paris at his behest. Artists who were not selected were furious; some who were invited refused to let their work be exhibited under government auspices, and the Women's Liberation Front was angry because only two of the seventy-two selected were women. The opening was notable for a particularly robust exercise of the police's talents for dealing with demonstrators, which impartially included members of *le tout Paris* invited as guests. Pompidou was deeply mortified.[9]

9. P. Cabanne, *Le Pouvoir culturel sous la Cinquième République*, Paris, 1981, pp. 278–80. Also P. Ory, *L'Aventure culturelle française, 1945–1989*, Paris, 1990.

During the five years of Pompidou's presidency three ministers held the culture portfolio – four if one includes Alain Peyrefitte, who was appointed on the eve of his death. None was given the time to make more than a modest mark. Michelet, the liberal Gaullist who succeeded Malraux, preserved the *maisons de la culture* from Right-wing hostility and established the Cultural Intervention Fund (which involved Matignon more closely in cultural affairs); Jacques Duhamel reorganised the ministry, reformed art education and the provincial museums, and rebuilt relationships with the arts community. Then Maurice Druon, popular novelist, member of the Academy, Gaullist and one of the authors of the 'anthem' of the Resistance, was appointed on Pompidou's express directive. Deeply traditionalist and unversed in ministerial politics, he cut himself off from his 'constituency' by attacking artists who had 'a Molotov cocktail in one hand and a begging bowl in the other', whose 'intellectual terrorism' 'confused liberty and opposition'. He achieved little or nothing.

Pompidou personally intervened relatively little outside two areas where his views were clear and influential. One was planning in Paris. As Prime Minister he had favoured expressways along the banks of the Seine; as President he encouraged the development of a 'forest of towers' on the western edge of Paris. As one observer put it, 'Consulted as a simple citizen, he was listened to as a monarch.'[10] Matters were not in fact so clear-cut; this was one of the rare occasions when his Prime Minister Messmer took a different line, the Academy of Architecture (predictably) was unanimously hostile, and the scheme foundered amid heated controversy.

The second owed everything to Pompidou. The idea that the space vacated by the transfer of the central markets to Rungis might be used for cultural purposes was not his, but the vision of a multi-purpose centre rivalling anything offered by New York or London as *la grande affaire* of his presidency apparently was. Beaubourg (or the Centre Georges Pompidou, as it became) was as much an assertion of his wider commitment to modernising France as a specifically cultural project.[11] He took the decision alone, envisaging it as encompassing a museum of modern painting and sculpture, with provision for the cinema and theatre research. A public library came later, compelling a financial contribution from a reluctant Ministry of Education, with a musical institute later still. Although Michelet was initially charged with fleshing

10. *Le Point* (undated), cited F. Chaslin, p. 151.
11. P. Cabanne, pp. 262–9.

out the scheme, it became part of Pompidou's *domaine réservé*. While he envisaged a thoroughly modern building, the winning design was utterly at variance with the kind of 'architectural gesture' he had hoped to make.[12] However, he accepted the jury's recommendation and, in the face of protests over its uncompromising modernism and the fact that none of the winning team was French, let it be known that he would tolerate no modifications that did not have the architects' approval. Thereafter he followed the project almost daily, now supervising the process of land acquisition, now bullying the Finance Ministry into meeting the capital cost, now deciding the colour scheme, now warding off attempts by traditionalists to divert or frustrate his plans. Still, he could not operate single-handed. Knowing little about contemporary music, he largely accepted proposals by Michel Guy and Pierre Boulez, which eventually took shape in the Institute for Musical-Acoustical Research and Coordination.

Pompidou also chose Beaubourg's first director, appointing a foreigner (Pontus Hulten of the Moderna Museet in Stockholm) because he felt that nobody in France had experience of running a thoroughly modern museum. As with the appointment of Boulez to head the Music Institute, he was determined to rout the conservative artistic establishment. His commitment was unwavering; among his last acts was to see that the building, its programme and the accompanying budget were approved. François Chaslin comments, 'If one remembers the virulence of the cabals opposed to the "Concorde of the arts and letters", the host of obstacles that accumulated during the long process of planning and building that extraordinary building, one realises the extent to which, in this country, it is essential to have a sponsor with complete authority, to counter the unending succession of cowardice, incompetence, jealousy, attempts at obstruction, lethargic administration and arguments for argument's sake that lead to impotence.'[13] Only Pompidou's unremitting application of presidential power could have seen Beaubourg to completion in anything like its final form. But 'What if the next head of state is not an art lover?'[14]

And indeed Giscard was not – at least, not in the sense that Pompidou was one. Beaubourg's fate hung in the balance. The very conception of this modernistic 'cultural supermarket' was utterly at variance with Giscard's tastes. Just as Pompidou's creation affirmed his commitment to modernisation, so Giscard's

12. *Ibid.*, p. 264.
13. F. Chaslin, p. 13.
14. Jacques Michel in *Le Monde*, 11 April 1974.

impulse to kill Beaubourg heralded the return to traditional values, which his presidency was to impose on cultural policy. In the event, work was so advanced that cancellation would have been prohibitively expensive. He demanded detailed changes, but was again too late. Through fidelity to Pompidou's memory rather than any liking for modern art, Jacques Chirac and Alain Peyrefitte, the new minister, pressed for the Centre to be completed. Giscard capitulated but remained unconvinced; he was reluctant even to attend the official opening. Beaubourg had few friends in high places, and Françoise Giroud, who by the time of the opening held the cultural portfolio, complained that it was an 'uneconomic' drain on her budget; even the Centre's defenders hoped for 10,000 visitors per day at best. In the event Beaubourg was an instant, runaway success. By the end of the 1980s it was averaging nearly 26,000 visitors per day, far outstripping all other museums and galleries; its problems were those of its almost embarrassing popularity. When proposals came forward to detach one of its functions to leave more space for the rest, Pompidou's widow successfully protected her husband's vision into the 1990s, an interesting instance of presidential power extending beyond the grave.

Giscard's much-publicised 1976 manifesto, *La Démocratie française*, contains only three lines on culture, which was demoted to having only a junior ministry assigned to it. Of the four holders of the portfolio during his presidency only one, Michel Guy (who implemented Giscard's pledge to abolish film censorship), was conspicuously fitted for it, deeply committed to it and enjoyed any substantial success. His three successors, Françoise Giroud, Michel d'Ornano and Jean-Philippe Lecat, were appointed more for reasons of political balance than for what they brought to the arts. They did not hold their posts long enough to achieve much. Yet although Giscard's interests were limited and frequently branded as 'reactionary' in artistic circles, he had a coherent vision and pursued it consistently. Pompidou's modern furnishings and paintings were banished from the Elysée in favour of more traditional styles; the arts and crafts of traditional France now enjoyed presidential patronage. His strongly-held views on urbanism and architecture were no less rapidly felt: 'Everything that has been done in the Paris region over the last ten years has been absurd.'[15] Pompidou had sacrificed some of the country's finest townscapes to motorists, property developers and an international architectural style out of harmony with French traditions. The left-bank expressway was abandoned, and tower blocks were banished to the capital's

15. P. Cabanne, p. 199.

periphery. Giscard vetoed plans for an international trade centre on the site of the old fruit and vegetable market, Les Halles, and ordered fresh plans. The City Council, which controlled the site and which Giscard failed to consult, was furious. Fearing the unpleasant surprises which open competition might hold, Giscard hand-picked the contenders, then went through the successful proposal to ensure that it met his requirements, which included gardens as the central focus. But he reckoned without the City Council. After Jacques Chirac resigned the premiership and became Mayor of Paris, this was hostile territory. Smarting from his autocratic intervention and objecting to the 'vulgarity' of Ricardo Bofill's 'greco-buddhist temple', the council dug its heels in. It held the whip-hand. Giscard had to reach an accommodation with Chirac. Bofill was sacked, and all that Giscard salvaged from a costly setback was Chirac's recognition that he had a free hand at the former meat market of La Villette and a much-reduced garden at Les Halles.[16] The antagonism between these rivals for leadership of the Right, between the Elysée and the *Hôtel de Ville*, bedevilled Giscard's progress for the remainder of his presidency.

Giscard was also responsible for a law requiring each *département* to set up a council for architecture, planning and the environment, reponsible for developing public appreciation of architecture. He established the *Institut Français d'Architecture*, to promote architecture in general and *architecture à la française* in particular, and backed the 'Thousand Days for Architecture campaign' to stimulate public interest. Above all, he was the first self-proclaimed builder-President. Giscard's monumental building programme – *'les grands chantiers du President'* – which he launched in 1977, envisaged turning the Gare d'Orsay into a museum of the nineteenth century; creating a new museum of sciences and industry and a 60-acre park at La Villette, so finding a use for the greatest of the Fifth Republic's planning disasters; an institute of the Arab world; and low-rise mirror-glass office blocks at the city's western edge.

Giscard involved himself closely in the application of his programme, especially the Gare d'Orsay. Pompidou had pondered turning it into an annexe of the Louvre, but Giscard decided that it should be an independent establishment devoted to 'nineteenth-century French art and civilisation'; it was his 'anti-Beaubourg', 'a fine museum in the traditional and enduring sense of the word'. He also decided that it should pay greater attention to the romantic period, its keynote furnished by Delacroix's painting celebrating

16. F. Chaslin, p. 99.

the 1830 Revolution, 'Liberty Guiding the People'. A competitioɪ.
was held, and Giscard personally chose the contenders; then, after
protracted cogitation, he selected the winning entry and specified
detailed amendments to be made to the successful scheme. He also
intervened to resolve the interminable disagreements between architects, museum designers and administrators.

Much the same happened with the other projects. Thus he added
a concert hall and school of dance at La Villette, the latter on
the urging of his sister.[17] However, the architects' scheme that he
accepted after lengthy reflection ran counter to his personal inclina-
tions; it had been pressed on him by Paul Delouvrier, whom he
had put in charge of the project. After a process incorporating
'wide consultation, the search for a consensus and the need for a
final decision' he took 'complete responsibility' for the decision,
prompting protests at this fresh example of an arbitrary *'fait du
prince'*. He also involved himself in the details of the Musée d'Orsay;
at the press presentation, the *maquette* was scarred by the last-
minute removal of a hemispherical stainless steel projection room,
following a note from the Elysée castigating 'this disgraceful pro-
tuberance, contrary to French taste'.[18] There were endless subsequent battles over modifications, while Chirac's Paris City Council
was furious over the failure to include the social housing development which it believed had been promised. The arguments were
unresolved when Giscard left power.

Giscard's fatal error was to overlook the political calendar. His
monumental building projects were not launched until his presidency was more than half spent. They were delayed by internal
quarrels and lack of cooperation from the City Council. Nobody
had overall responsibility for coordinating them, banging heads
together and forcing the pace. The result was that none of them
was complete when he left power, and all were left to the mercy
of his successor. The lesson was not lost on François Mitterrand.

Mitterrand took office firmly if imprecisely pledged to a 'cultural
renaissance'. 'Socialism', said his close associate Jacques Attali,
'is a cultural project.'[19] His party was eclectic in what it embraced
as 'culture', and its commitment reflected a humanistic and
ideological tradition dating back at least to Jaurès. But 'capturing'
culture was also important in the Socialists' strategy of attacking the
weakening ties of the Communists with intellectuals and artists, as
well as appealing to the young, educated middle class with

17. *Ibid.*, p. 67.
18. *Ibid.*, p. 87.
19. *Le Monde*, 21 May 1981.

cultural aspirations – the '1968 generation'. Under Right-wing governments, the Socialists argued, France had become a cultural desert, with the arts stultified by conformism, philistinism and financial asphyxia. However, although some areas were starved of funds, the Ministry of Culture's budget had in fact increased, in 1985 constant francs, from about 1.3 billion in 1960 to 4.1 billion in 1981. This nonetheless barely represented an increased fraction of the national budget.[20]

Mitterrand's key cultural decisions were to appoint and retain Jack Lang as minister; to double national cultural expenditure in real terms and maintain this even in hard times, and to be a 'builder-creator President'.[21] Lang, like Malraux, had no personal power-base, and depended on Mitterrand's backing for his immensely ambitious programme. Flamboyant, hyperactive, a self-publicist, eclectic and opportunistic in his enthusiasms, Lang saw culture as central to his party's commitment to transforming society, but his approach to culture was sufficiently pluralistic to appeal beyond the Socialist ranks. He readily acknowledged a debt to Malraux, and tinges of cultural nationalism spiked with attacks on American cultural imperialism touched a responsive chord among Gaullists.

Lang was as close as anyone ever came to Mitterrand, and he had none of Malraux's restraint about pressing his President for resources. His department's share of the national budget jumped from 0.44 per cent to 0.76 per cent in 1982 and was to reach 0.94 per cent in 1991, giving him the means to pursue an all-round cultural policy (while favouring 'creation' over 'preservation'). At one time more than 5,000 organisations were receiving grants. 'He subsidises everything that moves', commented *Le Point*. Whatever criticisms there might be of his policies – and there were many – it was unmistakably his. With two major exceptions Mitterrand let him have his head, even though the outcome was often far removed from his personal tastes. More than almost any other minister of the Fifth Republic, Lang showed what could be achieved by an energetic minister enjoying the President's confidence – and not subjected to his intervention.

The proviso is crucial. As in any system of court politics, Lang's power was highly contingent, as Mitterrand's handling of 'presidential projects' and key decisions on television amply showed. Like Giscard, Mitterrand claimed a long-standing interest in architecture and a conviction about its importance. 'There can be no great policy for France', he told an early Council of Ministers, 'without a great

20. R. Wangermee *et al.*, *La Politique culturelle de la France*, Paris, 1988, p. 70.
21. See also D. Wachtel, *Cultural Policy and Socialist France*, Westport, CT, 1987 and M. Hunter, *Les Jours les plus Lang*, Paris, 1990.

architecture.'[22] He was also moved by intimations of political mortality. A friend described him as 'very concerned about the mark he will leave in stone, for that may prove to be what best survives from this period of politics'.[23] Socialist rule might prove ephemeral; the *grands projets* would ensure a lasting monument. Conscious that the political calendar guaranteed him power only till 1986, he was determined that his programme would both outstrip Giscard's and avoid its fate, which now lay in his hands.

At his very first news conference Mitterrand announced that the scheme for La Défense, in northern Paris, the plans for which had been 'finalised' only eight months earlier, would be scrapped. The architect learned his fate from the next day's newspapers. The Institute of the Arab World would be built on a different site, entailing the writing-off of more than 5 million francs in abortive work, as the Cour des Comptes austerely noted. La Villette would proceed with a modified brief and the addition of a 'City of Music'. The Musée d'Orsay, which 'must not become a mere repository of past times', would now begin with 1848 – the year of revolutions – and emphasise realism in art and social history.[24] (However, the appointment of a Marxist historian to 'define a new historical orientation' stirred a furious storm in a teacup and an embarrassing climb-down.) Mitterrand also announced a world exhibition to celebrate the bicentenary of the Revolution in 1989, decreed the eviction of the Ministry of Finance from the Louvre that Malraux had advocated in vain, thus fulfilling his intention to make it 'the finest museum in the world'. The ministry fought a tenacious five-year rearguard action, assisted by the 1986–8 *cohabitation* interlude, before finally bowing to the presidential will.

Mitterrand's commitment to a fresh round of presidential projects came first; only then came the search to determine what these should be and where they might be sited. He announced in March 1982 eight major developments in Paris and several lesser ones in the provinces, with the declared aim of achieving a 'renewal of architectural creation in France'. He proposed a 'Popular Opera' at the Place de la Bastille, a 10,000-seat hall for jazz, rock and pop, an international communications centre in place of Giscard's defunct plans for La Défense, a new home for the Ministry of Finance, and an 'urban park' for La Villette. The provincial projects (some

22. F. Chaslin, p. 21. However, he was even prepared to choose the colour of the seats in the Opéra-Bastille. See Maryvonne de Saint Pulgent, *Le syndrome de l'Opéra*, Paris, 1991.
23. F. Chaslin, p. 18.
24. *Ibid.*, p. 52.

were abandoned in 1985 and others added) included a school of dance at Marseilles, a national comic-strip museum at Angoulême and a museum of photography at Arles. Amounting to only 4 per cent of the budget for *grands projets*, they prompted criticism that for all the Socialists' talk of decentralisation, the provinces were yet again being fobbed off with 'confetti'. Effectively Mitterrand subordinated the balance between Paris and the rest of the country to maintaining the capital's international standing and making it 'a model for the city of the twenty-first century'.

Most of these schemes had been canvassed in some form under earlier governments. The selection, by a cabinet sub-committee under Mitterrand's chairmanship, reflected a mix of personal and Socialist cultural priorities, tempered by hard-headed assessments about the availability of sites where work could be completed within the requisite five-year time-scale. This was less difficult than might have been expected, considering that Jacques Chirac was Mayor of Paris. The schemes would enhance the capital's facilities while respecting the consensus among planners about the desirability of shifting development in Paris eastwards and revitalising declining riverfront sites. Also, Mitterrand was more attentive than Giscard to securing Chirac's agreement, deferring to him on secondary points like the siting of the new Ministry of Finance. (While almost every scheme stirred fierce aesthetic arguments, the accident of being able to 'square' the principal opposition leader in this manner helps to explain why Mitterrand's plans roused little political controversy.) The sites were identified jointly during the early weeks of Mitterrand's presidency by Lang and members of his staff with officials of the Parisian Workshop for Urban Planning, an agency of the city with responsibility for Chirac's own urban strategy. Subsequently a senior member of the Workshop joined the team coordinating the projects. Despite occasional disagreements over the height of the new Ministry of Finance or the thorny issue of housing at La Villette, relations at the official level were remarkably good. At times, planning for presidential and city projects proceeded along complementary lines; this tacit complicity between the Elysée and City Hall via the Workshop was crucial to Mitterrand's chances of meeting the demanding timetable he had set himself. The only major clash was over the planned exhibition for the bicentennial of the Revolution. When it was dropped in 1983, each side tried to pin the blame on the other. The underlying reasons were financial: with austerity the order of the day and the bill for the presidential projects running at around 30 billion francs, they could not escape unscathed, and Mitterrand sacrificed the exhibition. The Opéra-Bastille, which from the start was a target

for a sceptical Finance Ministry and not greatly loved by either
Lang or Mitterrand, narrowly escaped the same fate, especially
once the architectural competition proved disappointing. Despite
Mitterrand's insistence on containing costs, they rose remorselessly
and several projects suffered pruning or rescheduling in the annual
budget negotiations at the combined insistence of the Prime
Minister's Office and the Ministry of Finance.

Initially the complex and at times turbulent task of coordinating
the projects was in the hands of a small group of ministers and
officials working from the Prime Minister's Office. Subsequently
this 'group of four' was restyled as the 'Coordinating Mission for
Major State Projects in Paris' and attached to the Elysée. It reported
directly to Mitterrand, who was never far away. He was dissuaded
with difficulty from breaching the law by choosing architects without a competition, with one exception – the Louvre Pyramid, for
which he personally selected I. M. Pei. This gave Pierre Mauroy a
difficult moment in the National Assembly, since he was compelled
to plead that 'by virtue of the constitution' the President was
'not accountable' for his actions. Otherwise the competitions were
held as prescribed. Several times the results were not to his taste,
notably the new Opera, La Villette and the Finance Ministry. He
preferred simple, pure forms like the cubic arch at La Défense, the
project which gave him greatest satisfaction, where he frustrated
attempts by a suspicious jury to constrain his freedom of choice.
However, even when disappointed he let the schemes proceed – to
some extent the captive of his own timetable. He frequently sought
the opinions of others, and characteristically kept his own counsel,
but the final decision was invariably his. Pondering his historic
responsibilities, he was at times even more indecisive than Giscard.
Once a particular scheme had been chosen, he remained closely
involved. We find him visiting La Villette, modifying the main
outlines of development, sacking the museum director appointed by
Giscard, restoring the hemisphere Giscard had banished, and
authorising the inclusion of a rock stadium dear to Lang's heart
that had not featured in the original conception.

Despite the relative harmony between Mitterrand and Chirac
the Mayor, Chirac the Prime Minister hoped to modify some of
the President's schemes, most of which had fallen behind schedule.
However, Mitterrand had anticipated this and seen that almost
every aspect of the programme, including key appointments, had
been brought under the control of the Elysée. Chirac had hoped
to halt the new Opera, leave the Ministry of Finance in the Louvre,
sell or let off its new offices and let out the space assigned to the
International Communications Centre. However, cancelling the

Opera would have been so costly that he had to settle for secondary changes. His Minister of Culture and Communication, François Léotard, thwarted him over the Louvre by threatening resignation. Although Chirac succeeded in turning the International Trade Centre to other uses, the buildings were now architecturally complete. Since the purposes to which the Socialists' intention of using them to embody the 'communications society' had never been entirely convincing, there was little complaint. While Mitterrand's projects emerged almost unscathed from the *cohabitation* period, his influence on other aspects of cultural policy was virtually nil – although much of Lang's work survived unscathed.

After the Socialists' return to power in 1988, Mitterrand restored Lang (who was hoping for better), flanking him with a pair of not entirely well-disposed colleagues, but despite his now more limited scope, he remained very much his own man. Mitterrand's *grands projets* moved forward with varying fortunes, coordinated on a more orthodox basis by a junior Minister for Major Projects, Emile Biasini. Mitterrand added the renovation of the Tuileries Gardens and a project in some respects capping all the others, a new National Library, universally referred to as the TGB.

Again this was not a new idea. The inadequacies of the old *Bibliothèque Nationale* had long been notorious, and in 1983 a report by André Chastel had called for a completely new library. Initial planning began under Léotard, and Mitterrand took the scheme over as his last big monument. Despite the appointment of Biasini his involvement was undiminished: he decided the site and set an opening date in 1995, just before his second term would end. Biasini underlined how intimately related to the political calendar such schemes had become: 'Experience has shown me that an undertaking of this kind can run into a certain number of difficulties linked to the developing political context. So it is more sensible for the period the project is to run to coincide with François Mitterrand's term of office.'[25] Mitterrand decreed that the TGB should be 'an entirely new kind of library', but nobody knew what that meant. Reversing the customary sequence to meet the deadline, the architectural competition was held and Mitterrand selected the winning design, featuring the simple geometrical style he favoured, before it had been decided what the library would hold or what services it would provide. Details like increasing the number of books to be held from 4 to 12 million came subsequently, requiring

---

25. *Le Monde*, 15 Sept. 1990. See D. Loosely, 'The *Bibliothèque de France*, last of the *Grand Projets*', *Modern and Contemporary France*, no. 46 (July 1991), pp. 35–46.

major modifications and fuelling prolonged polemics among architects, librarians and users. Mitterrand's hand remained evident in statements about the library's brief, in the working-through of the major details and the insistence with which work was pressed forward. A project which might well have hung fire for years proceeded at a pace that only a resolutely imperative President could achieve, albeit reflecting in a particularly acute form the 'undue reverence paid to Elyséen amateurism' inherent in placing such projects within the presidential domain.[26]

Mortality permitting, Mitterrand's projects should be completed or irreversible by the end of his presidency, so far outstripping Pompidou and Giscard in the mark he will have left on the capital that successors wishing to continue the tradition of presidential projects will have difficulty in finding sites. They will also find themselves committed to the substantial running costs of the new facilities, although this should not prove politically difficult so long as the consensus supporting a high level of cultural expenditure can be maintained. So, the *grands projets* stand among the purest expressions of sovereign presidential power in the Fifth Republic. Yet Beaubourg survived by the narrowest of margins, none of Giscard's schemes reached completion in the form he had envisaged, and Mitterrand had to drop the Bicentennial Exhibition and prune other projects for financial reasons, while he had no personal affection for the Opéra-Bastille and, like the new Ministry of Finance building, its architecture disappointed him. Indeed apart from the TGB, where judgement must still be reserved, the Grand Arch at La Défense and the Louvre Pyramid appear to be the only projects he would be proud to have associated with his name. Even at its zenith, presidential power may suffer constraints and frustrations.

Broadcasting

If cultural projects have become something of a regal hobby, broadcasting touches questions of power and rule so intimately that Presidents ignore them at their peril. This does much to explain why, although the Fifth Republic has innovated in cultural affairs, its handling of broadcasting shows such continuities with its predecessor. De Gaulle inherited a public quasi-monopoly, *Radio-Télévision Française* (RTF), which was technically a civil service department, with a Director-General appointed by the government and responsible to the Minister of Information, who appointed the Director of News. Successive governments colonised RTF with

26. F. Edelmann and E. de Roux, *Le Monde*, 3 Sept. 1991.

their supporters, constantly intervening in programming to hold the Fourth Republic's Communist or Gaullist enemies in check, keep Algeria French or simply bolster their own standing. As François Mitterrand put it, as Minister of Information in 1949, the broadcasters' task was to carry through a 'national policy of defending the interests of France' as laid down by 'the qualified representative of the French nation' – the government.[27] This notion that broadcasting should serve the interests of the government of the day was the Fourth Republic's legacy to the Fifth, and was a tradition successive Presidents sought to continue, initially by massive intervention, subsequently by controlling key appointments and later by creating tame regulatory agencies and assigning networks to friendly private interests. While the means varied greatly, the underlying aims did so much less.

Broadcasting could not safely be left alone. The Fifth Republic inherited a system in desperate need of reform. On the brink of tremendous expansion, its legal and administrative structures were hopelessly outmoded and its financial arrangements chaotic. It was riven by repeated strikes that demoralised the staff and infuriated the public. These problems have proved remarkably durable despite repeated intervention. On the contrary, since the first Gaullist ordinance in 1959 the future of broadcasting has been under almost constant discussion. Not one of the many 'reforms', inquiries and reports has produced a consensual, lasting solution. Presidents have a heavy responsibility for the resulting climate of uncertainty, damaging for staff morale, good management and programme quality.

De Gaulle embraced and intensified his inheritance of domestication and subjection. When his newly-appointed head of RTF suggested in 1959 that RTF have financial autonomy and be placed under the 'tutelage' of the Minister of Information rather than his direct authority, de Gaulle refused. He ruled that RTF must remain a state monopoly financed by licence fees, with very limited budgetary autonomy, under ministerial authority, with the Director-General, his deputy and the other directors appointed by the government. Both the accompanying Higher Advisory Council and the Watchdog Committee were constituted to reflect the government's wishes. Considering the press, for the most part, a 'noisy concert of doubt, criticism and frivolity', he was adamant that he must be able to rely on radio and television to convey the Gaullist message on every possible occasion, ignoring or traducing critics. 'Television

27. F.-O. Giesbert, *François Mitterrand ou la tentation de l'histoire*, Paris, 1977, pp. 134–8.

is mine,' he is reputed to have said. Whether the remark is apocryphal or not, his attitude to public service broadcasting was undeniably proprietorial. A 1964 memorandum stated: 'I cannot accept that French radio and television be put at the disposal of a critic or an author taking de Gaulle as his subject without my consent.'[28] Heads of RTF were invariably civil servants – disciplined by their very calling and dependent on government goodwill for advancement. There were five during his presidency. This succession of technocrats knowing little except where their duty lay did nothing to ease the perennial crises at RTF. Senior appointments had to be cleared with the Elysée, and the news and current affairs divisions were extensively colonised with loyalists – men like the head of television news in 1961, who is remembered for the egregious statement, 'A journalist should be French first, objective second.'[29] To make doubly sure, the Minister of Information and officials from other departments met the broadcasters daily to discuss the shape and content of news coverage. The heads of each network and the newsrooms had a direct line from the ministry on their desks so that instructions could be issued right up to the last minute. In the words of a Minister of Information of the period, 'Television is the government in the French people's dining rooms every evening.'[30] De Gaulle was an attentive viewer, and broadcasters soon became aware if anything had incurred his or Mme de Gaulle's displeasure (even non-political programming took account of the wishes, real or assumed, of the Elysée). The President did not greatly concern himself with broadcasting policy, although he fought hard and successfully for adoption of the French colour television standard in Eastern Europe – essentially for reasons of industrial and international policy.

But control of structures and appointments was not enough. De Gaulle, whose leadership of Free France dated from his radio broadcast of 18 June 1940, grasped that television was becoming the prime means of political communication and rapidly schooled himself in television techniques. The capacity of the new medium to reach the public over the heads of all intermediaries was particularly in keeping with his style of rule. His televised press conferences at moments of his own choosing, over which he took immense

28. Cited by A. Grosser, *Le Monde*, 23 Jan. 1990.
29. Cited by R. Thomas, *Broadcasting and Democracy in France*, London, 1976, p. 13. Or, as one of the best-known broadcasters of the time, Léon Zitrone, wrote, 'I am a State journalist at the service of the State.' *Le Canard enchaîné*, 6 Jan. 1971. See also P. Bourdon, *Histoire de la télévision sous de Gaulle*, Paris, 1990.
30. *Le Canard enchaîné*, 6 Jan. 1971.

pains, were the 'high masses' of the early Fifth Republic. His appeals to the French people at moments of high crisis were unforgettable and decisive. Great prose stylist though de Gaulle was, the regime would never have been dubbed 'the Republic of the word' had it not been for television.

De Gaulle's treatment of broadcasting could claim a semblance of justification while his regime was fighting for its life. However, he showed no disposition to change once the Algerian conflict had been resolved. In 1964, the Minister of Information, Alain Peyrefitte, hailed a new 'democratic and liberal' statute creating the *Office de Radio-Télévision Française* (ORTF). Broadcasting would have greater financial autonomy and be subject to the minister's 'tutelage' rather than his direct authority. However, the government would still control the purse-strings and appoint ORTF's chief executives. Attempts to liberalise the bill were rejected, apparently on de Gaulle's instructions. Although de Gaulle said that broadcasting should reflect without prejudice every current of opinion and be 'worthy of a democracy, worthy of France', the reform barely affected the level of political interference.[31] Yet, in a sense, the bill was a recognition that times were changing. Pressure for liberalisation, even from within the ruling majority, became increasingly difficult to resist in principle. Each succeeding reorganisation recognised the need to meet these pressures by proposing arrangements that appeared to concede greater independence, and although there arrangements still left ways in which the broadcasters could be brought to heel, each such occasion did produce real gains, however small.

The self-defeating character of this policy became clear in the 1965 presidential election, when the rules governing television during the campaign were fairer than in the past and viewers discovered that politicians who had been ridiculed or demonised for years were actually capable of talking sense. This had much to do with de Gaulle being unexpectedly forced to a second ballot. (1965 was France's first real 'TV election' with de Gaulle, who had declined to take up all his broadcasting time before the first ballot, being compelled to give an unprecedentedly freewheeling interview before the second.) Liberal Gaullist voices became more influential and new programmes were introduced, giving the opposition a fairer hearing, but old habits died hard. In the 1967 parliamentary elections fresh ingenuity was displayed in unbalancing coverage in the government's favour; this culminated in de Gaulle insisting, after the campaign had officially closed, on appealing

31. R. Thomas, p. 19.

to the nation on television to make the right choice. The Gaullist news director of a regional station said about this time: 'With only fifteen minutes of local TV news a day, do we have time to air local criticisms of official policy? We, the government, are doing all we can to promote regional progress. The time isn't ripe to let Bretons criticise us too openly on the screen. . . . They're too immature.'[32] Such arrogant condescension had its part in fuelling the explosion of May 1968 when de Gaulle's favoured weapon failed. The frustrations of a decade and the intensification of political intervention in the coverage of the 'events' precipitated a strike of news staff, including many Gaullists, for, among other things, guarantees of freedom from political interference.

Once normality had been restored, many strikers were dismissed or transferred to less politically sensitive posts despite categoric assurances from yet another new Director-General. This was at the insistence of de Gaulle, who was furious at being stabbed in the back in his hour of need. Yet another 'reform' offered apparently greater independence while perpetuating government control. However, these battles left their mark. In the 1969 presidential campaign all the leading candidates promised to abolish the post of Minister of Information. Georges Pompidou, who had suffered under the existing system after his dismissal as Prime Minister, pledged that television news would be 'objective, lively and open'. However, he was sceptical about the wish of his Prime Minister, Chaban-Delmas, to make ORTF independent of political pressures. Chaban-Delmas' reorganisation of TV news resulted in the appointment of a comparatively liberal journalist with links with the Prime Minister at one channel and a Gaullist close to the President at the other. Although there were signs of improvement, programmes were still dropped or cut for political reasons and Pompidou personally selected the sequences from his press conferences to feature in television news. 'A television journalist is not quite like other journalists,' he classically remarked. 'He has other responsibilities. Like it or not, television is seen as the voice of France.'[33]

Pompidou replaced Chaban-Delmas with the less liberal and less independent-minded Pierre Messmer at a moment when ORTF was being reorganised yet again after a scandal over clandestine advertising. There were renewed gestures towards the principle of independence, but the government still controlled the most senior posts. The new President-Director General, Arthur Conte, was a

32. J. Ardagh, *France in the 1980s*, Harmondsworth, 1982, p. 580.
33. *L'Année Politique 1970*, p. 430. For a time Pompidou banned ministers from televised debates with the opposition because of their poor showing.

friend of Pompidou. The new head of Channel Three was a 1968 blackleg recruited from the Elysée press service. Yet even this did not protect ORTF. When Conte was sacked after sixteen months amid allegations of mismanagement, he asserted that despite the minister's claim that ORTF was as free from political interference as the BBC (which he apparently imagined to be untroubled by such problems), he had demanded – on pain of freezing ORTF's budget – the dismissal of the head of radio, alleging that the *France-Culture* network was a 'permanent pulpit for the Communists'.

Characteristically, although the 1972 statute gave Conte a three-year term to ensure his independence, a loophole was found that violated its spirit (and probably its letter) in order to sack him. To Messmer the matter was simple: when minister and civil servant disagree, it is natural for the latter to lose his job.[34] It is doubtful whether it was the Prime Minister's decision; he was not a man to take controversial independent initiatives. Conte blamed the presidential entourage which, during Pompidou's last illness, attained exceptional power. According to Conte, they were angered by his independent-mindedness and resorted to dismissal when he failed to bow to subtler pressures or the minister's resort to financial blackmail.[35]

Giscard d'Estaing took office pledged to a new, liberal era. He contemplated privatising one of the state networks, partly because he considered ORTF unmanageable and partly because a private network might be politically more sympathetic than ORTF, which was packed with Gaullist placemen. But his Prime Minister, Jacques Chirac, was hostile, and this was one of those rare occasions when parliamentary opinion counted. Neither the Left nor Giscard's RPR coalition partners were prepared to end the monopoly. Instead Giscard decided to break ORTF into seven separate bodies. Yet again structures were devised which ostensibly provided independence and neutrality but preserved the government's right to appoint the president of each company. Predictably, those named to sensitive posts were predominantly government supporters, civil servants or otherwise 'reliable'.

However, Giscard repudiated Pompidou's position: 'It has always been my view that that was a mistake, because the voice of France meant some sort of official news. There never was official news and nobody ever said that ORTF should be an official news agency. . . For me, it is not the voice of France – simply Frenchmen and Frenchwomen expressing themselves.' He promised

34. R. Thomas, p. 48.
35. A. Conte, *Hommes libres*, Paris, 1973, pp. 16–20.

the new network heads that 'No special tutelage, no interventions
from outside must restrict or impinge on your responsibility.' Their
watchwords should be independence and quality.[36] His governments contained no Minister of Information. The direct interference
of earlier years ended; ministers no longer issued instructions to
news editors, interviews with ministers had a sharper edge, and
opposition views were heard regularly. National news was less
biased and livelier, though provincial newsrooms still deferred
obsequiously to the Prefects and the local 'barons' of the regime.
However, good intentions withered at moments of political difficulty, not least because the Elysée still involved itself in the
appointment of senior journalists. Thus when allegations that
Giscard had accepted gifts of diamonds from 'Emperor' Bokassa
of the Central African 'Empire' filled the press, television news
barely mentioned them. Two news presenters who gave the story
prominence were, respectively, moved and had their programme
cancelled. The blatant interference of earlier years ceased, but
conformism and self-censorship remained endemic. A Senate
report in 1979 spoke devastatingly of incoherence, inefficiency,
mismanagement and mediocrity.[37] Giscard had created seven mini-
ORTFs with all the failings of the old one. Worse, the enormous
expansion of the 1970s was under-financed, leading the networks
to resort to cheap American imports at the expense of the domestic
programme industry.

Giscard made one other major foray into broadcasting policy,
his 1979 agreement with Chancellor Helmut Schmidt of the Federal
German Republic to develop direct broadcasting satellites. Persisted
in by his successor, this was to be a costly failure. Risks are inevitable in high-technology ventures; what characterised this one
was that it was initiated for reasons of industrial policy and to
strengthen cooperation between countries but with no clear idea
of what the satellite would be used for. This failure to think the
policy through in all its aspects has dogged it ever since.

Like his predecessors, Giscard commanded television almost
at will for speeches, interviews or events like his appearance in a
popular programme playing the accordion to project himself as
a man of the people. However, he was not a very successful performer. His distant, rather tense intellectual manner did not readily
inspire rapport with his audience, and he had a weakness for dramatic gestures that did not quite ring true, most notably in his
petulant response to the voters' verdict when he ended his final

36. Cited in *Le Monde*, 7–8 Jan. 1990.
37. *Le Monde*, 13 June 1979.

broadcast as President with a long silence, then slowly rose and walked away, leaving viewers to contemplate the melodramatically symbolic empty chair.

François Mitterrand came to office pledged to liberalisation. Pierre Mauroy promised that there would be no witch-hunt, but Mitterrand's choice as minister, Georges Fillioud, a former radio journalist who had himself been victimised, was less forgiving. Within months, although he resisted pressures from zealots and the broadcasting unions for a widespread purge, all the network heads and a number of news directors and presenters had been induced by a variety of means to resign, along with the bosses of most of the peripheral broadcasting companies. Mitterrand reportedly counselled Fillioud, 'Better to keep a docile opponent in post than to put in an undocile friend', but did nothing to stop him. Presidential and ministerial telephone calls to broadcasters were now rare, although for some time the uncertainties engendered by the delays while the Socialists drew up their reform plans did much to foster docility.[38] Nevertheless, while many Left-wingers were recruited to news staffs, there was now greater emphasis on professionalism and the new appointees to senior positions were by no means all government sympathisers.

The 1982 statute ostensibly marked a new approach. Ministerial tutelage would end and a new High Authority would appoint the network heads, serve as a buffer between the broadcasters and external pressures and ensure fairness and pluralism. However, not only did the government still control the broadcasting budget but Mitterrand made a characteristic last-minute intervention in the Council of Ministers to modify the system of appointment, ensuring the Authority would be favourable to the government in its early years. So a new 'tradition' developed of placing broadcasting under an 'independent' agency so constituted as to be 'neutral-in-the-government's-favour'. Yet if political considerations weighed heavily in appointments, the new Authority was more than respectable in term of quality and professional experience. The first president, the journalist Michèle Cotta, a long-standing friend of Mitterrand, took her task seriously. Proclaiming that the birth of the Authority marked 'the separation of the state and the audiovisual', she set about making it genuinely non-partisan and collegial, with considerable success.

However, this was not how Mitterrand saw it. The government might no longer directly fill key posts, but the Authority was expected to produce the same outcome. Thus Mauroy had

38. F.-O. Giesbert, *Le Président*, Paris, 1990, p. 270.

appointed Pierre Desgraupes, who was very much his own man,
head of *Antenne 2*. Mitterrand, who could not abide Desgraupes,
told Cotta to get rid of him, but instead the Authority confirmed his
position. Furious, Mitterrand instructed Cotta to ensure that
Desgraupes retired the following year at the age of sixty-five, but
she refused. Mitterrand swore to have his way. Shortly afterwards
the 'Desgraupes Law' was passed, lowering the mandatory retiring
age for certain official posts to sixty-five. Desgraupes went and,
against Cotta's advice, the Authority promptly appointed a man
who had produced a favourable television portrait of Mitterrand.
Mitterrand reportedly clashed with Cotta again over press reports
of pressure from the Elysée over the affair. It is claimed that
his revenge took the form of making appointments to
the Authority that undermined its standing and collegiality and
by-passing it over major policy decisions.[39]

This was not the only such episode. The head of the *Société
Financière de Radiodiffusion* (Sofirad), a Socialist who formerly
headed Fillioud's staff and helped draft the 1982 statute, but
behaved too independently for the Elysée, resigned and was
replaced by a more pliant friend of the Prime Minister. There
was also an unsuccessful attempt to remove the head of *Radio-
Télévision Luxembourgeoise* (RTL) after Mitterrand took exception
to the station's news commentaries. RTL's resistance was allegedly
a factor in French hostility to Luxembourg's participation in the
French direct broadcasting satellite – a hostility which led to it
becoming the base for the far more successful Astra satellite.[40]

Mitterrand remained sceptical about the ability of any quasi-
autonomous agency like the Authority to ensure equitable treatment once the Socialists returned to opposition. Like Giscard in
1974 he saw the possible attractions of breaking ORTF's monopoly.
The first step was in radio. From their involvement with the illicit
'free radios' of Giscard's later years the Socialists inherited a commitment to authorise private FM stations. Fillioud austerely refused
to let these new stations accept advertising, and Mitterrand upheld
him over Mauroy's objections. Most of the idealistic (and mainly
Leftish) founders of the free radio movement went to the wall while
commercial operators flouting the law flourished. Mitterrand's
volte-face allowing the local radios to take advertising came too

39. *Ibid.*, p. 272.
40. Patrick Poivre d'Arvor in *Le Monde*, 13 March 1986. Also M. Harrison,
    'The Politics of Media Reform' in P. A. Hall *et al.*, *Developments in French
    Politics*, Basingstoke, 1990, pp. 237–52, and K. Dyson and P. Humphreys,
    *The Political Economy of Communications: International and European
    Dimensions*, London and New York, 1990.

late to save them, and the resulting dominance of networks offering predominantly foreign pop was far removed from the dreams of the pioneers. It did, however, produce a highly fragmented and thus less politically threatening system.

Mitterrand's next major decision followed logically. He authorised a subscription television channel, *Canal Plus*, headed by a long-standing friend, André Rousselet of Havas. Rousselet's ready access to the President during *Canal Plus*'s difficult early years, during which he gained concession after concession, was crucial to its survival to become the most successful innovation of the 1980s. It was again Mitterrand who, in 1985, gave the green light for private commercial television, temporarily paralysing negotiations over satellite and cable development and bringing *Canal Plus* close to bankruptcy. Political considerations were paramount. An opposition victory in the 1986 elections would deliver the new networks into hostile hands. While the Prime Minister, the Ministers of Culture and Communication and their advisers sought to reconcile Socialist audiovisual priorities with the realities of the market, the scarcity of frequencies, the desire to encourage domestic programme production and the difficulties of stimulating cable and satellite development, Mitterrand conducted his own negotiations, keeping his ministers in the dark. The result was a deal, on extraordinarily favourable terms, on a new privately-owned 'generalist' network headed by a friendly (this was crucial) French capitalist and an Italian media magnate whose notoriously down-market programming was invariably cited as precisely the model France must avoid. A music channel, while apolitical, would enhance the Socialists' appeal to youth. Mitterrand had brought off a masterly coup, at the cost of compromising his party's cultural policy, the prospects of satellite and cable and the industrial policies underlying them, undermining the programme production industry and creating an 'audiovisual landscape' afflicted by chronic instability and financial anaemia. Furious and humiliated, Lang contemplated resignation, but when confronted by the brutal reality that without Mitterrand his political career would be shattered, he conceded defeat.

With the 1986 elections, direct presidential power over broadcasting vanished. Jacques Chirac had a free hand to play Mitterrand's game, privatising the strongest of the three state networks, TF1, and reassigning the contracts with the private networks to friendlier hands (though leaving Mitterrand's concessionaires enough to stave off costly damages). His National Council for Communications and Liberties that replaced the High Authority predictably had an assured Right-wing majority. It promptly

appointed a bunch of politically acceptable nominees to head the
new networks – *en bloc*, on a single vote, in less than half an hour.
Despite pledges of no political victimisation, one of the surviving
state networks (FR3) embarked on a systematic packing of its
regional bureaux with editors favouring its new masters. Mitterrand
was unable to prevent this but his criticisms from the sidelines
further undermined the Council, making clear that its days were
numbered.

However, Mitterrand's 1988 victory did not give him a wholly
free hand. TF1 had become so successful he dropped the pledge
to renationalise it. Apart from *Canal Plus*, the other networks
were so demoralised and financially unstable that yet another cycle
of uncertainty and 'reform' might be fatal. While Mitterrand was
determined to replace Chirac's Council, caution was again essential
if the whole notion of quasi-governmental regulatory bodies was
not to sink into discredit. And he lacked the requisite parliamentary
support to write his new Higher Audiovisual Council into the Constitution as he had promised. The new Council was granted most
of the enhanced powers and resources of its predecessor, with
the inevitable pro-government majority. Although he was now
ostensibly more distanced, Mitterrand still followed developments
closely. Demonstrating its 'objectivity', the Council appointed the
'wrong' man head of the two public networks; the President's anger
rapidly became known. His Ministers of Culture and Communication set out to destabilise the new appointee, turning a deaf ear
to the networks' financial plight, until he resigned. The Higher
Audiovisual Council then appointed the candidate initially favoured
by the Elysée.

Nevertheless, there was progress. Some ministers grumbled that
they had too few opportunities to explain their policies on television.
Their complaints about Council decisions and indications that they
regretted having conceded so much power to it were no less significant. More programmes had a critical edge; the *Bébête* show poked
fun at politicians and survived. News coverage was fairer, notably
during the 1988 presidential election – the first election after which
no broadcasters lost their places following a change in the colour of
the government.[41] Perhaps inevitably the advance was uneven;
programmes were still occasionally dropped for political reasons
(albeit to a greater outcry than in the past), while coverage of the
1991 Gulf war relapsed into instinctive conformism. Interviews
with senior politicians remained deferential, and programmes marking Mitterrand's tenth anniversary were embarrassingly uncritical.

41. *Le Monde*, 14 April 1989.

It is difficult to gauge how far this uneven movement towards a system based more on 'professionalism' than on partisanship was consciously willed by Giscard and then by Mitterrand. Mitterrand's motives remained characteristically opaque. A charitable reading suggests a measure of liberalism qualified by prudently defensive bulwarks against less liberal opponents; alternatively, he was simply deploying devious means to extract partisan advantage in a period when older techniques had ceased to be acceptable. The truth probably lies somewhere in between, with the record inclining one to the second explanation. Meanwhile, competition between public and private networks was fostering greater professionalism, as Giscard had divined that it would. The old game seemed at last to be all but played out.

Like the power to dictate content, techniques aimed at externally manipulating the broadcasters assumed ever greater importance. Under Mitterrand they have blossomed as never before. His inauguration was memorably marked by a ceremony at the Panthéon drenched in republican symbolism, superbly *mise en scène* for television. His 1988 presidential campaign was to a startling degree packaged for television. He was not alone in this, but simply more successful. During the 1986–8 *cohabitation* he became adept at exploiting the institutional newsworthiness of the presidency (and television's tendency to personalise) to capture the headlines with wounding 'little phrases' that weakened the Chirac government and prepared the way for his subsequent victory. In his early years as President, Mitterrand's somewhat laboured traditional Socialist rhetoric and delivery hampered his effectiveness on television. Yet while never an outstanding performer – one reason why televised presidential press conferences were much rarer than in de Gaulle's day – he adapted himself to the medium's requirements to the point where, in his addresses to the nation during the Gulf war, he could command it to great political effect. Yet only months later he learned, through failing to strike the right note in responding to the attempted Soviet coup, that it is as easy to undermine as to promote oneself through television.

Successive Presidents have laboured hard to control or exploit broadcasting, but none has demonstrated a sustained concern for broadcasting as such. They have appointed ministers more for their docility than because of relevant interest or competence, and have alternated between sporadic regal intervention and distant neglect. The former style has resulted in isolated decisions with counterproductive consequences across a range of interlocking issues, damaging ministers' authority and destabilising decision-making processes. The second has allowed policy-making to drift, when what it required was a galvanising impetus (as distinct from imperious fiat) from the highest level. The outcome is a system which, while enjoying greater audience acceptance than in earlier years – no mean achievement – is rife with problems: both the public television networks, two of the commercial networks, the main national television production company and cable development were all in difficulties, the high-power broadcasting satellite was a costly failure, a massive increase in imported programming ran counter to the Socialists' commitment to defend the French language and culture, and an infant regulatory body was too weak and too limited to find the way forward. Neither regal intervention nor Olympian withdrawal seemed capable of producing the strategic overview that the situation needed and which presidentialism at its best might be expected to achieve.[42]

42. Since this chapter was completed, a well-documented article on President Mitterrand's cultural projects has been published by Sue Collard, 'Mission impossible: Les chantiers du Président', *French Cultural Studies* 1992, pp. 97–132.

8

PRESIDENTIAL COURT POLITICS

Jack Hayward

Of the three interrelated kinds of 'closed' politics that have survived into the late twentieth-century world of democratic mass politics – committee politics, hierarchical politics and court politics[1] – it is the last that emerges as the most distinctive feature of the presidency of the Fifth Republic. Committee politics allows the President and his staff to permeate the process of decision-making, notably through the various interministerial councils and committees whose activities reduce the Council of Ministers to a policy-endorsing rather than a policy-making role. Hierarchical politics allows the President to use the formal chain-of-command institutions to communicate his own decisions and to make the appointments to top posts of people whom he trusts to act in conformity with his own wishes. However, it is the concentration of prerogative power in the President's hands that has led to repeated accusations – by Mitterrand and others against de Gaulle and his successors before 1981, and against Mitterrand since 1981 – that there has been a 'monarchical drift' into court politics. The courtiers that pander to the President's wishes to secure political preferment or to exercise occult influence over political decisions are not endowed with either power or responsibility in their own right. They borrow their power and evade their responsibility by operating through the Elysée. Their personal fealty to the President means that he does not have to rely solely upon the impersonal state institutions. He can place his trust in devoted political and personal 'friends' who have often worked for and with him for years before his arrival at the presidency. The cold monster of the state assumes the human shape of a great impersonator: an individual's ambitions and whims, aspirations and animosities, capacity for far-sighted vision and short-sighted preoccupation with day-to-day survival. The Fifth Republic has reconstituted a court which sometimes risks comparison with the decadent democratic despotism of a

---

1. These distinctions were drawn by C. P. Snow in his Godkin Lecture on *Science and Government*, London, 1961, pp. 56–66.

Louis-Napoleon rather than with the resplendent royal absolutism of a Louis XIV.[2]

Having survived for a third of a century, as the longest-lived post-Revolutionary regime other than the Third Republic, the Fifth Republic has much more to its credit than its duration. France's emergence as a major European and world power, in economic as well as diplomatic matters, has been assisted by the fact that she has had as her successive spokesmen de Gaulle, Pompidou, Giscard and Mitterrand. Their relatively long periods in office have added to their influence as seasoned statesmen at the international summits where so much business is currently transacted. This makes it all the more strange that the French political class and by extension public opinion have become restive under the extended sway of the President, who is simultaneously criticised for excessive interference and blamed for everything that goes wrong. Perhaps this is the price of raising expectations that cannot be fulfilled, augmented by resentment against an inordinate authority which is nevertheless regarded as probably indispensable.

Given the French propensity to seek constitutional remedies for both their substantive problems and their insubstantial phantasms, it is characteristic that they search for a scapegoat in their institutions, starting at its apex. The current bout of 'constitutionitis' has returned to the project, set in train by Pompidou in 1973, of electing the President every five years rather than every seven. It was then conceived as a way of strengthening the authority of the President – who, it was assumed, would seek re-election. To minimise the problem of *cohabitation* which threatens to surface when a five-year Assembly of a hostile political complexion is elected (a prospect which at the time of writing is anticipated in 1993), Mitterrand revived the subject in 1991. It is not necessary to go into the complexities of trying to ensure coincidence between the terms of office of President and National Assembly[3] – which would imply abrogation of the President's power to dissolve the Assembly – to see that this would still not ensure partisan coincidence of views between the Assembly majority and the President. However, there is little disposition to go the whole way to an American-style rigid separation of powers, involving abolition of the office of Prime Minister and the accountability of the

2. As discussed in chapter 7 above, Mitterrand's use of presidential power to promote a series of major architectural projects may collectively bear comparison with Louis XIV's Versailles both in their *folie de grandeur* and their valued contribution to the public cultural heritage.
3. Olivier Duhamel, *Le Pouvoir Politique en France*, Paris, 1991, pp. 134–8.

government to the Assembly, as well as the end of the President's power to dissolve the Assembly. So one is left with the attempt either to weaken the President by confining him to a single seven-year term, or to reduce his term to five years – a proposal which would be supported by about two-thirds of both the French people and their deputies – this latter course would usually strengthen the President. However, the circumstantial support in 1991, both from Right and Left, for moving to a five-year term was to allow (without requiring) the premature exit of Mitterrand in 1993, reluctant to face a second, more abrasive period of *cohabitation* as he concludes his political career. He would wish at all costs to avoid being compelled to resign, like Millerand in 1924, because of the unwillingness of any Prime Minister capable of commanding an Assembly majority to serve under him.

The 'court politics' character of French presidential practice is exacerbated by the President's constitutional non-accountability for actions in which he clearly played a major part. Although he shares with the Prime Minister and Finance Minister a general oversight of public policy, he leaves them to 'face the music' in parliament when things go wrong. When the Prime Minister and Finance Minister are at loggerheads, as Pompidou and Giscard were in 1963–5 and Cresson and Bérégovoy in 1991–2, the President is inclined to intervene surreptitiously. However, the public are not duped by this political sleight of hand and persist in blaming him. Thus Giscard could not shift the responsibility for his short-comings on to the shoulders of Barre, his Prime Minister from 1976, when competing against his previous Prime Minister (Chirac) as well as Mitterrand in the 1981 presidential election. The Habash affair in January 1992 (see above, p. 100) demonstrated that Mitterrand was able to avoid his Ministers of Foreign Affairs and the Interior accepting ministerial responsibility for decisions apparently taken by the directors of their personal staffs. Prominent members of Mitterrand's court were spared, just as so many ministers in France have previously avoided resignation for mistakes made by them personally or by their closest collaborators. However, the price is confirmation of public cynicism about prominent politicians, who as a result are frequently blamed even when they are not responsible. Whether one is an experienced former Finance Minister of long standing like Giscard, or a President who, like Mitterrand, has never – despite assiduous tuition by an Elysée adviser (Jacques Attali) – been able to muster more than a semblance of economic grasp, an inability to prevent mass unemployment remains in France a major disqualification for continuing to hold the highest office.

The European Community has bulked ever larger in the activities of the French Presidents during the Fifth Republic. De Gaulle's crucial 1958 decision not to treat national independence as antithetical to the EC, like Mitterrand's decision in 1983 to sacrifice his domestic Socialist programme to France's Community commitments, were landmarks in France's European policy. With the exception of Pompidou's flirtation with Edward Heath, France's EC policy has been based upon the personal ties of de Gaulle and Adenauer, Giscard and Helmut Schmidt, and Mitterrand and Helmut Kohl. However, the increasing tendency of a reunified Germany to refuse the role of deferential junior partner means that French Presidents can no longer rely upon German power in support of Paris-based policies. As long as Jacques Delors is President of the EC Commission, this dramatic shift in power within the Community is partly compensated by the dynamic role which this Frenchman plays in Brussels. However, a 'presidential' head of the Commission is no substitute for democratic leadership. Whether the incapacity of France any longer to provide the leadership that has given the EC its impetus since the Second World War simply means that it will be essential to reform the EC's political institutions is a crucial issue for the 1990s. France having had recourse to a directly-elected President to transcend its divisions in 1962, the EC may have no constructive alternative to adopting a French institutional model to make up for the lack of French political leadership in the years after 1992.

The need to reform the Constitution before ratifying the Maastricht Treaty allowed Mitterrand to retrieve in 1992 the political initiative that he had lost in the previous year owing to the unpopularity of a Socialist Party soiled in the morass of corruption and a Prime Minister, Edith Cresson, who seemed to maximise rather than minimise the problems faced by her government. Knowing the unresolved divisions between Chirac's RPR and Giscard's UDF over European integration, Mitterrand exploited his advantage to the full. He chose the parliamentary rather than the referendum road to constitutional revision, relying on PS-UDF votes to carry the day against the RPR and the PCF. (Because the Communists have become so marginal a force in French politics, the split on the Left was much less serious than that on the Right.) At the price of concessions to the Senate, where the UDF is especially strong, the President secured the majorities for identical texts in both Chambers of parliament, followed by a majority in excess of the three-fifths required in the Congress of Versailles in June 1992.[4] Thereafter, it remained to secure popular ratification of the

---

4. *Journal Officiel*, 26 June 1992. Three articles of the Constitution (2, 54 and 74) were modified and four new ones (88–1/4) were added under the heading 'The European Communities and European Union'. *Le Monde*, 27 June 1992, p. 8.

Maastricht Treaty by referendum to complete the political discomfiture of his 1988 presidential election rival, Chirac. After an impassioned campaign, in which Mitterrand made a forceful intervention on television, the 'Yes' to the European Union Treaty was carried by the narrow but decisive margin of 51 to 49 per cent on 20 September 1992. The post-Mitterrand presidential election may well precipitate the partisan realignment which the 1992 clash over increasing European integration has foreshadowed. That this is a possibility is one more indication of the presidency's pivotal place in both the exercise of French state power and the broad partisan coalition necessary to win political control over it. Thus, the commitment to European integration, which has been a constant feature of Mitterrand's political convictions, provided him simultaneously with the opportunity to give his second term a powerful theme, to promote 'discord among the enemy', and to assert presidential leadership.

Just as Napoleon was condemned continuously to win battles to remain Emperor, unlike the hereditary monarchs who could survive repeated defeats, the late twentieth-century French President must rely on at least the appearance of sustained success to retain pupular confidence and electoral support. To that extent, the presidency remains insufficiently institutionalised, in that its incumbents can be treatened by particular failures. While such retribution may be a desirable incentive to Presidents, whose sense of insecurity may lead them to deploy all their political capacity in the service of the state as a matter of personal prudence as well as out of public spirit, it embodies a threat of instability that recalls a turbulent past that was thought to be buried. Because no institutional arrangement is immune to disruption, the inherent dangers embodied in a directly-elected head of state should not dissuade the European Community from considering adopting a French-style model. This would equip Europe's closer political union with a tried and tested instrument of effective political action to counterbalance the monetary power of the Governor of a European Central Bank. That a directly-elected President of the European Community might be a possibility is remarkable testimony to the success of an institution that has restored the credibility of France's political system by reconciling its national traditions with contemporary international necessities. However, the mid-1990s are more likely to be concerned with preventing the morose economic context from reversing the impetus of European advance than with undertaking bold initiatives to achieve closer political integration.

INDEX

225

www.ingramcontent.com/pod-product-compliance
Lightning Source LLC
Chambersburg PA
CBHW032131020426
42334CB00016B/1116